Such a Woman

The Life of Madame Octavia Walton LeVert

Unveiling long-hidden evidence reveals fascinating,
unknown facts about Octavia Walton LeVert,
a singular woman.

Paula Lenor Webb

Paula Lenor Webb

An Intellect Publishing Book

Copyright 2021 Paula Lenor Webb

madamelevert@protonmail.com

www.SuchaWomanBook.com

ISBN: 978-1-954693-09-8

Cover design and by Michael Ilacqua
www.cyber-theorist.com

FV-7

Intellect Publishing, LLC
www.IntellectPublishing.com

Dedication

My family members, friends and companions have endured many tales about Octavia as I worked on this book.

You wonderful people know exactly who you are when you read this – know that I am ever grateful

Paula Lenor Webb

Foreword

by

Editor, Mary S. Palmer

Octavia Walton LeVert came from good stock. Her grandfather signed the Declaration of Independence. This multi-talented lady was a woman extraordinaire who accomplished many things in her lifetime. In this book, Paula Webb describes her as an author, wife, and mother known for being a gracious hostess who entertained famous poets and politicians. Her intelligence and ability to converse in several languages drew them to her.

Octavia ventured far from her hometown of Mobile, Alabama. Extensive travel in the United States and abroad expanded her horizons, as did being accepted into wide circles of society, meeting a president and the Queen of England.

Contrary to the norm of the era, this woman was accepted by males who sought her opinion and advice. She was a person first and a female second.

Webb outlines the many facets of Octavia's personality, showing how she dealt with tragedy, adversity, and success. She takes readers through changing times leading up to the Civil War, illustrating how this Southern woman was torn by long-held loyalties conflicting with those of the region where she lived.

Extensive research provides valid documentation from primary and secondary sources. Those specific, proper details prove Octavia was—as the title suggests—*Such a Woman*, a woman for all ages and seasons.

The book is a page-turner and a must-read. It is timely and timeless, combined with an appealing style. When you have finished reading it, you will *know* Octavia.

Introduction

'Tis strange that the feelings of Life's early Spring
Will linger so long - aye, ever will cling,
So close to the heart, with their earliest power
Their first gushing freshness, 'till Life's lastest hour.[1]

How exactly do you introduce a woman like
Madame Octavia Walton LeVert? I imagine there are
many ways. If she was introducing herself, she might
launch her introduction with a poem or two, embellished
with large words, maybe a foreign verse or so thrown in
for good measure. Her methods were well-practiced,
subtle ways to let those around her know she was a lady
of Society, but with a touch of the exotic.

I can see her strumming on her guitar the Spanish
tunes she learned in Pensacola, Florida, and lure you into
her web with tales of meeting Queen Victoria and Prince
Albert. In her Mobile residence, her ever-patient husband,
Dr. Henry S. LeVert, and her enslaved person and
rumored half-sister, Betsey Walton, silently watched as
Octavia worked the room. Octavia had that effect on
people. I see the Salon of her Federal-style home lit with

massive silver candlesticks[2], twirling and spinning through the night air. I see the Victorian chairs and settees filled with Mobile influential families, actors from the local theatre, and those well-known people who traveled to the city to attend one of her "Mondays." She was the ultimate hostess to all visitors during those cotton years of growth.

When she lived in Mobile, her peak of fame and connections took her family to a unique Society level, one well beyond the usual Southern stratosphere. According to Corinne Chadwick Stephens, "Throughout her entire life, these family connections were responsible in a large measure for her social importance, and even, indirectly, for her travels abroad and her literary effort."[3]

However, it is one thing to talk about perfect things, but not talk about things when they were not quite so. Madame Octavia Walton LeVert did not always smile, greet, or meet with the Society she loved. The real Octavia encountered emotional struggle, a challenging home life, and family so intent on using her for their gains, they sometimes put her welfare aside. It is even possible she did the same thing with her own family when her fame grew beyond what most people ever experience.

The Octavia you will meet in this book is different than the one you think you know. She is an endless number of conflicts, but she never intended to be so. How does a Unionist rectify the owning of slaves? How does she survive in a city where most of her friends and neighbors supported the Confederacy, a cause she opposed? You would think this contradiction in personhood would be her downfall, but instead, I feel it is the thing that attracted everyone to her more. It is most certainly why she attracted me as a subject for a book.

When women had limitations placed on them and rarely ventured outside the home, Octavia did the opposite. Yet how did she manage this? Even during her time, the ability to charm was confusing to those who met her. In *Women of the South*, Mary Forrest, a well-known writer herself, recognized Octavia's different impressions conveyed to other minds. This author expressed, "We had read many of the newspaper sketches of her, and listened to the countless relations of her varied accomplishments, but had failed to recognize her specific charm, until a little child, who had been sitting, one day, in her presence, thinking a child's "long, long thoughts," came to whisper softly in our ear: "She isn't a fine lady at all: she is just like me, and I love her!" The darling! Through all the éclat and circumstances of the famous, flush woman, this six-summered soul had discovered and paid tribute to its sweet counterpart."[4]

The reader can glance at her significance in the book by W. Brewer, *Alabama: Her History, Resource, War Record, and Public Men*.[5] In this relatively large printing in 1872, a few glaring points reveal themselves. First, it emphasized men, one only has to read the title to see, and despite this, it does mention a few prominent women. The inclusion of women indicates their achievements were significant. Two of these ladies were from Mobile, Alabama. Augusta

Evans Wilson, who spent her life in Mobile, and Octavia Walton LeVert, who left in dubious circumstances in 1865.

Much like her exodus for various reasons, her information seems to have made the same journey in the years that followed, yet the breadcrumbs still exist. In discovering her, I have traveled to many archives, museums and visited valuable personal collections. I have exhausted all known resources about her with this book's writing, but there must be more to discover. I am sure there are at least two journals, possibly a manuscript and other such relics lurking in an attic or basement somewhere waiting to see the light. If they are not, then the research world should weep, for they have experienced a severe loss.

Those who inherited some of her letters and remains of her wealth live and thrive in Georgia. The city of Pensacola, Florida, still has a few interesting bits it wants to share. Of course, there is a clue of her travels to Europe; her one published book, *Souvenirs of Travel*, exists today online and is available for everyone to use through the public domain.

While Octavia's fame did fade after her death in 1877, she remained a part of Alabama history until around the 1930s when a struggling country no longer needed to hear about socialites and Society but how to survive every day. However, her time has now come once more. She is a significant figure in history whose story still matters, and she needs rescuing from disappearing.

Thank you, reader, for investing a few hours of your time learning about a woman who was unlike any other in a time unlike any other. I hope you to will see the difference she made in the world of those around her, marvel at how she has managed to wrap you around her heart and know of her sincerity despite the circumstances.

Works cited and Notes

1. Octavia Walton LeVert, *Octavia Walton Le Vert Journal 1846-1860*. Journal/Diary. SPR638, Closed Stacks, Alabama Department of Archives. Note: This entry is titled "Stanzas" and dated November 10, 1846.
2. Note: The silver candlesticks are located at the History Museum of Mobile.
3. Corinne Chadwick Stephens, "Madame Octavia Walton Le Vert" (PhD diss., University of Georgia, 1940, Collection #837, University of Georgia Libraries, *John Donald Wade Papers*.
4. Mary Forrest, *Women of the South Distinguished in Literature* (New York: Charles B. Richardson, 1866).
5. W. Brewer, *Alabama: Her History, Resources, War Record, and Public Men* (Tuscaloosa: Willow Publishing Company, 1964).

Paula Lenor Webb

ɪ

Prologue

To Octavia

When wit, and wine, and friends have met
And laughter crowns the festive hour
In vain I struggle to forget
Still does my heart confess thy power
And fondly turn to thee!
But Octavia, do not strive to rob
My heart, of all that soothes its pain
The mournful hope that every throb
Will make it break for thee![1]

A great mystery to modern minds arises when visiting the back parlors at Oakleigh Place in Mobile, Alabama. It is not unusual to see old paintings and portraits in centenarian houses in this city, but artists whose work continues to draw the eye rise above the norm. One such artist was Thomas Sully, and his subject for the painting was Miss Octavia Walton of Pensacola, Florida.

Boucher, Jack. *Oakleigh, House & Slave Quarters, 350 Oakleigh Place, Mobile, Mobile County, AL*. Photograph. Washington, D.C., 1933. Library of Congress Prints and Photographs Division Washington, D.C. 20540 USA http://hdl.loc.gov/loc.pnp/pp.print.

When you learn Sully and Miss Walton's stories, one cannot help but wonder how the painting got there.[2] Octavia entered the world while the United States was still determining what kind of country it was to become. This painting was the start of her influence, her official introduction to Society as a young woman entering adulthood, and Sully had the honor of capturing it.

In Miss Walton's portrait, she dressed in a shimmering pink silk gown that powerfully attracts the eye across the open room, distracting the viewer from the surrounding antiques. The shift appears expensive and well-made, perhaps by the hands of Chloe, her grandmother's slave. Another set of skilled hands might have helped, and they belonged to Betsey Walton, possibly Chloe's granddaughter. She could have been there as a twelve or thirteen-year-old child, perceiving her grandmother make each careful stitch while learning her role in the Walton household. She soon began to care for the young woman to whom she would have no choice but to be a servant for most of her life.

The dress is of the finest quality and shines in the portrait, but Miss Walton is not adorned with any jewelry to indicate established family wealth or position. She was the direct descendant of George Walton, a signer of the Declaration of Independence. Since this rendering was in honor of her formal introduction into Society and her eligibility to wed, maybe adorning her with jewels was a responsibility that fell to the man she married.

She was a blossoming young woman at the time, a mere twenty-three years old, and it bespeaks her power as only the famous portrait artist Thomas Sully could do. Sully titled the work "Miss Walton of Pensacola,"[3] but he already had a reputation for painting those figures in history, Thomas Jefferson, for example, who molded the United States' early years. Why else could Octavia have a portrait made by such an esteemed artist? Like George Washington and Andrew Jackson, and other Sully subjects, Octavia Walton impacted our infant country in her unique way. Her sometimes quiet and sometimes not so quiet influence would reach further than the other ladies he would paint, with one notable exception, Queen Victoria.

Sully, Thomas. Queen Victoria. Photograph. New York, 1838. The Met collection.

In many ways, Octavia, as the Queen of Society in the United States and Victoria as the Queen of England, profoundly influenced the culture in which they lived.

When Octavia traveled to Europe in 1853 and visited with Queen Victoria before the American Civil War, her letters home was published in newspapers all over the country. Readers were in awe of how Octavia handled herself in the British Court, speaking to each foreign dignitary in their native language.

Things of the past often bespeak things of the present, and there has always been a power in placing things where they belong. However, the efforts made by Historic Mobile Preservation Society to bring home to Oakleigh the LeVert collection, which included the painting by Thomas Sully, cannot be overstated. Indeed, Octavia did not have a close relationship with the Roper family or the Irwin family, owners of Oakleigh during her time in the city; still, this fine old home was the best place to house her memories. Octavia Walton LeVert needed to be back in Mobile, where she ruled as queen of its Society for many years, despite her dramatic exit from the city.

A 1953 *Mobile Press-Register* article opens the story of the portrait's return to Mobile, "According to Caldwell Delaney, Mobile Historian and a member of the Historic Society, who unearthed the treasures in a cluttered old house in Kansas City after detective work which took him into several states and over several years, these things were just the cream of a crop of other LeVert relics which included valuable personal papers and the portrait of Edwin Booth which the actor said he liked best."[4]

Only when the niece of an admirer who built the collection died were arrangements for the sale.

Correspondence between Mrs. Lucile L. Ghormley, who inherited the priceless items and lacked the proper facilities to care for or display them in her home, and Mrs. John F. Lyle, then president of Historical Mobile Preservation Society (HMPS), showed great insight and stated, "these things belong in Mobile."[5] While the Sully portrait was the most valuable piece in the collection, included in the bundle of items was the portrait of Octavia's mother, Sally Walton, by Rembrandt Peale, and the woman responsible for educating the Octavia known today. The collection included two silver Christening mugs and three miniatures of Octavia and her two surviving daughters, plus the small black inlaid writing desk Octavia used to write her famous book, *Souvenirs of Travel*. In 1954, these items were returned, and a part of Madame Octavia Walton LeVert finally was in the city where she had once spent the majority of her years.

The Thomas Sully painting is the most substantial piece in the bundle and is rather large and looming. Like all portraitists, Sully charged his clients based on the size of the work. The painting's size indicates Octavia had some wealth at the time, possibly the money she inherited from her grandmother, Dorothy Walton's recent death. Despite the painting's massiveness, in reality, Octavia was a very petite woman. One may surmise she was sitting on a stool since she gave an even stare to the painter. A writer's observation, but in discovering the hidden messages all too common with these sorts of paintings, it seems Sully's focus was not upon his subject's hair or dress but on her eyes. He seems to make her eyes the direction of the work; they are almost piercing; their gaze hints of the brilliant mind within.

There are other points the viewer can easily see through a further study of the painting. The subject does not appear formal but rather casual. The Spanish guitar she is holding indicates an ability to play the instrument, but she is not strumming; perhaps she was not a professional player. She is sitting as if away from the painter, not upfront. The young Miss Octavia Celestie Valentine Walton sat on a simple red chair. She appears relaxed amongst a great countryside, possibly Saratoga Springs or a close approximation by Sully, complete with a large oak tree and an expanse of water behind. In reality, she was enduring a rather chilly 1833 Washington D.C. winter, and she spent those days either in Sully's studio or at the gallery at Congress.[6]

However, do not be distracted from the lack of authenticity that surrounded her. Instead, it would be best if you took in the brightness of the light that shines on her face, her luminous white skin tones, the soft curve of her body, sloping shoulders, and small waist. She displays a perfect complexion from the peak of her head to the curve of her shoulder. She was the focus of the painting, and she revealed a unique yet straightforward smile. She was intelligent, and it shined through in this work of art.

What you see was a mere reflection of what there was about her and the world she knew. Yet during her life, it was effortless to discover her because she was always in the newspapers. She was a well-known writer and the ultimate hostess at home and abroad. She was well-loved and celebrated until she was not. The Civil War changed everything, and a note from the Union commander who took over the city of Mobile would seal her fate.

She was indeed the Belle of the United States, America's Belle, but the Civil War eliminated that version of Society forever. Octavia, her daughters, and Betsey, even, would be among the last.

Works Cited & Notes

1. Edgar Allen Poe, "To Octavia," The Edgar Allen Poe Society of Baltimore, last modified March 13, 2011.
2. Note: Oakleigh House is located in Mobile, Alabama at 300 Oakleigh Place, Mobile, AL 36604. The painting is owned and maintained by the Historic Mobile Preservation Society.
3. Edward Biddle and Mantle Fielding, *Life and Works of Thomas Sully (1783 - 1872)* (Philadelphia: Wichersham Press, 1921). Note: The title of the of the painting by Thomas Sully indicates she was not married. In addition, at the time of the painting, Florida was a very young state, and Pensacola was where her father, George Walton, Jr., was the Governor of the West Florida Territory (previous to statehood).
4. Untitled Printed article located at the Minnie Mitchell Archives, Oakleigh Place, Mobile, AL. Note: The painting of Edwin Booth is located at Oakleigh.
5. *Correspondence from the Historic Mobile Preservation Society to Lucile L. Ghormley*, January 15, 1954, Minnie Mitchell Archives, *Le Vert Collection*. Note: HMPS purchased the Le Vert Collection from Mrs. Ghormley for $4000.
6. Elswyth Thane, *Mount Vernon is Ours: The Story of its Preservation* (New York: Duell, Sloan and Pearce, 1966).

Such a Woman

The Life of Madame Octavia Walton LeVert

Unveiling long-hidden evidence reveals fascinating, unknown facts about Octavia Walton LeVert, a singular woman.

Paula Lenor Webb

Chapter 1

Generation Before

When in the Course of human events
It becomes necessary for one people to dissolve
The political bands which have connected them with another
And to assume among the powers of earth,
The separate and equal station to which
The Laws of Nature and of Nature's God entitle them,
A decent respect to the opinions of mankind requires that
They should declare the causes which impel them to the separation.[1]

The United States of America started as a bundle of British Colonies whose young people were still indebted to a country they had never seen. Before the significant year of 1776, the parents and grandparents of this progeny immigrated and longingly remembered their home countries, complete with the legal system. This new generation of those born in American colonies did not share these unswerving feelings and did not feel the same loyalty. As if the resenting young group of individuals was not enough of a catalyst to challenge England, they began imposing taxes. These young colonists felt they would receive little if any benefits.

Currier, N. Destruction of Tea at Boston Harbor. Photograph. Washington, D.C., 1846. Library of Congress. Library of Congress Prints and Photographs Division Washington, D.C. 20540 USA http://hdl.loc.gov/loc.pnp/pp.print.

Taxes placed on everyday necessities provided reminders of who controlled the colonies—the Sugar Act of 1764 established duties on importing sugar. The Stamp Act of 1765, of which Georgia was the only colony that complied with the Act, required newspapers in America to be printed on paper produced in Britain and stamped with a revenue stamp. Through the 1770s, tensions resulted in the Boston Massacre, the Boston Tea Party, and the Intolerable Acts; Parliament's response to the famous Tea Party moved the colonies towards revolt. Those next-generation Americans were seekers of something else, something greater than themselves that would last beyond their lifetime. The Walton family and all their relations fell into this category.

George Walton, Octavia Walton LeVert's grandfather, was the rebel who led the Walton family to social prominence. He entered the world on December 1749 in Cumberland County, Virginia; his birth circumstances gave little indication of what his future would become. The episode was rather sad in one respect; he was born without a father. Robert Walton, Jr. must have had an inkling of his impending death, for he wrote a will to manage his family's affairs before George's birth. According to the book, *Geo. Walton of Meadow Garden*, "George's father's will in Cumberland County referred to his unborn son as "the child my wife now goes with." George Walton, Sr. was named for the uncle, who over sawed his education, but did not play a fatherly role.[2]

When young George was sixteen years old, he began his apprenticeship under carpenter Christopher Ford, but Ford soon realized George did not enjoy this life. He noticed George was more interested in studying law. One famous story is as follows, "Unable during the day to give any attention to his books he read faithfully by night, his light being obtained from light-wood knots burned in the fireplace." George was relieved of his apprenticeship and moved to Savannah to study law. He was admitted to the bar in 1773, and in 1774 was employed to legally advise in many important cases.[3]

According to the book *Signers of the Declaration*, "among those who were prominent in those germinal revolutionary movements...He was President of the Council of Safety, Secretary of the First Provincial Congress of Georgia, and delegate of the Second Continental Congress, which met in Philadelphia in 1776."[4] He joined the Liberty Boys, a group openly protesting the British in Savannah and the surrounding area.

George Walton and twenty-five other men entertaining freedom from Britain met at Savannah's Tondee's tavern on August 10th, 1774. According to Jones and Dutcher, "When several gentlemen attempted to go in, the tavern keeper, who stood at the door with a list in his hand, refused them admittance because their names were not on that list." When word of this assembly reached the Governor of Savannah, he declared their group was punishable by law. On that fateful day, Georgia decided to join with ideas expressed in the other American colonies and began to participate in the adoption of measures that would bring about the Revolutionary War.[5]

Among this group of protesters, George Walton quickly rose in position, and in 1776, he joined Button Gwinnett and Lyman Hall as delegates to the Second Continental Congress. A letter Walton wrote to Col. Lachlan McIntosh on June 17th, 1776, shows how eager he was to join other patriots in declaring freedom for the United States, "He had been detained...with fever while on his way to Philadelphia, but he rejoiced that he was "not too late for the great American question if question it may now be called." The spirit of Virginia inspired him, and he exclaimed, "O, America! Did this happy spirit equally animate all thy sons, the inhabitants of all Europe, transformed into devils, could not hurt thee!"[6]

George Walton Sr. was a signer of the Declaration of Independence. Binns, John. *Declaration of Independence.* Photograph. Washington, D.C., 1819. Library of Congress Prints and Photographs Division Washington, D.C. 20540 USA http://hdl.loc.gov/loc.pnp/pp.print.

While George worked to form a revolution, he was also seeking a wife, and he set his eyes on Dorothy Camber. He could have known her and her family in Savannah.[7] During this time, Dorothy blossomed into a beautiful young woman, but she had much more to offer. When Thomas Camber, her father, died, Dorothy was around fifteen years old. She was said to be very mature for her years and enticed George Walton, who was twenty-five years old at the time.[8] Dorothy, unlike George, was from a longtime slave-owning family. She would inherit from her father's estate three slaves: Newberry, Polladore, and Chloe. After the estate was settled, Dorothy would receive little else.[9]

When George learned of Thomas Camber's death, he quickly returned to Savannah and paid his respects in hopes of pursuing Dorothy. According to Leora Sutton, "She was described as a decorous, posed, well educated, mature teenager...George felt an urgency to protect the attractive young lady. As a token of his affection for her, he presented her with an oval, gold locket with a cross on

top, engraved on the back where she would wear it next to her throat, "To Dorothy from George 1776."[10]

Painting of George Walton, Sr., Octavia Walton LeVert's grandfather. Peale, Charles Willson. *George Walton, American, 1749(?)–1804.* Photograph. New Haven, 1777. Yale University Art Gallery.

He followed this gift with another priceless heirloom. In the fall of 1777, he had a miniature self-portrait painted by one of the Peale artists for two dollars, his bride's wedding gift. The priceless piece became the most-known portrait of George Walton, Sr. At some point,

George asked for Dorothy's hand in marriage, and she said, "Yes." George married Dorothy at her family home in September 1778.[11]

Their marriage was soon interrupted. England was not quick to give up on the possession of the American colonies. In 1778, they set their sights on recapturing Savannah, Georgia. When British soldiers appeared within the city's view, the town's atmosphere quickly went from theaters and balls to the citizens proceeding in haste to evacuate the women and defend their homes.[12]

One of the harrowing stories Dorothy Walton, Octavia's grandmother, told was when the British first began their attack on Savannah, George arranged passage for Dorothy, family members, and enslaved on a ship to South Carolina to protect their lives. Dorothy, like many women during the Revolutionary War, became a refugee. It disrupted their life as a family before it started.[13] George Walton remained in Savannah to fight the British attack. On January 9th, 1778, he was commissioned as colonel of the First Georgia Regiment of Militia and a part of the Battle of Savannah. He found himself posted on Savannah's south common to guard the road leading the Great Ogeechee ferry. George was familiar with all the ways of travel in the area, possibly due to his days as a member of the Liberty Boys, and he knew of a secluded path in the swamp area southwest of town.[14]

According to *The Walton House*, General Howe did not pay any attention to George's warning and chose to reinforce where they expected the enemy. Walton proceeded to protect his post with only one hundred men. The English, tipped off by an old enslaved man, learned of the seldom-used path. When they gained a strategic hill, they encountered Walton's men. According to Leora Sutton, "While leading his men on horseback, George Walton received a severe wound in his thigh. Two of his men helped him to a porch of a house occupied by two Jewish ladies who bound his bleeding leg. Two Englishmen pursued him and drew their bayonets in an all-out attempt to spear Walton, but, remaining as calm as possible, he gave the Masonic sign. One of the two bayonet men was a Mason. He called for an officer who rescued Walton and took him to the English surgeons."[15]

Walton wrote his young wife from his bed of pain on January 4th, 1779, telling her, "I was very happy to hear just this minute by a flag that you have safely arrived in Carolina...The day you left your brother and myself, my dear Dolly [Dorothy], in the chances of it I received a wound in the thigh. The bone is broke, but of cures of this kind are quite common. I have every possible comfort from my conquerors - their hospital surgeon to attend me... And they tell me they expect to see me do well. Be therefore of good spirits; and let me not hear by every flag that you are inconsolable, which will only operate to depress mine. At any rate, you ought to recollect that in these troublesome times you have no right to expect a life of superior tranquility to your neighbors... God bless you, my dear, and remember that you are sincerely loved by a man who wishes to make honor and reputation the rule of all his actions."[16]

George Walton sent the letter to his wife, neglecting to mention that the surgeons suggested his leg's amputation. They decided to delay the amputation for a few hours, and the skilled surgeons were able to save his leg.[17]

Walton recovered as a British prisoner of war in the town of Sunbury, forty miles south of Savannah. His wife, Dorothy, and her enslaved could return from exile to be with him while he recovered as a prisoner of war. Walton's recovery from the dangerous wound took almost a year before he was released from doctors' care, and he was lame for the rest of his life.[18]

Towards the end of 1779, George Walton wrote a letter to John Houston, seeking a prisoner of war exchange. He told him about his wound, indicating he was hoping to be out of danger but still confined to the bed and expected to be so for some time since an injury of this sort took time to heal. He also asked Houston to help the peaceful exchange of his men on board prison ships.[19]

General George Washington felt George Walton was valuable and arranged an exchange in October 1779, and he was moved from his British confinement in Sunbury to the American camp in Savannah. The camp did not have accommodations for Dorothy and her enslaved, so arrangements were made to return to her family in North Carolina by ship.[20] Dorothy was probably brokenhearted to leave her husband but did so to protect her life and those of her servants.

George Washington. Photograph. Washington, D.C., 1854. Library of Congress Prints and Photographs Division Washington, D.C. 20540 USA http://hdl.loc.gov/loc.pnp/pp.print. Art Gallery.

Another tale from the Revolutionary War Dorothy Walton must have shared with her grandchildren was when the ship on which she and her enslaved, Clarissa,

Chloe, and Chloe's son, Charles, rode was captured by the English and became a war prize. When those who took over the ship discovered Dorothy's identity, they allowed her to keep Chloe and sold her Chloe's son for five English guineas. Clarissa was separated from Dorothy and sold.[21] Dorothy Walton and her remaining enslaved were British captives on the island of St. Eustatia, where she was taunted by her captors to return to England and abandon her husband and the American cause. She held firm, and her entourage was exchanged for two British Colonels and sent back to Georgia.[22]

Dorothy Walton did not know the ship she was on when she left Georgia sank as it swept to sea. Mary Winter commented, "In the meantime, it was reported that she had been drowned at sea because the sloop in which she started from Charleston had gone down in the hurricane. The news brought much sorrow to her many friends, who later rejoiced as at a miracle when they learned that she had been saved because of the transfer to the British ship."[23]

Shortly after George Walton's release from prison, he was appointed Governor of Georgia in 1779. After only two months in the position, he was re-elected to the Continental Congress.[24] The Walton's, now united, returned to Savannah but did not have the home or possessions they held previously. George's appointment to the Continental Congress took him and Dorothy to Philadelphia. She told Octavia of being awakened one night by the town watchman. He yelled joyously to anyone who would hear, "Post midnight and a pleasant good morning. Cornwallis is taken!"[25] The Walton's encountered great victories, but also significant challenges. They welcomed their first son, Thomas Walton, not long after the war.

George Walton, Sr., moved his growing family to Georgia's Plantation Belt, where most slaveholders and enslaved people lived in central Georgia.[26] He had made many attempts to support his wife and son in Savannah, but he returned to his law practice. His attempt to profit from a rice plantation did not work out. He decided to sell everything in Savannah and moved to Augusta, where his family remained for many generations. Dorothy would give birth to a second son, George Walton, Jr., on January 19th, 1789.[27]

George Sr. was surrounded by his own family as well as that of his wife. Augusta was quickly growing into a commercial hub. The doorway to the new unsettled land to the west and the jumping-off place where settlers followed the old trails blazed by Native Americans and traders. Augusta was designated the capital of Georgia. After the war, Georgia expanded from a strip of land along the ocean to a virtual empire, stretching to the Mississippi River. The city of Augusta continued to grow, and by 1790, the population was over a thousand people.[28]

When George Walton moved to Augusta, this became his chosen home, and he wanted to influence it and shape it into a significant part of Georgia. Edward Cashin stated, "Since 1779, when he was Governor in

Augusta, Walton had envisioned a rapidly expanding back-country with Augusta as its hub."[29]

Meadow Garden, the home of George Walton, Sr. and his family. Johnston, Frances Benjamin. *Meadow Garden, Augusta, Richmond County, Georgia.* Photograph. Washington, D.C., 1944. Library of Congress Prints and Photographs Division Washington, D.C. 20540 USA http://hdl.loc.gov/loc.pnp/pp.print.

While he and his family lived in various locations in and around Augusta, he finally built his home, Meadow Garden. Martha Belton recounted, "The farm consisted of two hundred acres of land, and no doubt gained its name from the level meadow of which it was a part. He surrounded the place with a grove of mulberry trees and filled the modest home with books."[30]

One of the most significant events in the history of the Walton family and a story passed down was George Washington's visit to Augusta in May of 1791 when George Walton, Augusta's first citizen, greeted him. According to *The Story of Augusta*, "The President noted in his journal that "Judge Walton" came out to meet him in the company of officials he named only by title. Walton's name headed a committee including John Meals, Thomas Cumming, Peter Carnes, and Seaborn Jones, who greeted Washington on behalf of the people of Augusta."[31]

Washington was the guest of honor at many dining events throughout Augusta. Mrs. Telfair hosted a ball that the President attended and a reception for the President, where Washington duly noted the presence of "between 60 and 70 well-dressed ladies." Among these ladies in attendance certainly had to be Dorothy Walton, Octavia's grandmother.[32]

In 1796, Dorothy had experienced many successes and tragedies. George's work for the United States frequently took him away from home, leaving Dorothy to handle home affairs. George wrote Dorothy a letter from Philadelphia on January 26th, 1796, indicating how much she had matured during her years as his wife. She was now directing business affairs at home, sending a statement of such to her husband, and he was content with her management skills.[33] A letter to George Walton Jr. in 1801, while he was away at Hampden Sidney School in Prince Edward, Virginia, indicated Walton's efforts to work Meadow Garden as a farm, despite past struggles.

Meadow Garden was finally prosperous, with seventy acres of excellent corn and ninety acres of the best corn.[34]

Judge George Walton was at the peak of his career. He was known to issue fatherly advice that included urging Georgians not to practice gouging eyes and biting noses when there was a disagreement. Clearly, this was a problem in this area because it came to the notice of a visiting Scotsman, "In their quarrels, they use the horrible custom of gouging (a mode of busting out the eye with the thumb) and hence the number of people with one eye only to be met within the Interior of this State & in Carolina."[35]

George Walton, Sr.'s last days were not nearly as grand as some of his actions in life. According to the *Augusta Chronicle*, George Walton Sr. died unexpectedly on February 2nd, 1804, at fifty-five. His illness was relatively short, but those around him could see that something was not right. The death of his oldest son, Thomas, could have made his condition worse in 1803.[36]

Thomas Camber Walton, the firstborn son, was noted as one who had genius, talents, and agreeable manners, died unmarried, in 1803, as a young lawyer in Augusta.[37] There is no mention of George Jr., his namesake, but one could imagine his feelings regarding this, even at such a young age. George Walton, Sr. breathed his last at Meadow Garden and was buried at the plantation of his nephew, Robert Watkins. Forty years later, his body was re-interred beneath the Signers Monument in Augusta, Georgia.[38]

George Walton, Sr., had been elected to Congress six times, to the U.S. Senate, and he had served as Governor of Georgia twice. He had been selected as a Judge four times.[39]

Dorothy Walton had lost her husband and her oldest son in rapid succession when her remaining son, George Walton, Jr., was only fifteen years old. On April 2nd, 1804, she would receive twenty-five thousand dollars from his estate. In today's money, it equals between six-hundred and fifty thousand to seven-hundred and fifty thousand dollars.[40]

Dorothy's skills at managing money and estates benefitted her survival, and that of her son, George Jr. It was standard practice for the male heads of the household to handle estates, but young George was gradually showing himself to be a poor manager of personal finance.[41]

After the death of her husband, George Sr., and her oldest son, Thomas, Dorothy had her only remaining child, George Walton, Jr. Since her husband left her enough money to survive upon in the will but not enough to maintain their lifestyle for an extended period, she must have been dependent upon her Walker and Walton family relations to remain at Meadow Garden, the family home northwest of Augusta, Georgia.

In a letter from Dorothy to George as he was setting up to begin his studies at Princeton University in New Jersey on September 9th, 1805, she encouraged him and advised, "We must look up to him who has promised to raise up friends to the fatherless and widow who put their trust in him." She further lets him know that Sally Minge Walker, the woman he would one day marry and become the mother of Octavia and Robert, was with her, as well, and joined with her in love.[42]

The sixteen-year-old George Walton Jr. began his studies at the University in November of 1805. He was a member of the Cliosophic Society and progressed to the rank of Sophomore in 1806. He would not make it to the position of Junior. On March 31st, 1807, he participated in what was known at Princeton as the Rebellion of 1807.[43]

When three fellow students were suspended, one-hundred and fifty students, including Walton, signed a petition asserting that the faculty had not appropriately acted according to the crime. The faculty felt the students were trying to control the governing of the college. According to James H. Moorhead, "When angry, jeering students stomped out; the faculty regarded them as part of the illicit conspiracy, took down their names, and promptly suspended them - 126 in all. Some of the rebels smashed doors and windows, armed themselves with clubs and stones, and prepared to defend themselves against the local militia who had been summoned to eject the rioters."[44] Instead, the faculty decided to send the militia away and closed the school until the start of the summer session. Though there were a few students who repented and were allowed back to complete their degree, George was not one of them.

Dorothy Walton had to cope with her son when he returned home from Princeton in 1807. He returned to

Augusta, Georgia, and studied to become a lawyer. He prepared for entry into his chosen profession of law through apprenticeship but interrupted it briefly to marry Sarah (Sally), Minge Walker.[45]

George Walton, Jr. and Sally Minge Walker were married on January 10th, 1809. Sarah Minge Walker was the seventeen-year-old daughter of one of Georgia's most distinguished jurists, neighbors, and friends of George Walton, Sr. and Dorothy. Corinne Chadwick Stephens commented, "By all accounts, the new Mrs. Walton was an exceptional person. Beautiful, witty, and intelligent, she was a member of one of the proudest Georgia families. The Walkers, like the Waltons, have come from Virginia to Georgia around 1750 and have settled near Augusta. Sally Minge's father, George Walker, was a member of the law firm of Walker and Walker, had married Elizabeth Talbot."[46]

After the wedding, George moved his new wife into his home, Meadow Garden, with himself and his mother. The following December, the Acts of the Georgia General Assembly published in the Augusta Chronicle listed George Walton among those admitted to ". . . plead and practice in any court of law or equity in this state."[47]

George settled into a steady life by working as a local attorney and representing Richmond County in the Georgia Legislature, serving under his wife's uncle, Freedman Walker.[48] He served in the Georgia Legislature as the Representative for Richmond County but still survived off the fame of his father. George's future

20

decisions revealed his longing to achieve fame and notoriety equal to his father, but he was not the same type of man.

Works cited and Notes

1. Thomas Jefferson, *Declaration of Independence*. Manuscript/Transcription. National Archives Digital Collection, *America's Founding Documents*. Last modified July 24, 2020. Note: Octavia's grandfather, George Walton, signed the Declaration of Independence with Button Gwinnett and Lyman Hall as representatives for Georgia.
2. Marie Derry DeLamer, *Geo.Walton of Meadow Garden*, (The Georgia State Society: Daughters of the American Revolution, published date unknown).
3. Brenner, "Master of Meadow Garden."
4. John Bakeless and Katherine Bakeless, *Signers of the Declaration* (Boston: Houghton Mifflin, 1969), 297.
5. Charles C. Jones and Salem Dutcher, *Memorial History of Augusta, Georgia: From its Settlement in 1735 to the Close of the Eighteenth Century* (Augusta: D. Mason, 1890).
6. George Walton, *George Walton to Col. Lachlan McIntosh* in "Madame Octavia Walton LeVert 1810 – 1877," ed. Caldwell Delaney (Master's Thesis, University of Alabama, 1952), 17; Note: According to the dissertation, it is part of the Josephine Walton Collection. Miss Walton copied these letters when they were in the possession of Madame LeVert's grandson, George Walton Reab, but their present location is not known. As of November 2019, the location of this material is still not known.
7. Mary C. Winter, "Dorothy Camber Walton, Signer's Wife had a Romantic Life Marked by Great Adventure," *Augusta Chronicle*, September 5, 1954, 3. *GeneologyBank*. Note: Also a part of: Mylius, Virginia S. *Our Southern Cousins*. n.d. Online. June 2nd 2019.
8. Winter, "Dorothy Camber Walton," 3.
9. Leora M. Sutton, *Walton House* (Pensacola: Elite Mimeographing Service, 1968),; *Will of Thomas Camber Will, 1772, Will Book* Vol. 16, 1774-1779, 113, Court of Records, St. Peter's Parish Court House.
10. Sutton, *Walton House*.

11. Sutton, *Walton House; Book of Realty H, Folios,* 168-172, Clerk's Office of Superior Court, Richmond County Courthouse.

12. Sutton, *Walton House.*

13. Linda K. Kerber, *Women of the Republic: Intellect and Ideology in Revolutionary America* (Chapel Hill: University of North Carolina Press, 1997), 47.

14. Sutton, *Walton House.* Note: Personal note found in the collection of Madame Octavia LeVert. As of 2019, this collection appears to be lost. The only record is in this book.

15. Sutton, *Walton House.* Note: Personal note found in the collection of Madame Octavia LeVert. As of 2019, this collection appears to be lost. The only record is in this book.

16. Brenner, "Master of Meadow Garden".

17. *Letter to Savannah,* January 4, 1779. Letter. University of West Florida, *Satterfield Collection.* Note: Frances Gibson Satterfield, author of *Madame LeVert, A Biography of Octavia Walton LeVert,* visited Augusta, Georgia and accessed the collection of Josephine Walton in the 1970s. In this collection was a scrapbook and Satterfield made copies of the pages in the scrapbook. The copy of this letter is housed at the University of West Florida Library. The location of the scrapbook and the original letter is unknown as of November 2019.

18. Sutton, *Walton House.*

19. Sutton, *Walton House.* Note: According to the transcribed letter in the book. She cites the <u>Chronicle and Constitutionalist</u>, (Augusta, GA), "Interesting Documents of more than a Hundred Years Ago. George Walton of Georgia, Letters Furnished by Madame Octavia Walton LeVert, Article appeared during the summer of 1877. The original article cannot be found at the time of this note. The actual letters were at one time in possession of Octavia Walton LeVert. According to family history she inherited them from her grandmother, Dorothy Walton. The current location of these letters is also unknown."

20. Sutton, *Walton House.*

21. Sutton, *Walton House.*

22. Sutton, *Walton House.*

23. Winter, "Dorothy Camber Walton," 3.

24. Charles C. Jones Jr,. *Biographical Sketches of the Delegates from Georgia to the Continental Congress* (Cambridge: Houghton, Mifflin and Company, 1891), 168-198.

25. Sutton, *Walton House.*

26. Sutton, *Walton House.* Note: Sutton writes this information is located in the unpublished personal notes of Octavia Walton LeVert. The author can only assume this is part of the Josephine Walton collection, but the location of the collection is unknown as of November 2019.

27. Sam Carnley, "Who Was George Walton Jr, The Man Whose Name the Florida County of Walton Shares?," *Walton Relations & History* 8, no. 1 (October 2016): 2-6.

28. Edward J. Cashin, *Story of Augusta* (Spartanburg: Reprint Co., 1991).

29. Cashin, *Story of Augusta.*

30. Martha Brown Benton, *Sketch of Meadow Garden Home of George Walton Signer of the Declaration of Independence* (Augusta: Daughters of the American Revolution, Augusta Chapter, 1922).

31. Cashin, *Story of Augusta.*

32. Cashin, *Story of Augusta.*

33. Sutton, *Walton House.*

34. *George Walton Jr. to George Walton Sr,* July 31, 1801. Letter. University of West Florida Archives, *America's Founding Documents.* Note: A copy of the letter is located at the University of West Florida Library, Satterfield Collection. The location of the original note is unknown.

35. Raymond A. Mohl, "A Scotsman Visits Georgia in 1811," *Georgia Historical Quarterly* (Summer 1971): 259-274, JSTOR.

36. Marie D. De Lamar, *George Walton of Meadow Garden* (Augusta: Georgia State Society Daughters of the American Revolution, 1979).

37. Virginia S. Mylius, "Our Southern Cousins". n.d. Accessed June 2, 2019.

38. Cashin, *Story of Augusta.*

39. Lucy Henderson Horton, "Family History," *Press of the News,* 1922.

40. Sutton, *Walton House.*

41. Sutton, *Walton House.*

42. Sutton, *Walton House.* Note: According to the transcribed letter in Sutton's book, page 15. She cites the <u>Chronicle and Constitutionalist,</u> (Augusta, GA), "Interesting Documents of more than a Hundred Years Ago. George Walton of Georgia, Letters Furnished by Madame Octavia Walton LeVert, Article appeared during the summer of 1877. The original article cannot be found at the time of this note. The actual letters were at one time in possession of Octavia Walton LeVert. According to family history

she inherited them from her grandmother, Dorothy Walton. The current location of these letters is also unknown.

43. *Walton, George (1809)*. Ledger. Princeton University Library, *Undergratue Alumni Records, 19th Century*. Note: The author contacted the Princeton University Library and had copies made of the records. They are in her personal collection.

44. James H. Moorhead, *Princeton Seminary in American Religion and Culture* (Grand Rapids: Eerdmans, 2012).

45. Carnley, "Who Was George Walton Jr," 2-6.

46. Stephens, *Madame Octavia Walton Le Vert*.

47. Carnley, "Who Was George Walton Jr," 2-6.

48. "For the State Legislatue," *Augusta Chronicle*, September 29, 1810, *GenealogyBank*.

Chapter 2

And so She Came into the World

I saw on the top of a mountain high,
A gem that shone like fire by night
It seemed like a star that had left the sky,
And dropped to sleep on the lonely height.[1]

Augusta, Georgia, was a flourishing city in its early years. Politicians, judges and lawyers realized this and moved to the city with their families. The fledgling United States spread outward from the original thirteen colonies to the South and the West. Thomas Jefferson's Louisiana Purchase on May 2nd, 1803, nearly doubled the size of the country, causing a rush to newly discovered lands by citizens. Augusta was one of the routes taken to the undiscovered West.[2]

One visitor, John Melish, traveled through the city in 1809 and remarked, "The inhabitants are in general well-informed and have a considerable taste for literature. They are affable in their deportment and polite and hospitable to strangers."[3] The feeling of acceptance appeared to be common amongst travelers encouraging people to choose the same route to the wilds of America.

Augusta also played an intermediate role as an early capital of Georgia and its growth and development were supported by those traveling West to newly acquired portions of the country. People passing through Augusta purchased the supplies they needed to experience this new world. They traveled to exotic locations such as the wilds of Alabama, Missouri, and other places beyond the Mississippi River.

The Walton family survived in this environment after losing the family patriarch and the oldest son, Thomas. Dorothy Walton managed to maintain the Meadow Garden estate but the details are scarce. She most likely had help from her family, and according to Laura F. Edwards, "Wealthy families willed sizable estates to wives and daughters throughout the Antebellum Period." Among them were widows appointed as guardians of property for their children."[4] Dorothy did not look to remarry after the death of George Walton, Sr. After her son's problems at Princeton, he interned in a law office in Augusta, and became a lawyer. He was already rumored to have disagreeable habits, but the most concerning one was gambling.

On August 11th, 1810, a beautiful baby girl graced the Walton family. Octavia Celeste Valentine Walton was born at Belle Vue, the estate of Sally's mother, Elizabeth Talbot Walker, just outside Augusta in the Sand Hill area.[5] Belle Vue remained in the hands of the family for many

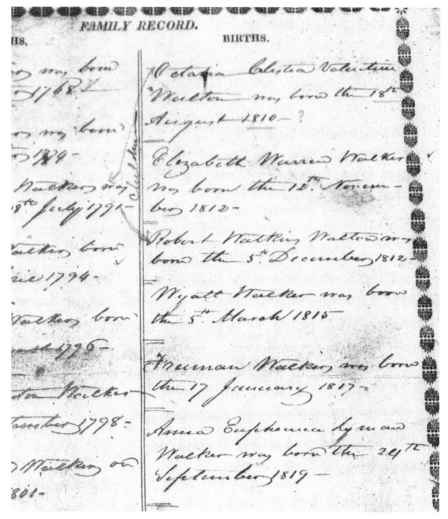

Walker Family Bible where they listed the birth of Octavia Walton LeVert and Robert Watkins Walton. Walker Family Bible - Births. 2019. Photograph. University of West Florida Archives and West Florida History Center. Satterfield, Frances Gibson Collection. Also in courtesy of Betsy Evans.

years, eventually under the care of Sally's uncle, Freeman Walker. He considered it his summer residence until November 1826 when he sold the house and property to

President John Quincy Adams for the new location of the Augusta Arsenal.[6]

While the Walton family most certainly celebrated the birth of Octavia, an official announcement did not appear in the *Augusta Chronicle*, the local newspaper. Little information concerning the early years of many people, much less Octavia, existed during the early 1800s. However, readers can surmise a few things from the information discovered.

Sally Walton chose a unique name for her firstborn daughter, not as common as the "Elizabeths" and "Sarahs" of past family relations. She wanted something different for her daughter and chose a name accordingly. According to Virginia Tatnall, "She was named by her mother after the Roman Octavia, the beloved and noble sister of Augustus and the deserted wife of Marc Anthony, and was taught to revere the beauty of a character that possessed, as Pope Pius IX said, when Madame Le Vert told him for whom she was named, 'every virtue and grace should adorn a woman.'"[7]

The confirmation of her unique name lies within a loved and well-worn copy of the book, *Female Biography*, by Mary Hays, published in 1807.[8] The inside page, discolored from time, still carries a powerful inscription, "Octavia C.V. Walton from Her affectionate Gran Mother - Mrs. Eliza Walker - Belle Vue Nov 1821."[9]

Inside the book, Female Biography, the inscription to Octavia from her grandmother, Eliza. Inscription to Octavia from Eliza. 2019. Photograph.
Augusta University, Greenblatt Library,
Historical Collections and Archives.

These lines bespeak the educational level of the women of the Walker family; it is when the page is flipped to the Table of Contents and two very special references are checked clearly with a faint grey pencil mark, "Octavia, wife to Antony" and "Octavia, wife to Nero." It is hard not to see the influence of the women within the Walker and Walton family. Octavia kept this book with her as she journeyed from Augusta, Georgia, to Pensacola, Florida as a young girl, and all points between. Like her, it eventually found its way home to Augusta.

ourable Roger North, esq. whom she left her sole executor. She had made a valuable collection of books, which, after her death, were presented by her only surviving brother, the lord North and Grey, to the parochial library, at Rougham in Norfolk, founded by the honourable Roger North, for the use of that parish and the neighbouring clergy.

Ballard's British Ladies—Biographium Fœmineum.

OCTAVIA.

WIFE TO ANTONY.

OCTAVIA, grand-niece of Julius Cæsar, and sister to Augustus, was the daughter of Caius Octavius and Atia, Romans of distinguished birth and virtue. She received in the house of her parents a strict and exemplary education; she was early accustomed to control her feelings, to discipline her imagination, to sacrifice her inclinations to others, and to impart the benefits she received. The modesty of her deportment, her unaffected ... the beauty of her person, her virtues and

Inside the book, Octavia wife of Anthony.2019. Photograph. Augusta University, Greenblatt Library, Historical Collections and Archives.

The level of education achieved by both Walton children was a testament to Sally Walton's and Eliza Walker's character as their history unfolds. There is an understanding Sally Walton was formally educated, a situation designated for elite women.[10] It is also possible she attended a private school for females because of the skills she had and those she taught to Octavia. According to Chirhart and Wood, "All children at such schools were taught reading, writing, and arithmetic, but beyond those rudimentary skills, the curriculum became more gendered. For the young girls of prosperous families, specialization could be pursued in needlework...dancing, music, and languages."[11] Sally was also well-read and shared her love of learning with her daughter and son.

In 1811, George Walton was elected to represent Richmond County in the Georgia House of Representatives and maintained some honorable man's semblance. In a paradox, during this same time, he was sued by Seth John Clayborn to repay a debt and sold off segments Meadow Garden property to satisfy the debt.[12] His method of dealing with debt became a common theme for George Walton, Jr., much to the family's frustration.

The Walton family participated in the War of 1812 and worked to keep the Meadow Garden tract of land from being taken by debtors. Alex Juhan, a person seeking repayment from George Walton Jr., posted in the *Augusta Chronicle* that he had claimed the land. George was quick to post in the same paper that Juhan's claim was false and was "seen with some little astonishment by the subscriber."[13]

The Walton's continued to live by selling parts of Meadow Garden land and their enslaved to family members, keeping slave families intact. In one instance, Sally sold an enslaved girl named Pratt to a family member, Augustus G. Walton, covering some of the debt incurred by her husband. In the same year, George levied four of his enslaved people, Jim, Elsey, Dianah, and Tener, to cover another debt. This was described as "to satisfy sundry executions" to Zachariah Lamar.[14] George's behavior continued to negatively impact the family.

On November 12th, 1812, the Walton's had a son, Robert Watkins Walton, named in honor of George's grandfather. According to Caldwell Delaney, "The children grew up in the aristocratic environment of Belle Vue and its neighboring estates. Most of the settlers on the Sand Hills were Virginians, and they had brought with them to Georgia the Old Dominion's tradition of gracious living. The Sand Hills cottage, of which Belle Vue was an example, was not pretentious, but it was graceful in proportion and refined in design. Furnished with old family pieces, it was comfortable and sometimes even elegant."[15]

Sharing a home with both grandparents, Octavia and Robert were well cared for and grew into healthy children. It is also apparent they both showed early signs of mental quickness. It was expected with Robert since his father and grandfather were prominent within the Augusta area. The discovery of Octavia's cleverness as a child seemed to be noted as different from what was expected of a girl. Caldwell Delaney continued, "Octavia developed into an attractive child with golden hair and blue eyes. She had inherited her mother's vivacity and her father's charm of manner. At an early age, she showed signs of unusual mental quickness, and she was encouraged to develop her gifts."[16]

Octavia found herself in a fortunate situation; her grandmother and mother were educated women who enjoyed teaching. They were able to see her intelligence and that she harbored the skills to begin her education early. They could direct her in a positive way without interference from male family members who might object.[17]

The year 1816 saw the growth of different church denominations in the area, and the Walton family played a role. According to Edward Cashin, "In 1816 the Augusta Episcopalians were ready to support their church, and the following were constituted trustees: John Milledge, John Carter, Valentine Walker, George Walton, Jr., Thomas Watkins, Richard Tubman, Edward F. Campbell, Augustine Slaughter, Freeman Walker, Joseph Hutchinson, William M. Cowles, John A. Barnes, Milledge Galphin, and Patrick Carnes. The cornerstone of the new church, the third on the same site, was laid in 1819, and the building was finished in 1820."[18] It was clear that the Walker and the Walton family wanted their own place to worship. However, Octavia's father and his family had little time to enjoy the new church.

Augusta maintained steady growth, and by 1818, the town had a defined pattern of streets, a busy commercial center with numerous shops and warehouses near bridge row.[19] Eight-year-old Octavia most certainly visited these shops with her mother to choose fabric for new dresses, shoes, and other things the daughter of a successful Augusta lawyer would need.

While George Walton, Jr. practiced as a lawyer, not a plantation owner, he still needed to follow plantation standards to social success. He continued to be a member of the Legislature, representing Richmond County with the help of Sally's uncle, Freeman Walker, but was not moving to higher positions within state government.[20] It is possible his financial and moral issues kept his fortunes from changing. A depression in 1819 crippled Augusta, followed by several years of severe summer fevers and a rash of fires could have been instrumental in his decision to reroute the lives of his family shortly .[21]

Octavia and Robert spent their early years in Augusta's Sand Hill area, which contained the Belle Vue and Meadow Garden properties. Even though George Walton, Sr. had passed away six years before she was born, according to Frances Gibson Satterfield, "her grandmother, fourteen years his junior, taught Octavia American history at the age of her contemporaries were listening to fairy tales. She made it so interesting and exciting that she planted the seeds for Octavia's lifelong love of her country and her firm conviction that her grandfather was a national hero."[22]

Octavia carried this pride into her adult years. Later she wrote in her journal, "I frankly confess that I have respect for family pride. If it be a prejudice, it is a prejudice in its more picturesque shape. But I hold that it is connected with some of the noblest feelings in our nature. Is it nothing to be connected with the history of one's country, and to feel that: "The name of every noble ancestor, a bond upon your soul upon disgrace? No one who admits the rule can deny the exceptions, but I believe the pride of blood to have a beneficial influence. It is much to feel that the high and honorable belong to a name that is pledged to the Present by recollections of the past."[23]

It proved beneficial that Octavia took pride in the accomplishment of her grandfather and the Walton women focused their energies on developing their two children's lives. Eliza, Dorothy, and Sally, women of status in their community who wanted to maintain it, could see George was probably not going to be the means to achieve their goal. Time showed them to be correct.

Works cited and Notes

1. Autograph Album of Octavia Walton Le Vert. Album. Columbia University Libraries Rare Book & Manuscript Library, *Poe Collection.*

2. Jan Goldberg, *The Louisiana Purchase: A Primary Source History of Jefferson's Landmark Purchase from Napoleon* (New York City: Rosen Pub. Group, 2004).

3. Daniel Blowe, *A Geographical, Historical, Commercial, and Agricultural View of the United States of America* (Liverpool: H. Fisher, 1820).

4. Laura F. Edwards, *Scarlett Doesn't Live Here Anymore: Southern Women in the Civil War Era* (Champaign: University of Illinois Press, 2000).

5. Delaney, "Madame Octavia Walton Le Vert.". Note: While Octavia's gravestone has her date of birth as 1811, it is written as 1810 in the Family Bible. I am in agreement with Delaney on the date of birth. A copy of the pages of the Family Bible are located at the University of West Florida, Satterfield Collection. The location of the original pages are unknown as of November 2019.

6. Walter A. Clark, *Lost Arcadia: or, The Story of My Old Community* (Brothersville: Walter Clark, 1909), Digital Library of Georgia, *Georgia Historical Books..*

7. Virginia Tatnall Peacock, *Famous American Belles of the Nineteenth Century* (Hardpress Publishing, 2012).

8. Mary Hays, *Female Biography, or Memoirs of Illustrious and Celebrated Women, of All Ages and Countries* (London: Forgotten Books, 2016).

9. Hays, *Female Biography.* Note: The 1809 edition of this book is located at Augusta University, Summerville Campus, in the Reese

Library Archives. The special markings within this book were discovered by the author, Walker relative, Stacy Plooster, and Archivist, Maranda Christy.

10. Ann Short Chirhart, *Georgia Women: Their Lives and Times* (Athens: University of Georgia Press, 2014).

11. Chirhart, *Georgia Women*, 66.

12. "Sheriff's Sales," *Augusta Chronicle*, August 30, 1811, 3.

13. "Notice," *Augusta Chronicle*, February 28, 1812, 3.

14. "Sheriff's Sale," *Augusta Chronicle*, October 30, 1812, 3.

15. Delaney, "Madame Octavia Walton Le Vert."

16. Delaney, "Madame Octavia Walton Le Vert."

17. Peacock, *Famous American Belles*.

18. Cashin, *Story of Augusta*.

19. Cashin, *Story of Augusta*.

20. Cashin, *Story of Augusta*.

21. "State Legislature," *Reflector*, November 12, 1817, 1, *GenealogyBank*.

22. Cashin, *Story of Augusta*.

23. Frances Gibson Satterfield, *Madame LeVert* (Edisto Island: Edisto Press, 1987).

24. Stephens, "Madame Octavia Walton Le Vert." **Note**: This information was taken from extracts from Madame Le Vert's unpublished journals in Mrs. Lucia Starnes Monroe's Scrapbook, labeled "Pride of Birth." As of the publication of this book, the original resource is missing.

Chapter 3

The Floridas

Go and in Friendships hallowed name,
Where ere they wanderings may be.
A tribute fond of feeling claim,
A few brief lines for memory.[1]

Shortly after the colonies joined together and formed the United States, the Founding Fathers looked Southward, towards the Gulf of Mexico. Alexander Hamilton saw Spain's occupation of the Floridas as a threat and he hoped the United States would acquisition the area. Before Hamilton's hopes were realized he died in a duel with Aaron Burr. Andrew Jackson, tasked with the duty by Congress, took over Pensacola and demanded the cession of Florida.[2]

Rarely does one receive a second opportunity to improve their lives politically, but this happened to George Walton, Jr. In 1821, he received the appointment to Governor of the West Florida Territory. He was given a chance to make his mark in newly conquered territories, not unlike his father.

Alexander Hamilton. Photograph. Washington, D.C., 1895. Library of Congress Prints and Photographs Division Washington, D.C. 20540 USA https://hdl.loc.gov/loc.pnp/pp.print.

The failure at Princeton haunted him. George had a chance to strive for something better. Practicing law helped him support his family with Dorothy's sources of income. Still, his nefarious habits kept him from living up to the esteemed level of his father. When George Walton, Sr. signed the Declaration of Independence in 1776, the family's social standing changed dynamically, providing them a seat in the world of American Society. The marriage to Sally and her wealthy connections indicated George Walton, Jr. wanted to maintain this social standing, but not at great personal sacrifice.

George Walton, Jr. was a part of the social class where elite men affirmed their honor through the practice of business and political actions, but he was a failure at both. The family still owned Meadow Garden, but the land had to be sold in parcels to cover his debts. The constant threat of complete loss suggested bad business decisions and did not help the rumor of his gambling addiction.

The *Augusta Chronicle* published advertisements about the new United States Territory of Florida, showing it a place of extreme promise, enticing many residents. The local newspaper stated, "The Provinces of Florida having now become part of the territory of the United States, is believed that the tide of emigration will set rapidly towards her shores increasing her wealth, and filling her ports with our enterprising and industrious fellow citizens of the old States, and offering a home and a refuge to the exile and fugitive from the oppression of European thralldom." [3]

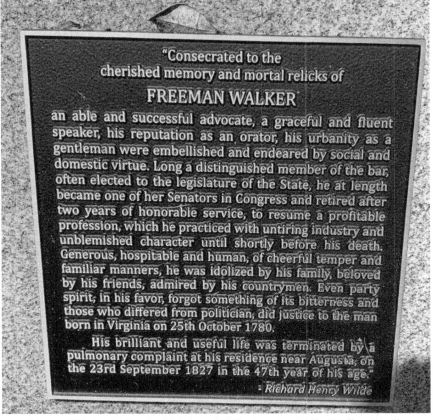

"Consecrated to the
cherished memory and mortal relicks of

FREEMAN WALKER

an able and successful advocate, a graceful and fluent
speaker, his reputation as an orator, his urbanity as a
gentleman were embellished and endeared by social and
domestic virtue. Long a distinguished member of the bar,
often elected to the legislature of the State, he at length
became one of her Senators in Congress and retired after
two years of honorable service, to resume a profitable
profession, which he practiced with untiring industry and
unblemished character until shortly before his death.
Generous, hospitable and human, of cheerful temper and
familiar manners, he was idolized by his family, beloved
by his friends, admired by his countrymen. Even party
spirit, in his favor, forgot something of its bitterness and
those who differed from politician, did justice to the man
born in Virginia on 25th October 1780.

His brilliant and useful life was terminated by a
pulmonary complaint at his residence near Augusta, on
the 23rd September 1827 in the 47th year of his age."

Richard Henry Wilde

*Photo of Plaque in front of Freeman Walker's grave at the Walker Family
Cemetery in Augusta, Georgia. 2019. Photograph. Photo courtesy of
Stacey Plooster.*

George retained his appointment as the representative for
Richmond County in the Georgia Senate. However, Sally's
uncle, Freeman Walker, a rising star in Washington D.C.,
working to make the right connections, recommended to
John Quincy Adams, then-Secretary of State, to appoint
Walton Secretary of the West Florida Territory in February
of 1821. George received notification of his commission
from President James Monroe on June 27th, 1821. He
served under General Andrew Jackson, the Florida

Photo of Freeman Walker's grave at the Walker Family Cemetery in Augusta, Georgia. 2019. Photograph. Photo courtesy of Stacey Plooster.

Territories appointed Governor, until Florida's official state could be formed.[4] George might have seen the new position as an exciting adventure. Still, he could not anticipate the struggles of rural life in the Floridas.

The move South was a drastic one, not only for George but also for the family. They took belongings they could carry by wagon and forced the immigration of their enslaved to the Florida Territories' wilds. The move from Augusta, Georgia to Pensacola, Florida, was difficult for all the women, but not unexpected. They knew when George accepted this new position; they were obliged to follow him to the frontier's unexplored territories.

Dorothy and Sally had managed George's wanderlust and advised settling near the Walker relatives for years, but not any longer.[5] It was also evident this branch of the family attempted to distance themselves from George by arranging an appointment thousands of miles away in Pensacola. The Walton women realized they had to make allowances for him and their family. In a surprising show of strength, Dorothy Walton rose to the occasion.

The travel from Augusta, Georgia to Pensacola, Florida, appeared more of a worry for the women than for George. He quickly packed for the trip, leaving the liquidation of the household to the family remaining in Augusta. He arrived in Pensacola on August 4th, 1821, missing the formalities. He did not arrive in time to attend Florida's transfer from the Spanish to the United States on July 17th, 1821, with Andrew Jackson, Henry Brackenridge, Richard Keith Call, and Dr. James C. Bronaugh, Jackson's physician, and confidante.[6]

Life in the new American city of Pensacola was different from the Colonial establishments of the North. Rachel Jackson, Andrew Jackson's wife, in a letter to her friend, Elizabeth Kingsley, described the conditions while she lived there with her husband, "Pensacola is perfectly plain; the land nearly as white as flour, yet productive of fine peach trees, oranges in abundance, grapes, figs, pomegranates, etc... all the houses look in ruins, old as time. Many squares of the town appear grown over with the thickest shrubs, weeping willows, and the Pride of China; all look neglected. The inhabitants all speak Spanish and French. Some speak four of five languages. Such a mixed multitude, you, or any of us, ever had an idea of. There are fewer white people far than any other, mixed with all nations under the canopy of heaven, almost in nature's darkness." [7] Clearly, colonial Florida was much wilder than established Georgia of the same time. Florida contained only two white settlements, and these were separated by four hundred miles of Indian territory. Pensacola's population was around fourteen hundred people of all races.[8]

George Walton, Jr. could rough these new conditions, but his family could not. Before they arrived, he searched for a home ideal for all of them. Also, he could not run the Florida Territories from a soldier's barracks or a shared home.

George arrived at another concern; he was barely in town before Andrew Jackson prepared to leave for his home, the "Hermitage" in Nashville, Tennessee. He stayed in Pensacola long enough to get the government securely organized. Then Jackson and his wife, true to his word, left for Tennessee on October 4th, 1821. The interim government fell under the responsibility of George Walton and W.G.D. Worthington.[9] According to Herbert J. Doherty, Jr., "Before leaving, the retired governor had communicated his ideas about the territorial government

Andrew Jackson. Photograph. Washington, D.C., 1896. Library of Congress Prints and Photographs Division Washington, D.C. 20540 USA.

and its officers to President Monroe and Secretary of State John Quincy Adams." Congress was to make the two Floridas one and suggested that Colonel William King is appointed Governor and George Walton as Secretary.[10] An Act of Congress would terminate this brief provisional regime on March 30th, 1822.[11]

George Walton, Jr. began his term as Governor of West Florida positively, and his work with Andrew Jackson resulted in good connections, and a ball held in his honor. Society in Pensacola was not as grand as Augusta, but it still elevated George in a position of integrity and trust. According to the *Floridian*, "In honor of Col. Walton...the citizens of our town, in conjunction with the gentlemen of the army, stationed at this place and Barrancas, gave a splendid Ball at M. Lavalett's... The ball was numerously attended and graced by nearly all the beauty and fashion of Pensacola." [12]

The Jackson family left the Floridas before the arrival of the rest of the Walton family, but the departing Governor still sought the kind regards of the Walton women. Andrew Jackson stated to George in a letter, "Present me although unacquainted, respectfully to your Lady & mother, and accept for yourself Mrs. J. and my kindest salutations." [13] Jackson arrived at the Hermitage in November and resigned as Governor of Florida shortly thereafter. The Jackson's never returned to Florida. [14]

Despite the distance from Kentucky to Pensacola, Andrew Jackson did maintain correspondence with George Walton, advising on various gubernatorial issues. Jackson left Walton in charge of a growing town and he needed help. According to Dibble, "During Jackson's last short visit in Pensacola, the town's population jumped from a total of 695 (441 white and 254 black) free people shown in the last Spanish Census in 1820 to about four thousand settlers before the end of 1821." [15]

It is unclear how George Walton, Jr. felt regarding the move to Pensacola, Florida, but according to Satterfield, it was a place "where there were no schools, one doctor, one innkeeper, and inexplicably, twenty-one shoemakers (apparently indicating the main means of transportation.) Of course, there were fishermen, grocers, bakers, a few seamstresses and tailors, and prostitutes." [16] He could manage, but what about his family?

The home the Walton family lived in while in Pensacola. 2019.

Unlike the affluent Augusta, the lack of schools resulted in home education for the Walton children: Octavia and Robert. Fortunately, both Dorothy and Sally

Walton were highly educated and could properly instruct the children. The Walton children were very fortunate to be cared for by these two women, and time would show their ability to educate was exemplary. According to Kerber, "Motherhood was discussed almost as if it were a fourth branch of government, a device that ensured responsible motherhood, prospective mothers needed to be well informed and decently educated."[17]

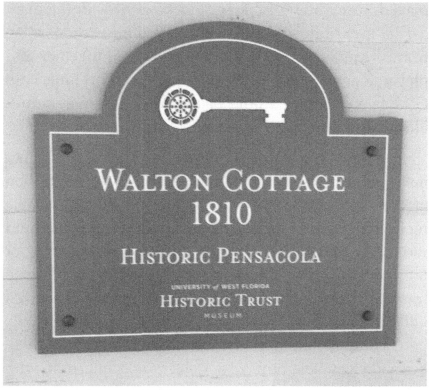

Walton Cottage 1810. 2019.

George decided to keep running the Florida Territory, much like the model Andrew Jackson had created. He did differ in a few aspects: he chose to mingle with the local population while the Jacksons' were more distant, and he continued the habit of visiting billiard parlors and taverns. He did arrange a suitable home for his family on a street with a pleasant view of Pensacola Bay.[18] Octavia later remembered, "fragrant acacia, oleander, and Cape jasmine trees, which filled the parterre sloping down to the sea-beach; of merry races with my brother along the white sands, while the creamy waves broke over my feet, and the delicious breeze from the gulf played in my hair; of the pet mocking-birds in the giant oak by my window, whose songs called me each morning from dreamland." [19] They attended school together and played together prior to adolescence. In a short time, both Octavia and Robert would begin to take on more adult-like responsibilities.[20]

In the book *Women of the South*, Octavia shared her memories of those early days in Pensacola. As a reflection of the intelligence of the Walton women, Octavia recollected before she was twelve years old, she could write and converse in three languages with facility. Her father utilized her ability by taking her to his office to translate from French or Spanish the letters connected with the affairs of state. According to Forrest, "There, perched upon a high stool - she was too tiny in stature to be made available otherwise - she would interpret, with the greatest ease and correctness, the tenor and spirit of foreign dispatches, proving herself, thus early, quite worthy of her illustrious descent." [21]

Despite Walton's role as acting Governor of the Florida Territory, he was not appointed to the position of Governor. Instead, on March 3rd, 1822, the role would fall to W.P. Duval of Kentucky, who soon arrived, and George was appointed as the first Secretary for the new State of Florida. By June 1822, George was once again struggling with finances.[22]

He wrote the Secretary of State, John Quincy Adams, thanking him for his commission as Secretary of the Territory of Florida, but he had a problem. Andrew Jackson had left and made it clear he was not coming back. George had not received any money, which would allow him to operate in his new role as Secretary and Acting Governor of West Florida. He struggled with the rent of the house his family currently resided in and extra expenses. The appointed Governor, Duval, had not yet arrived.[23]

Henry Marie Brackenridge was one of Octavia's tutors. Portrait of Henry Marie Brackenridge. Photograph. Tallahassee, 1870. State Library and Archives of Florida.

Henry Brackenridge, a multilingual lawyer assigned to help Walton, did not think much of George Walton, Jr. He wrote, "The person who fills the office of Governor is a young Georgian who has run through a handsome fortune,

49

without the capacity of habits of business. I have been compelled to do everything for him since General Jackson went away...he is a wastrel, a despicable character...unfortunately, he is totally wanting in that weight of character and dignity of manners which become the station he fills. No one respects him or confidence in him. His companions are persons of no character or the subalterns of the army with whom he passes almost every night over the gaming table...He is in truth, an object of universal contempt." [24]

Despite Brackenridge's feelings for Walton, he could not feel the same way for the entire family. He became close to Octavia and recognized her extraordinary intellect and her ease in learning languages. He filled in the role as her tutor and continued the training with her mother and grandmother.

In less than a year, the Walton family and the new state of Florida encountered a devastating blow. On August 13th, 1822, the Pensacola Board of Health announced the dreaded arrival of yellow fever and warned all inhabitants able to remove to retire to the country. Many felt the fever would pass, but others thought it wouldn't. The disease spread quickly throughout the town. McMahon, an Army assistant surgeon, described the symptoms of yellow fever for those in the North, "a sensation...in the thoracic and abdominal regions; the tongue became yellowish black...; the stools are involuntary, liquid and dark green; the urine is small in quantity and passed with great difficulty; the pulse becomes imperceptible at the wrist; then follow...

convulsions, and hemorrhage from the mouth, nose, eyes, and ears...- the immediate precursor of death; and finally, black vomit, that ever fatal symptom, puts a period to the patient's sufferings. If prominent symptoms are not...relieved by active depleting measures, all hopes of recovery may be abandoned." [25]

The establishing of the government for the new State of Florida would have to wait until the epidemic was over. George shared with Andrew Jackson, "It is unnecessary to state to you the situation of things in this section of Florida, in consequence of the dreadful pestilence which has prevailed in Pensacola. The sickness of my family, and of an esteemed friend (Doctor Bronaugh) who was confined to my house, detained me considerable time in the city after the Legislative Council adjourned to Emmanuel's. As soon as it was in my power to leave Pensacola, I was compelled to provide a shelter for my family in the woods, to which their safety urged me to retire." [26]

Dorothy Walton wrote to a niece in September 1822 and told of their situation, "You will no doubt know before this reaches you...the yellow fever is in Pensacola, and be anxious to hear from us...Yes, my dear, that place has been visited with an overwhelming calamity. All those that did not leave the City at the first commencement have been swept off. (The American population I mean) We are the only family that remained any time after the commencement of the fever that have been spared. That we are spared is owing to the superintending hand of a merciful God."

Dorothy continued to tell her niece they did not leave like everyone else because they had a large family of black enslaved they could not remove due to the expense, but they also felt they could not leave them behind to suffer. They kept them close in hopes everyone might escape since the house was located next to Pensacola Bay. According to her letter, everyone had experienced a fever to some degree, but Octavia was among those very sick.

Dorothy continued, "I should have observed that at the same time that the lady who died first ill Octavia and a little girl I had in my room also a [black] woman in the kitchen was taken very suddenly ill, all with the same symptoms, we did not think the yellow fever then, but I am now sure that it was, they recovered and did not take again." She finished the letter telling her niece her eyes were very bad and Octavia's health was very delicate, and she was fearful of her health.[27]

Yellow Fever would not leave the city before taking the life of Dr. Bronaugh and threatening the lives of Sally, Robert, and Octavia. Only George and Dorothy would escape the symptoms. In a letter to George Walton on November 26th, 1822, General Andrew Jackson expressed his sorrow over losing many friends from the "dreadful calamity." [28]

The newspapers reported on the Yellow Fever cases in Pensacola and the drastic number of deaths, but by December, when the weather cooled, the fever stopped spreading. A letter from one of Pensacola's residents told of the situation, "We improve the present opportunity of informing you that we have escaped its effects and that Pensacola is entirely restored to its former state of health. More than 200 persons have fallen victim to the disease since its commencement, among whom are several of our most valuable citizens: a great number, perhaps, in proportion to the population than was ever before known. But few Americans who were so hardy as to remain in town have escaped. The fever was introduced from Havana, by the brig Franklin, of Boston; which vessel, owing to the negligence of our board of health, was not quarantined. We have resided during the sickness, on a small plantation, 20 miles from town, and have enjoyed excellent health." [29]

Governor William P. Duval, who left Pensacola in a hurry to escape the Yellow Fever epidemic, returned to the city on April 28th, 1823, ready to manage the new state of Florida. He wrote John Quincy Adams, "Sir, I have the honour to inform you of my arrival at this city on the 28th ultimo with the public records and documents under my charge - I was compelled to perform the journey from Pensacola by land - as a vessel could not be procured for St. Augustine. Colonel Walton was left in Pensacola. His family was unwell, and his only daughter was dangerously ill at my departure. If the situation of his family will permit, the Secretary will attend the council, after which I shall direct him to return to West Florida as

First Governor, William Pope Duval. Photograph. Tallahassee, 1870. State Library and Archives of Florida.

his presence will be more necessary there than in this quarter...I find all peace and quietness here. The excitement against me was confined to a few disappointed men, who have succeeded in imposing themselves on our delegate, as the majority of the people."[30]

In the struggle to establish the state of Florida, another issue was the placement of a capital city. While the most developed city was Pensacola, connected to the Federal Road, it still was not central to the new state; therefore, other places needed to be considered. St. Augustine was one location investigated by George Walton and other members of the legislature. It was even suggested members move their families to St. Augustine. George Walton wrote Andrew Jackson on April 18th, 1823, advising him this was not a good idea. His family, including Octavia, was still recovering from the horrible yellow fever outbreak. To move everyone who had just moved from Augusta a year previously, was too much. George told Jackson his family was to stay in Pensacola until a permanent seat of government was located and established.[31]

George Walton, Jr. and other men in the Florida Legislature explored the wilds of Florida, seeking a location for the new capital. They searched for an area between the two most populous portions of Florida; Pensacola and St. Augustine. In the end, under the recommendation of Governor Duval, Tallahassee was suggested and established as the new seat of government for Florida.[32]

The establishment of Tallahassee, Florida. Baldwin & Cradock, 1834.
Photograph. Tallahassee, 1834. State Library of Florida,
Florida Map Collection.

Octavia also had a story about naming of the new capital of Florida. In *Women of the South*, she shared, "During her father's administration, as Governor of Florida, he located the seat of government, and, at the earnest request of his little daughter, Octavia, called it by the Indian name of "Tallahassee." Its signification ("beautiful land") fell musically upon the ear of the imaginative child; she was greatly interested, too, in the old Seminole king, Neamathla, who, in the days of his power, struck his tent-pole in that ground, made it his resting-place, and called it first by this sweet name." [33]

George Walton was the only member of the family to leave Pensacola to for the new city, Tallahassee. In contrast, the rest of the family stayed in Pensacola. According to Johnson, "He never moved his family to the village of log buildings, although the Tallahassee Census of 1825 shows him as a resident with seventeen slaves." [34] Octavia and Robert remained in Pensacola and grew into the roles they filled as adults.

The United States was a young country and needed to look to its defenses. President James Monroe suggested this during his 1823 Annual Message. In 1825 Gulf Coast defenses were established in Pensacola, Florida, bringing a steady stream of the military to the remote city.[35] The young soldiers who visited the city were attracted to the young ladies they saw in town.

In this environment Octavia was fifteen years old and growing into a beautiful young woman. She learned the ways of managing a drawing room as her family entertained visitors to the port city. Pensacola became a place where a gala was held when Navy ships returned from their cruises - balls and parties at the Governor's house, onboard the vessel, or other areas throughout Pensacola. According to Mary Forrest, "The well-educated and chivalric officers were a large element in the society to which our author was thus early accustomed; and while yet a mere child, she had little to learn in the way of drawing-room ease and elegance." [36]

In 1824, General Lafayette took his final tour through the country he helped to form. While he traveled south, including Georgia, Alabama, and Louisiana, he spent time visiting friends and family of those he fought

Lafayette. Photograph. Washington, D.C., n.d. Library of Congress
Prints and Photographs Division Washington, D.C. 20540 USA.

beside during the Revolutionary War, including the
Walton's. According to *Women of the South*, Octavia
relayed another story from her childhood. She shared with
the biographer that her grandmother, Dorothy Walton,

was Lafayette's friend, and he had sent a letter begging her to meet him at Mobile.

At Dorothy Walton's advanced age, possibly blind, she felt she could not make the trip. Instead, she sent Octavia to meet Lafayette. According to Mary Forrest, "After the arrival and grand reception of Lafayette at Mobile, Octavia and her mother were quietly presented by the committee of arrangements, and the little fair-haired girl envoy then placed in his hands the miniature of her grandfather, to which she bore a striking resemblance. For some minutes, he gazed upon both pictures in silence; then, bursting into tears, caught the child to his heart, exclaiming: 'The living image of my brave and noble friend!' A long and interesting interview ensued, the young Octavia, seated upon the knee of the old hero, holding him spell-bound with her piquant and fluent use of his native tongue. He then folded her again to his heart and blessed her fervently, remarking to one of the committees, as she left the room: 'A truly wonderful child! She has been conversing all this while with intelligence and tact in the purest French. I predict for her a brilliant career.'" [37]

As the Walton family established themselves in Pensacola, so did the enslaved who they brought with them. In 1824, the exact date unknown, one particular enslaved person was born into the household, and she was called Betsey Walton.[38] A baby, a possible relative, that in time impacted everyone's life for generations to come.

By 1826, the Walton family was poised to move up within their social circles. Octavia had grown into an intelligent and beautiful young woman and attracted the attention of young Navy men in port at Pensacola. Octavia later recalled, "The presence of the Navy officers at Pensacola gave a great charm to the society there, and under the most propitious auspices, the young flower expanded to light and beauty." [39] Octavia was in her mid to late teens, when young Southern women assumed their adult gender roles and moved from a little girl to a lady.[40]

Florida's Governor, Duval, also dispatched the newly appointed Secretary for Florida, George Walton, Jr., to Key West to collect salvage revenue. According to Sam Carnley, "Walton wrote Duval on February 22, 1826, advising that he had collected for the Territory the sum of $9,879.10. He arrived in Washington in early April 1826, as evidenced by his letter from there on the 8th to Georgia U.S. Senator John M. Berrien regarding the settlement of the land claims in Florida." [41]

What George Walton did with the money he had collected between Florida and Washington D.C. became a source of embarrassment for himself and his family. Any hope of rising into governmental positions like his father was dashed entirely with losing the large amount of money. While his daughter, Octavia, flourished in her rise into the same society he aspired to, George fell from its graces, haunted possibly by his gambling addiction.

The following year saw Walton's humiliation complete; he was removed from the position of Secretary of Florida and replaced with William M. M'Carty of Virginia on March 3rd, 1827.[42] He returned to the port of Pensacola by March 3rd, 1827. George Walton returned home amid intense humiliation and embarrassment.

Works Cited and Notes

1. Octavia Walton Le Vert Autograph Album; 1827. MS#1009. Columbia University Libraries Rare Book & Manuscript Library, *Edgar Allan Poe papers, 1827 – 1908.*

2. Ernest F. Dibble, *Ante-bellum Pensacola and the Military Presence* (Pensacola: Mayes Printing Company, 1974).

3. Augusta Chronicle, March 15, 1821, GenealogyBank.

4. Satterfield, *Madame LeVert.*

5. Catherine Clinton, *Plantation Mistress: Woman's World in the Old South* (New York City: Pantheon, 1984).

6. Sutton, *Walton House.*

7. *Rachel Jackson to Elizabeth Kingsley,* July 23, 1821, in *Papers of Andrew Jackson: 1821-1824,* ed. Andrew Jackson, Sam B. Smith, Harriet Chappell Owsley, and Harold D. Moser (Knoxville: University of Tennessee Press, 1980).

8. Stephens, *Madame Octavia Walton LeVert.*

9. Satterfield, *Madame LeVert.*

10. Herbert Doherty Jr., "Andrew Jackson's Cronies in Florida Territorial Politics: With Three Unpublished Letters to His Cronies," *The Florida Historical Quarterly* 34, no. 1 (Jul. 1955) pp. 3-29, JSTOR.

11. Doherty "Andrew Jackson's Cronies in Florida Territorial Politics," 3-29.

12. "In Honor of Col. Walton," *Augusta Chronicle & Georgia Gazette,* November 15, 1821, 3. Digital Library of Georgia, *Georgia Historic Newspapers.*

13. Doherty "Andrew Jackson's Cronies in Florida Territorial Politics," 3-29.

14. Carnley, "Who Was George Walton Jr," 2-6.

15. Dibble, *Antebellum Pensacola and the Military Presence.*

16. Satterfield, *Madame LeVert.*

17. Kerber, *Women of the Republic*, 200.

18. Sutton, *Walton House*.

19. Forrest, *Women of the South Distinguished in Literature*, 16.

20. Anya Jabour, *Scarlett's Sisters: Young Women in the Old South* (Chapel Hill: University of North Carolina Press, 2009).

21. Forrest, *Women of the South Distinguished in Literature*, 17.

22. Sutton, *Walton House*.

23. *Acting Governor George Walton Jr. to Secretary of State (John Quincy Adams)*, June 16, 1822, in *Territorial Papers of the United States*, Volume 22. ed. Clarence Edward Carter and John Bloom Porter (Washington, D.C.: U.S. G.P.O., 1934).

24. Satterfield, *Madame LeVert*, 5.

25. George F. Pearce, "Torment of Pestilence: Yellow Fever Epidemics in Pensacola," *The Florida Historical Quarterly* 56, no. 4 (Apr. 1978): 448-472.

26. Sutton, *Walton House*.

27. *Dorothy Walton to Unknown Niece*, September 22, 1822. History Museum of Mobile, *Octavia Walton LeVert Collection*. Note: According to Chuck Torrey, the researcher historian for the History Museum of Mobile, it was probably part of Caldwell Delaney's Octavia LeVert collection. The location of the original letter is currently unknown. This copy is a typed document.

28. Pearce, "Torment of Pestilence," 448-472.

29. "Yellow Fever; Improve; Informing: Escaped, Pensacola, Former Victims, Commencement," *Evening Post*, December 14, 1822, 2.

30. *Governor William P. Duval to Secretary of State John Quincy Adams*, April 28, 1823, in *Territorial Papers of the United States*, Volume 22. ed. Clarence Edward Carter and John Bloom Porter (Washington, D.C.: U.S. G.P.O., 1934), 675.

31. *George Walton to Andrew Jackson*, 1823. Letter. Library of Congress, *Digital Collection*.

32. Doherty "Andrew Jackson's Cronies in Florida Territorial Politics," 3-29.

33. Forrest, *Women of the South Distinguished in Literature*, 17-18.

34. Malcolm Johnson, *Red, White, and Bluebloods in Frontier Florida* (Tallahassee: Rotary Clubs of Tallahassee, 1976).

35. Dibble, *Antebellum Pensacola and the Military Presence*.

36. Forrest, *Women of the South Distinguished in Literature*, 18.

37. Forrest, *Women of the South Distinguished in Literature*, 18.

38. U.S. Census Bureau, United States Census, 1880, Betsy Lamar, Georgia, Richmond, Augusta, 096, Ancestry.com.
39. Le Vert, Octavia Walton. *Souvenirs of Travel*. Mobile: S.H. Goetzel and Company, 1857. Google Books.
40. Jabour, *Scarlett's Sisters*, 27.
41. Carnley, "Who Was George Walton Jr," 2-6.
42. *Commission of William M. McCarty as Secretary*, 1827, in *Territorial Papers of the United States*, Volume 23. ed. Clarence Edward Carter and John Bloom Porter (Washington, D.C.: U.S. G.P.O., 1934), 784.

Paula Lenor Webb

Chapter 4

The Debut into Society

Lady this pure unsullied page
Seems like thy youthful mind
Where all that's best of love & truth
In brightness gleams combine.[1]

With the guidance of her mother and grandmother, Octavia Celeste Valentine Walton focused her studies on adulthood and what it meant to become a young woman.[2] Her father's ability to influence the social standing of the Walton's was falling, but her own was shining. Unlike most young women of Octavia's status who spent their late teens and early twenties living with their parents in one location, the result of George Walton's decisions left an unsettled home life in Pensacola.[3]

Octavia and her health were mentioned in early family letters and her father's correspondence. Still, the earliest expression of what others thought about Octavia and how she related to her contemporaries is in her

Autograph Journal.[4] What is the catalyst in the life of a young girl in Pensacola, Florida, that resulted in the start of her autograph book?

The collection of autographs from famous people and those in power and position was not uncommon during the time Octavia began her album. While not everyone who wrote the borrowed verses and stylized prose in her album are known, it does outline a set of experiences and emotions that could "serve as the basis for a distinctive female community."[5]

The first dated entry into Octavia's Autograph Journal is June 29, 1826. At this time, she was a young girl, newly seventeen years old, and the documentation reveals the type of attention she attracted by the summer. There is a poem of farewell written for her. It is unknown if it was in honor of her leaving Pensacola, Florida to visit the watering places of the North, from a young Navy man leaving town, or a dear friend wishing her well. It is clear the person regretted her departure.[6]

Another possibility for these solemn notes lies in Sally Walton's solution to a problem. Her husband, George Walton, Jr., as Secretary for the state of Florida, lost a large amount of money that belonged to the state, and it resulted in his removal from the position. He formally submitted his resignation to Henry Clay, the U.S. Secretary of State, on Dec. 14, 1826. He then returned to Pensacola in March of 1827.[7]

The local writer, J.G. Drake wasted little time reaching out to young Octavia and expressing his sorrow

Haas, Philip. *Henry Clay / A. Gibert Del. from a Daguerreotype by P. Haas; Lith. and Published by P. Haas, Washington City.* Photograph. Washington, D.C., 1844. Library of Congress Prints and Photographs Division Washington, D.C. 20540 USA. http://hdl.loc.gov/loc.pnp/pp.print.

over the situation until March 9th, 1827, he wrote the poem, *Pensez a Moi*, quoting, "When sorrow clouds they dream of mirth, And promised joys fade too soon."[8] By April, we find the family had traveled to Baltimore, Maryland.

Sally Walton's reasons for making such a trip are not known. She might not have wanted to deal with the situation her husband had placed her in or the new influx of attention her daughter was receiving from bachelors in Pensacola. Many of these men might be seeking an opportunity to court her daughter in a moment of family strife, but one thing is clear, she took her daughter and left town. Sally Walton attained funds from her sources, Dorothy Walton, most likely. Dorothy, who never remarried and had a gambling son, probably survived by renting out the enslaved from Georgia and then utilized those funds to support their lifestyle and invest in land.[9]

Sally Walton left Pensacola with Octavia, escorted by her brother, Robert Watkins Walton. He was a young man of sixteen years, and since they needed to have a male escort during these journeys, he was perfect. It is also possible he visited or enrolled at the University of Virginia, where he was to complete his law degree.[10]

After this visit North, the Walton family traveled throughout the South and the Northeast. All the locations they visited to introducing Octavia to Society cannot be determined from her Autograph Journal, but some of them are revealed. According to Caldwell Delaney, "indications are that Octavia spent the time in "trial flights" at Mobile, New Orleans, and Augusta."[11] Research also indicated additional locations such as Baltimore, Tuskaloosa, and Erie, Alabama.

David Crockett. Photograph. Washington, D.C., n.d. Library of Congress Prints and Photographs Division Washington, D.C. 20540 USA.

It is certain by April 1827, Octavia was in a position to meet David Crockett and Sam Houston while they were in Baltimore, Maryland. David Crockett later wrote, "I

Meade. *Sam Houston / Lith. of E.C. Kellogg, Hartford, Conn. from a Daguerreotype by Mead [I.e., Meade] Brothers*. Photograph. Washington, D.C., 1852. Library of Congress Prints and Photographs Division Washington, D.C. 20540 USA http://hdl.loc.gov/loc.pnp/pp.print.

take great pleasure in recording my name in Miss Octavia Walton's Album as a testimonial of my respects for her

Success through life, and I hope she may enjoy the happiness and pleasures of the world agreeable to her expectation as all Ladys of her sterling worth, merits."[12]

Edgar Allan Poe. Photograph. Washington, D.C. , 1848. Library of Congress Prints and Photographs Division Washington, D.C. 20540 USA.

Another young man Octavia met during her time in Baltimore grew into one of the greatest poets of all time. On May 1st, 1827, Octavia and Edgar Allen Poe were introduced, and he left two of his earliest known poems in her Autograph Journal. According to Louis Leary, "They are not signed by him, and the date attributed to them "May the 1st, 1827" - is written in Miss Octavia's hand, But, again, the tradition which has followed the album describes these verses as having been written by Poe, and the handwriting in which they appear has in our time been identified by the leading Poe authority, Dr. Thomas Ollive Mabbott, as being that of Poe, and of an early period."[13]

Octavia must have reconnected with her father, George Walton, Jr., by early May, possibly to escort his family back to Pensacola and leave his son, Robert, at the University of Virginia to begin his training as a lawyer.[14] She was back in Pensacola, Florida, by July 21, 1827.[15] She remained in Pensacola until August of 1827 where she left town and possibly met Sarah Haysworth Gayle in Greensboro, Alabama. In her journal, she describes a Miss W., "Miss W. Is an unaffected, pious, quite pretty girl - small and delicate. She is a member of the Church."[16] During the same time she was out of town, the local paper, *Pensacola Gazette*, began to increase their attacks on George Walton and the missing funds he had yet to return. The article on August 24th did make allowances for his family:

> *While on this subject, it may not be improper for us to notice an erroneous idea...it is, that in the remarks we have made with regard to the detection, by the Ex-Treasurer, to the Territorial*

72

funds, we have unnecessarily harassed and wounded the feelings of his family. This we have certainly had no intention of doing, and we think that every candid person who reviews our course in this business, will acknowledge that we have said no more than our duty to the Public absolutely required.[17]

She returned to Pensacola by September 1827,[18] in time to attract the eye of young Naval Lieutenant Franklin Buchanan. He fell under her spell when he arrived at the Pensacola Port in October of 1827.[19] He was serious about marriage, but she did not love him. He wrote in her album, "Love is by no means necessary in marriage, but as a woman giving herself a master when she marries, she ought to fix upon a man when she can revere and admire, and her happiness is proportionate to the degree of admiration which she feels for him."[20] He accepted her rejection in stride, and he was among the first she refused during her unusually extended time as a single lady. It was a common tactic of hers. In a Rhode Island newspaper death notice many years later, stated, "She would tell them in the harsh or musical accents of their individual countries that she loved them, but not with a love like theirs, and this so declaring it better to be refused by her than accepted by another."[21]

Buchanan, after returning to sea, wrote the following description of her to a friend: "Nothing could exceed the brilliancy of her eyes or the fascination of her smile...Dazzlingly beautiful, wherever she moves, there is a light in her path...She is encompassed by grace and

Franklin Buchanan courted Octavia when she lived in Pensacola. [Com. Franklin Buchanan, C.S.N., Half-Length Portrait, Standing, Facing Right.] Photograph. Washington, D.C., 1865. Library of Congress Prints and Photographs Division Washington, D.C. 20540 USA.

splendor… Rank, talent, beauty--all contribute to aid the enchantment and render the tenure of her power secure…She possesses in the highest perfection all the tender, graceful, retiring attributes of women. Being almost nature's masterpiece, it is impossible to wish her different."[22]

Susannah Claiborne Clay and Octavia were close friends. Bell, C.M. *Clay, Mrs. C.C.* . Photograph. Washington, D.C., 1873. Library of Congress Prints and Photographs Division Washington, D.C. 20540 USA. http://hdl.loc.gov/loc.pnp/pp.print.

Octavia also developed a close relationship with many significant women. One such person was Susannah

Claiborne Clay. Susannah wrote a poem in Octavia's Autograph Journal about their friendship on November 22, 1827.

Female Friendship
Joy cannot claim purer bliss
Or grief a dew from stain more clear.
Than female friendship's meeting kiss,
Than female friendship's parting tear.[23]

By April of 1828, Octavia had achieved enough of a reputation in the North to attract the attention of many young sailors who later filled in roles in the U.S. military and, in the upcoming years, those in charge of both Union forces and Confederate forces. When the Navy schooner, *Shark*, arrived in Pensacola on April 11th, 1828, the first actions of at least three sailors was visit Octavia and leave poems in her Autograph Album.[24]

One sailor, Charles Stedman, who later became a Rear Admiral, wrote of an early visit to Pensacola. He recalled the town to be one of the most pleasant of Southern cities. He considered society to be relatively small but excellent and a lot of pretty girls of Spanish parentage. He also visited the Walton household. He described the home as open to officers and how they were entertained with tea, dancing, and music. He also described an early Octavia. He stated, "Their daughter, the celebrated Octavia Walton...was just sweet seventeen, and, although so young, she had all the tact and attractiveness of a woman who had been years in society."

He remarked a young midshipman received the same treatment from her as the captain or commodore. Charles became friends with Octavia's brother, Robert, and was treated like family.[25]

Octavia related her past experience in the book *Women of the South*, "Pensacola, situated on a noble bay, was the rendezvous of the United States vessels of the Gulf station. It was a gala time when they returned from their cruises; balls and parties at the governor's house - splendid entertainments on board the ships - moonlight excursions upon the bay, and picnics in the magnolia groves. The well educated and chivalrie officers were a large element in the society in which our author was thus early accustomed; and while yet a mere child, she had little to learn in the way of drawing room ease and elegance."[26]

While the Walton family considered Pensacola the residence where they always returned, Dorothy's poor eyesight limited her ability to travel, but not that of her daughter-in-law or granddaughter. These ladies visited many locations in the old and new South during the winter months. In 1828, they traveled to New Orleans[27] and to Mobile, where a Mrs. Buckley told of having a very gay winter in consequence of Mrs. Sally Walton and Octavia from Pensacola.[28]

Also, several river towns started in cotton country: Tuscaloosa, Claiborne, Cahawba, Selma, and Montgomery. In these towns were pockets of people who knew the Walton's by family relations, political status, or religion. The introduction of the steamboat along the Alabama river eased the time and cost of travel for men visiting the cotton market in Mobile and women visiting their friends and family in the Alabama Black Belt, eligible daughters in tow. [29]

Robert Walton attended the University of Virginia in 1828 and 1829, completed his education, and became a lawyer, practicing law alongside his father.[30] The Walton family and their enslaved continued to live in Pensacola and frequented the Methodist Church when they were in town,[31]but this did not mean George Walton, Jr. resolved all his problems regarding the missing funds. One issue resulted in a duel.

George Walton, Jr.'s reputation continued to acquire negative attention. He was served a warrant in Tallahassee, Florida, in August of 1827, but he was released on his recognizance, and trial did not occur till April 1828. According to the Walton County Historical Society President, Sam Carnley, Dorothy Walton feared this trial might hurt the family and took necessary measures. She was confident she had to sacrifice the land she purchased in Tallahassee to cover the missing funds, but she did not want to lose anything else.[32]

In January of 1828, before the trial started in April, she wrote her Will. She left Robert and Octavia all the enslaved and their children. To Octavia, she left, "Nancy and her two daughters Cornelia and Fanny Rosetta and her two children Chloe and John, together with the future increase of the said female [black] slaves the said [blacks] to be delivered to her when she reaches the age of eighteen years or on the day of her marriage."[33]

The terms of this will reveal the cleverness of Dorothy. She added her son as executor of the will, but not the only person. She added a family friend, John H. Walker of Alabama. Also, Octavia's eighteenth birthday was in August of 1828, and she would inherit the enslaved after the trial, but the window of time was too small for her father to to sell them or his creditors to attempt to take them. Robert, Octavia's brother, inherited his portion outright, and the enslaved she left to both Octavia and Robert was to ensure the protection of this specific portion of the enslaved.[34]

George went to trial in April of 1828 and was required to repay the money taken with interest. Dorothy offered her land in place of the money he owed. According to Sam Carney, "It was accepted, and the Legislative Council adopted a resolution assigning to Mrs. Walton the judgment against her son for the land and granting a full discharge of all claims of the Territory against him."[35]

It appears George continued to struggle with personal and financial issues after the settling of this debt. Still, the most notable consequence of all of this was his duel with Dr. J.P.C. McManon on May 27th, 1828. Within days of his trial, he returned to Florida politics. George ran for election to one of the Legislative Council seats available for Escambia County, Florida. Ironically, despite his past troubles with the state, he won. Dr. McManon was insulted by his win and challenged him to a duel.

Florida's most colorful founding father could not keep the duel a secret since he was wounded. On June 2nd, 1829 a group of his friends gave formal notice of the events to the *Pensacola Gazette*. Colonel Walton and Dr. McMahon met on St. Rosa's Point at 5 pm.

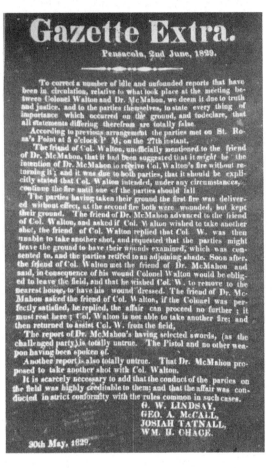

The notice in the Pensacola Gazette. Photograph. 1829. University of West Florida University Archives and West Florida History Center. Satterfield Collection.

Gazette Extra.

Pensacola, 2nd June, 1829.

To correct a number of idle and unfounded reports that have been in circulation, relative to what took place at the meeting between Colonel Walton and Dr. McMahon, we deem it due to truth and justice, and to the parties themselves, to state every thing of importance which occurred on the ground, and todeclare, that all statements differing therefrom are totally false.

According to previous arrangement the parties met on St. Rosa's Point at 5 o'clock P M, on the 27th instant.

The friend of Col. Walton, unofficially mentioned to the friend of Dr. McMahon, that it had been suggested that it *might* be the intention of Dr. McMahon to receive Col. Walton's fire without returning it; and it was due to both parties, that it should be explicitly stated that Col. Walton intended, under any circumstances, continue the fire until one of the parties should fall

The parties having taken their ground the first fire was delivered without effect, at the second fire both were wounded, but kept their ground. The friend of Dr. McMahon advanced to the friend of Col. Walton, and asked if Col. Walton wished to take another shot, the friend of Col. Walton replied that Col. W. was then unable to take another shot, and requested that the parties might leave the ground to have their wounds examined, which was consented to, and the parties retired to an adjoining shade. Soon after, the friend of Col. Walton met the friend of Dr. McMahon and said, in consequence of his wound Colonel Walton would be obliged to leave the field, and that he wished Col. W. to remove to the nearest house, to have his wound dressed. The friend of Dr. McMahon asked the friend of Col. Walton, if the Colonel was perfectly satisfied, he replied, the affair can proceed no further; it must rest here; Col. Walton is not able to take another fire; and then returned to assist Col. W. from the field.

The report of Dr. McMahon's having selected swords, (as the challenged party)is totally untrue. The Pistol and no other weapon having been spoken of.

Another report is also totally untrue. That Dr. McMahon proposed to take another shot with Col. Walton.

It is scarcely necessary to observe that that the conduct of the parties on the field was highly creditable to them; and that the affair was conducted in strict conformity with the rules common in such cases.

G. W. LINDSAY,
GEO. A. McCALL,
JOSIAH TATNALL,
WM. H. CHACE.

30th May, 1829.

According to the *Gazette*, "The parties having taken their ground the first fire was delivered without effect, at the second fire both were wounded but kept their ground. The friend of Dr. McMahon advanced to the friend of Col. Walton and asked if Col. Walton wished to take another shot, the friend of Col. Walton replied that Col. W. was then unable to take another shot and requested that the parties might leave the ground to have their wounds examined, which was consented to, and the parties retired to an adjoining shade. Soon after, the friend of Col Walton met the friend of Dr. McMahon and said, in consequence of his wound, Colonel Walton would be obliged to leave the field, and that he wished Col. W. to remove to the nearest house, to have his wound dressed. The friend of Dr. McMahon asked the friend of Col. Walton if the Colonel was perfectly satisfied, he replied, the affair can proceed no further; it must rest here; Col. Walton is not able to take another fire, and then returned to assist Col. W. from the field."[36] All honor satisfied, Walton remained in this office till the move to Mobile, Alabama.

It appears the family visited Mobile in 1830, previous to the move, during one of Octavia's trial flights. In April of 1830, Sarah Haynsworth Gayle wrote in her journal about Mr. Bowman and his perspective on the belles of Mobile. Those young girls available for marriage included: Harriet Gayle, Miss Leslie, and Octavia Walton. In 1831, Sarah's husband, John Gayle, was elected governor of Alabama.[37]

Another friend, Dr. Wither's, brought Sarah more information on the status of belles in Mobile when he visited on May 21, 1830. She commented in her journal, "Caroline Leslie is greatly changed, in their manner more than person tho' that is thin. Her native fondness for argument & her satirical powers render her an object of fear to society. This may be true, but I cannot believe she evinces a jealousy of the admiration Miss Walton receives. Caroline is inferior to few women, to none in Alabama, so far as my acquaintance extends. If she be envious she has too much policy to let it be known." Octavia was still

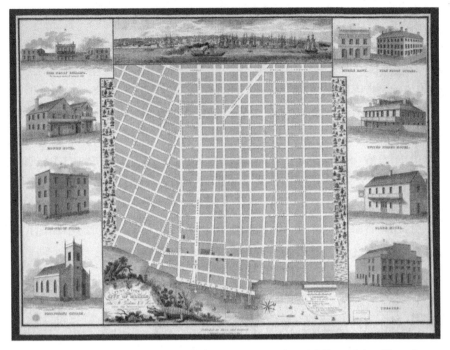

Map of Mobile, Alabama. Goodwin, Jas M. *Plan & View of the City of Mobile.* Photograph. Washington, D.C., 1824. Library of Congress Geography and Map Division Washington, D.C. 20540-4650 USA.

attracting attention at twenty years old, not married, and someone who brought out jealousy in other ladies. A common occurrence as she rose in the ranks of society.[38]

Octavia's life changed dramatically when her grandmother, Dorothy Walton, passed away on September 12, 1832. Octavia inherited her portion of Dorothy's enslaved and the income from their rental, a miniature painting of George Walton and the collection of letters between Dorothy and George Walton, Sr. during the Revolutionary War. These letters were all that remained after a house fire at the Walton residence in 1825 burned the valuable historical letters.[39] Dorothy was buried in a marble-topped grave at St. Michael's Cemetery, located in the downtown district of Pensacola.

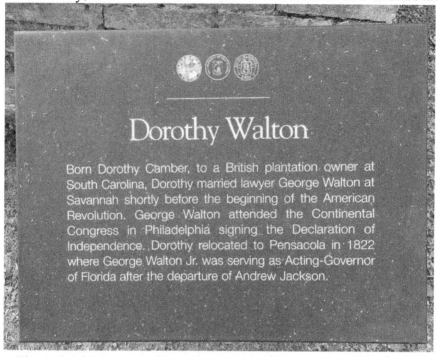

Dorothy Walton

Born Dorothy Camber, to a British plantation owner at South Carolina, Dorothy married lawyer George Walton at Savannah shortly before the beginning of the American Revolution. George Walton attended the Continental Congress in Philadelphia signing the Declaration of Independence. Dorothy relocated to Pensacola in 1822 where George Walton Jr. was serving as Acting-Governor of Florida after the departure of Andrew Jackson.

The marker for the grave of Dorothy Walton in Pensacola, Florida. St. Michael's Cemetery. 2019. Photograph.

At the death of Dorothy, the resources used to support the Walton family went on to the surviving family. Also, time had passed, and so had the memory of George Walton's deeds.

It was time to truly introduce the available young woman in the family to Society. According to *A Southern Odyssey*, by John Hope Franklin, "No grand tour was completely successful without the visit to one or more of the fashionable watering-places - Saratoga Springs, Balston, Newport, or Cape May. Some Southerners spent

The grave of Dorothy Walton in Pensacola, Florida. St. Michael's Cemetery.
2019. Photograph

their entire time away from home at Saratoga or Newport, while some were there for only a few weeks or days."[40]

Octavia was twenty-three years old and still not married. The reasons she remained so in an age where young women in Society tended to marry early are numerous. Some considerations include the fact she was so popular. Eligible bachelors, young and old, continuously courted her. Her family might have seen her status as a method of developing the necessary connections in society and politics. Another consideration may rest in the development of Octavia's way of thinking. When men held the majority of the power, Octavia learned her advanced status in society allowed her advantages, which many other women did not have. She might have had pronounced reservations about men due to the situation between her mother and father. Despite her love for him, her exposure to his negative vices did not mean she wanted to marry a man like her father. She did not want to deal with a man who did not respect the sanctity of marriage and security of home by gambling, drinking, and possibly womanizing.[41]

Octavia's natural position in Society allowed her to meet significant people in Pensacola, Mobile, and New Orleans. She was about to meet someone who helped steer the direction of her life toward a more literary influence. The chance meeting can be called a variety of things: happenstance or the good fortune to be at the right place at the right time, but the results were the same.

Sally and Octavia, escorted by her brother Robert, were riding a coach North from Mobile. They had taken a riverboat up from the city and had transferred to a stagecoach.

It was the Spring of 1833, and they were on their way to Augusta, Georgia, where they were expected in April.[42]

Their earlier travels throughout the South and the connections they made were paying off. They went through various cities where they now had friends or introductions, and they received the well-known Miss Octavia Walton into society as a belle. During this trip, the Walton's shared a carriage with a very distinguished-looking man, dark-haired and dark-eyed, also destined North, but not much for conversation.[43]

Virginia Tattnall's account of this incident explains best what happened next, "They speculated frequently upon his identity, for his appearance was unusual, his manner courtly, and his language that of a most cultivated man. While she (Octavia) was talking to her brother in Spanish one day, he joined in their conversation and related some incident in connection with a bull-fight he had seen when in Spain. Octavia had already heard the identical story from another source, and, connecting the two narrations, she exclaimed, quickly and quite unconsciously betraying the fact that his identity had been a matter of curiosity to her, "I know who you are! You are Washington Irving. Mr. Slidell, who related that story to me, told me that Washington Irving was standing beside him when it happened." Thus began a friendship that had an extensive influence upon her life."[44]

It was not unusual for Octavia to know who Washington Irving was when she made her statement. The Walton's were people of some wealth and their

Washington Irving. Photograph. Washington, D.C., 1859. Library of Congress Prints and Photographs Division Washington, D.C. 20540 USA https://hdl.loc.gov/loc.pnp/pp.print.

extensive travels allowed them to buy books, subscribe to English reviews, and meet their counterparts in Newport or Saratoga, or Paris.[45] The publication of Irving's book, *The Sketchbook,* and the viral short story "Rip Van Winkle" in 1819 allowed Irving fame he had not encountered in the past. It easily could have found itself in the hands of Octavia.[46]

Many years later, in 1857, when Octavia's fame was at its highest and Washington Irving had retired peacefully at his home called Sunnyside, she wrote to him about their encounter when she was a young woman. He confirmed their meeting and called her his "fellow traveler." He also recalled the "much more civilized and brilliant scenes thus, we once witnessed together in Alabama."[47]

The Walton's first stop was in Augusta, Georgia, where they spent the early part of the Summer of 1833[48] and parted ways with Washington Irving, though he continued to influence her later in life. This clandestine meeting resulted in a relationship that helped guide her toward a more literary path and provided an avenue to exercise her education and skills.

According to a letter discovered by Caldwell Delaney, she was popular in Augusta before they had arrived. It was to a friend, a young man describing the current Season. He was quick to note, "I am the only man in this place who waltzes and Miss Walton, the great Florida Belle, who is here, and I have fine sport in astonishing the natives and making the men envious."[49]

Octavia and the Walton family arrived in New York around June 28th, 1833.[50] Her activities are currently unknown during her visit to New York, but since it was so important for her arrival in town be announced in the paper, it is a good guess she was introduced to the social scene in New York. It is also possible she visited Washington Irving at home for the first time at Sunnyside, the tiny castle he had built on the east bank of the Hudson.[51]

The family soon moved on to where Octavia had the largest influence due to her status as the granddaughter of George Walton, Sr.; Washington D.C. She arrived in the winter of 1833, where she was officially introduced to Society and chaperoned by no other than her dear friend from Alabama, Susannah Whithers Clay, the wife of Clement Comer Clay. According to the book, *A Belle of the Fifties*, "At a time when a knowledge of the foreign tongues was seldom acquired by American women, Miss Walton, who spoke French, Spanish and Italian with ease, speedily her fame which afterward became international."[52]

Elswyth Thane, author of *Mount Vernon is Ours*, summarizes her activities in Washington D.C. nicely, "In Washington that winter, she sat each day in the gallery at Congress, taking notes in her journal while Clay, Webster, and Calhoun debated President Jackson's unpopular policies, and she was highly regarded by all of them as a reporter. She was painted by Thomas Sully, wearing a rose-pink silk gown and accompanied by her guitar - being listed in his register as "Miss Walton of Pensacola."[53]

The season Octavia spent in Washington D.C. was a success. It is unknown where they traveled during the early part of 1834, but there are hints. For example, much like they did when traveling along the Gulf Coast region, the family moved to other fashionable areas to introduce Octavia; this time, it was Saratoga and Newport. A society reporter attending Octavia's reception at Saratoga reported, "Amid the charming representatives of the various states, she stands the most distinguished, having no rival. Her colloquial talents, her tact, emanating from a kind heart, captivate all who approach her."[54] The Waltons, riding on a wave of social success, arrived in Newport where it was reported that "No queen could have met with a more enthusiastic reception."[55]

Accounts of the Walton family and Octavia's continued impact on society are scarce the early part of 1834, but she does make her way back to Alabama, and we can find an account in the journal of Sarah Haynsworth Gayle in Tuskaloosa on December 1st, 1834, "A separate paragraph must mention the arrival of Mrs. and Miss Walton - the admired of all eyes - the theme of all tongues - the admiration of all hearts - a very witch - a sorceress whose spells there is no revisiting. She must be a remarkable girl, tho' I am not yet able to settle upon the particular trait which win all to admire & love her. She is quite low, with the round French figure - not a pretty complexion - grey eyes, large mouth, full of the finest teeth ever seen - but there is an animation, a fullness of life, perfectly indescribable. Her intellect seems to be fine, & her mind is said to be well cultivated. She has traveled all over the United States, spending her winters in the cities & her summers at the Lakes, the Springs, in Canada, & indeed wherever nature deals in the grand, the beautiful

& the wonderful; or wherever society could lay the brightest & largest trophies at her feet." She continued to comment, "Tuskaloosa will require time to recover from the ecstasy into which she has thrown it."[56]

The Walton family finally returned to Pensacola by April of 1835, and Octavia, specifically, was greeted home by a poem in the *Pensacola Gazette*. The poem acknowledged the extensive travels and the success she had with Society. It also implored her to wander no more and stay in her "native bower,"[57] though this advice was not heeded.

Sarah Haynsworth Gayle mentioned Octavia again in her journal about Sally Walton and Octavia. Still, she noted something was appearing unusual to her when she was called upon by Mrs. Walker, "...the importance of the whole family is derived from the young lady."[58]

Sometime in 1835, when Octavia, Sally, and Robert returned to Pensacola, the family moved to Mobile, Alabama, and George Walton, Jr., with his son, began practicing as a lawyer in Alabama.[59] Mobile was in the middle of a building boom. Many new houses and stores appeared downtown, and it grew one-fourth larger physically than it had been just one year before.[60]

One can only be introduced to Society and be its queen for so long, and Octavia's time was waning. She was twenty-five years old and among the older group of young ladies who had not yet married. If her status of remaining single so long was the choice of her family or a personal one, it mattered not. If she was to have a successful match, the time had to be soon.

Works Cited and Notes

1. Octavia Walton Le Vert Autograph Album, 1829, MS#1009. Columbia University Libraries Rare Book & Manuscript Library, *Edgar Allan Poe papers, 1827 – 1908.*
2. Jabour, *Scarlett's Sisters*, 27.
3. Jabour, *Scarlett's Sisters*, 27.
4. Octavia Walton Le Vert Autograph Album, Columbia University Libraries Rare Book & Manuscript Library, *Edgar Allan Poe papers, 1827 – 1908.*
5. Anya Jabour, "Albums of Affection: Female Friendship and Coming of Age in Antebellum Virginia," *The Virginia Magazine of History and Biography* 107, no. 2 (Spring 1999): 125-158.
6. Octavia Walton Le Vert Autograph Album, 1826, MS#1009. Columbia University Libraries Rare Book & Manuscript Library, *Edgar Allan Poe papers, 1827 – 1908.*
7. "Ship News, Port of Pensacola," *Pensacola Gazette* IV, Issue 1, 9 March, 1827, 3, Genealogy Bank.
8. Octavia Walton Le Vert Autograph Album, 1827, MS#1009. Columbia University Libraries Rare Book & Manuscript Library, *Edgar Allan Poe papers, 1827 – 1908.*
9. Stephanie E. Jones, *They Were Her Property: White Women as Slave Owners in the American South,* (London: Yale University Press, 2019), 33.
10. Jabour, *Scarlett's Sisters*, 27.
11. Delaney, "Madame Octavia Walton Le Vert."
12. Paul Williams, *Jackson, Crockett and Houston on the American Frontier: From Fort Mims to the Alamo, 1813-1836* (Jefferson: McFarland & Company, 2016), 132.
13. Lewis Leary, "Miss Octavia's Autograph Album and Edgar Allan Poe," Columbia Library Columns 17, no. 1 (1967): 9. Friends of the Columbia Library.
14. Octavia Walton Le Vert Autograph Album, 1827, MS#1009. Columbia University Libraries Rare Book & Manuscript Library, *Edgar Allan Poe papers, 1827 – 1908.*

15. Octavia Walton Le Vert Autograph Album, 1827, MS#1009. Columbia University Libraries Rare Book & Manuscript Library, *Edgar Allan Poe papers, 1827 – 1908.*

16. Sarah Haynsworth Gayle, *The Journal of Sarah Haynsworth Gayle, 1827 - 1835,* ed. Sarah Woolfolk Wiggins (Tuscaloosa: University of Alabama Press, 2013), 5.

17. "Territorial Treasury," *Pensacola Gazette* IV, no. 25, August 24, 1827, Genealogy Bank.

18. Octavia Walton Le Vert Autograph Album, 1827, MS#1009. Columbia University Libraries Rare Book & Manuscript Library, *Edgar Allan Poe papers, 1827 – 1908.* Note: In the autograph journal belonging to Octavia Walton Le Vert. Author indexing, page 64.

19. "Shipping news," *Pensacola Gazette,* IV, no. 29, page 2, October 8, 1827, Genealogy Bank.

20. Octavia Walton Le Vert Autograph Album, 1827, MS#1009. Columbia University Libraries Rare Book & Manuscript Library, *Edgar Allan Poe papers, 1827 – 1908.*

21. "A Notable American Woman," *Rhode Island Press,* April 21, 1877, Genealogy Bank.

22. Mrs. Thaddeus Horton, "Madame LeVert and Her Friends," *Uncle Remus's Magazine,* 1907, 1.

23. Octavia Walton Le Vert Autograph Album; 1828; Edgar Allan Poe papers, 1827 – 1908. MS#1009. Columbia University Libraries Rare Book & Manuscript Library, New York City, New York, United States. Note: I compared the handwriting from the journal to the handwriting of S.C.C. in the LeVert papers from UNC Chapel Hill Library and they are a match.

24. *Pensacola Gazette,* April 11, 1828, 3; Octavia Walton Le Vert Autograph Album; 1828; Edgar Allan Poe papers, 1827 – 1908. MS#1009. Columbia University Libraries Rare Book & Manuscript Library, New York City, New York, United States.

25. Charles Steedman and Amos Lawrence Mason, *Memoir and Correspondence of Charles Steedman, Rear Admiral 1811-1890* (Cambridge: Riverside Press, 1912), Hathitrust.

26. Forrest, *Women of the South Distinguished in Literature,* 17.

27. Octavia Walton Le Vert Autograph Album; 1828; Edgar Allan Poe papers, 1827 – 1908. MS#1009. Columbia University Libraries Rare Book & Manuscript Library, New York City, New York, United States.

28. Gayle, 53.

29. Charles Grayson Summersell, *Mobile: History of a Seaport Town* (Tuscaloosa: The University of Alabama Press, 1949), 16.

30. Students of the University of Virginia. A Semi-centennial catalogue with Brief Biographical Sketches. Manuscript. Baltimore: Charles Harvey & Co. Publishers, 19.

31. Marion Elias Lazenby, *History of Methodism in Alabama and West Florida* (Alabama and West Florida Conferences, 1960), 130.

32. Carnley, "Who Was George Walton Jr," 2-6.

33. Will of Dorothy Walton. Will. University of West Florida Archives, *Satterfield Collection.*

34. Will of Dorothy Walton. Will. University of West Florida Archives, *Satterfield Collection.*

35. Carnley, "Who Was George Walton Jr," 2-6.

36. *Gazette Extra,* June 2, 1829. 86-1, Box 7, University of West Florida Archives. *Sutton Collection.*

37. Gayle, 128. Note: April 1830 entry.

38. Gayle, 134. Note: Friday, May 21, 1830.

39. *Miss Octavia Walton LeVert to Mr. Leach*, 1885. Letter. University of West Florida Archives, *Satterfield Collection.*

40. John Hope Franklin, *A Southern Odyssey: Travelers in the Antebellum North*, (Baton Rouge: LSU Press, 1979).

41. Jabour, *Scarlett's Sisters*, 27.

42. Delaney, "Madame Octavia Walton Le Vert."

43. Horton, "Madame LeVert and Her Friends," 1:19.

44. Peacock, *Famous American Belles.*

45. Anne Firor Scott, *The Southern Lady: From Pedestal to Politics, 1830-1930* (Charlottesville: University Press of Virginia, 1995).

46. Peacock, *Famous American Belles,* 109. Note: Uncle Remus Magazine, the person was Mr. Slidell of New Orleans.

47. *Washington Irving to Madame LeVert*, September 22, 1857. Letter. The University of West Florida Archives. *Satterfield Collection.*

48. List of Letters, Walton Mrs. George, Walton Miss Octavia, April 9, 1833, Georgia Constitutionalist, Georgia Historic Newspapers.

49. Delaney, "Madame Octavia Walton Le Vert." Note: J.V. to George Tyler Olmsted, Esq. "Augusta, May 20, 1833." Note: In the Josephine Walton collection. As of 2019, the collection titled Josephine Walton is missing since the time Delaney saw it.

50. *Evening Post,* no. 9628, June 28, 1833, 2. Genealogy Bank. Note: In copying the list of David Brown's passengers, the names of Mrs.

Geo. Walton and Miss Octavia C.V. Walton were accidentally left out.

51. Thane, *Mount Vernon is Ours*, 52.

52. Virginia Clay-Compton and Ada Sterling, *A Belle of the Fifties: Memoirs of Mrs. Clay, of Alabama, covering Social and Political Life in Washington and the South, 1853-66*, (New York: Doubleday, Pay & Company, 1905), 35.

53. Biddle and Fielding, *Life and Works of Thomas Sully (1783-1872)*. Note: Portrait began October 25, 1833, finished December 12, 1833. Whole length price, $300.00. This was one of his most expensive paintings.

54. Delaney, "Madame Octavia Walton Le Vert," 6.

55. Elizabeth Fries Ellet, *Queens of American Society* (New York: C. Scribner, 1867), 412-413.

56. Gayle, 300. Note: This entry is from December 1, 1834.

57. "Passengers," *The Pensacola Galette*, April 6, 1835, GenealogyBank.

58. Gayle, 310. Note: This entry is from Wednesday, 15 April, 1835.

59. Thane, *Mount Vernon is Ours*, 52. Note: according to the document, Octavia Walton LeVert The Belle of the Union by Beverly, "When Governor George Walton came to Mobile, he lived at No. 7 North Conception street, which must have been near Dauphin, on the west side, approximately in the two story brick, which had an iron lace rail and it is reached by a stairway, as all of the lower stories have been used for business for 80 years or more."

60. Harriet Elizabeth Amos, "Social Life in an Antebellum Cotton Port" (Master's Thesis, Emory University, 1976).

Chapter 5

Man Not Like Her Father

Woman oh woman! Whose form and whose soul,
Are the spell and the light of the path we pursue;
Whether sunn'd in the tropics or chill'd at the pole,
If woman be there, there is happiness too.[1]

The dramatic growth of Mobile, Alabama, in the 1830s, turned the old port town into a larger city, attracting wealthy cotton dealers and plantation owners who meandered downriver from the Alabama Delta to sell cotton and purchase supplies for their upriver plantations. The increase in traffic resulted in a good income for professional doctors and lawyers.

George Walton Jr. was almost fifty years old and ready for a less dramatic life. His son, Robert, had completed law school and was practicing by his side. The pull to migrate to Mobile was strong, and when George's tenure of office expired in Florida in 1835, the Walton's changed their residence yet again, moving to Mobile.[2] The years of bad blood, traveling through jungle-like climates, and surviving a duel seemed to feed George's need for a comfortable life, and maybe he could find such comforts in this city.

Sarah Minge Walton, his ever-patient wife, took up the role of matriarch of the family and filled in where George often fell short. It is most likely she took up the same practice as the women before her and rented out the skilled enslaved she inherited from Dorothy Walton and Elizabeth Talbot Walker. Slavery, and ever challenging and disagreeable practice, was an early avenue for affluent women who could not easily own land to garnish a reliable income. It was an unfortunate necessity when the men in their lives were not always above reproach and could endanger their family's livelihood and status in society.[3]

The move from Pensacola, Florida, to the larger city of Mobile was ideal for a family seeking great access to Southern Society. The Walton's visited Mobile frequently during their travels to see friends, and attend balls in the Alabama Delta. The city was an excellent place to continue introducing Octavia to potential suitors. They saw Mobile's growth with the increase in cotton crop coming down the river in every visit. Between 1820 and 1830, the city's population increased dramatically from 2762 residents to 6267.[4]

In 1835 the Walton family resided in Mobile and living in a raised cottage, typical for the affluent, on St. Anthony Street at the north west corner of Conception Street. The family liked it well enough, for they resided here for many years.[5] According to Summersell, "When the famous Irish actor, Tyrone Power, visited Mobile in 1835, he observed, "This little city was to be one of the most attractive spots I visited south of the Potomac...I found here...the best conducted and best appointed hotel in the Southern country, and society congenial and amiable; all these combined go a good way to prejudice a man in favor of a place which in itself may have little to recommend it."[6]

Time also came for Octavia to settle down and take the next life-altering leap for one in her station in society: marriage. In later years, those who interviewed Octavia in her role as "Madame LeVert" sought an exciting story associated with her meeting Dr. Henry S. LeVert, and Octavia obliged. As described by Caldwell Delaney, "Octavia engaged in charity work which was expected of young ladies of good family and served as a volunteer nurse. In this activity, within a year after her arrival in the city, she met a young Doctor Henry Strachey LeVert."[7] While this is commonly told, evidence shows introductions between these two prior to this time and the tale is probably more interesting.

Dr. Henry S. LeVert, the youngest son of Claude and Ann LeVert, was thirty-one years old in 1835, had lived in Mobile for over five years, and his practice was growing as part of the dramatic increase in population. His family had called Alabama home for many years.[8] He and his older brothers and sisters lost their father not long after Henry's birth. Claude LeVert, their father, was a native of France and had come to America to fight in the

Revolutionary War along with Rochambeau as his ship's surgeon. He chose to remain in the newly formed United States and start a family.

Claude's Will gives an idea of his character; he was a man who focused on a sense of fairness, for the time, and education. He wanted all his debts paid out of the Estate, each girl to have an enslaved girl each as part of their increase, and the sons to have a funded education.[9] Henry, himself, was not an owner of slaves by inheritance, like Octavia, but the lifestyle was one very familiar to him.

Henry attended the School of Medicine of the University of Pennsylvania from 1826 to 1828 and received his degree in 1829 after an internship at the Alms House.[10] He submitted his dissertation on the use of Metallic Ligature of Arteries. Simply put, he devised a new method of closing arteries using metal wire.[11] After he passed his exam, he told his brother, Francis, "I felt very much flattered by the compliments passed on me by the professors." He added regarding his thesis, "You will see it, for it has been published. The subject was one altogether novel, and being experimental, and my experiments succeeding remarkably well, it has excited a good deal of interest."[12]

After graduation and spending time in Philadelphia, the new Dr. Henry S. LeVert was ready to begin his practice. In 1829, he started working in Mobile, Alabama, and had a letter of introduction from his sister's husband, Dr. Francis T. Martin of Huntsville, Alabama. His first year in Mobile, he chose to remain in the city instead of going to the surrounding country as the other practicing physicians since he was already exposed to yellow fever and immune. Eager to put his degree to work, he was available to help with diseases and fevers that arrived during the summer months.[13v]

In 1832 Dr. LeVert started working for the city and was sent by the mayor of Mobile, John Stocking, Jr., to Norfolk, Virginia, to study an outbreak and treatment of cholera.[14] This information was valuable to prepare for when the disease came into the city. His studies soon took him on to Philadelphia when the plague was dying out in Virginia.[15]

In all of Henry's travels North, it is hard to imagine he did not know about the young woman from Florida who attracted eligible men throughout the South. According to one news article Octavia was famous for teasing her suitors, "She would tell them in the harsh or musical accents of their individual countries that she loved them, but not with a love like theirs, and this so prettily that they would leave her presence, declaring it better to be refused by her than accepted by another." She was also recognized as an incorrigible flirt, and her offers of marriage were in the hundreds.[16]

One early meeting might have taken place in April of 1834 when a public dinner was arranged for Lieutenant Ogden, of the U.S. Corps of Engineers. He superintended the construction of the military works at Mobile Point[17] and, after completing the job, retired from the station. At this farewell dinner, Col. George Walton officiated as president, and Dr. Henry S. LeVert was one of the organizers. A true Society event, despite none of the ladies mentioned in the account, Lieutenant Ogden specifically toasted, "Woman!" followed by a poem originally written by Thomas Moore. It is almost certain Octavia was at this event with her father.[18]

Octavia was twenty-four years old, and her popularity among Society was not denied despite her age being more significant than other young ladies. When new music was released in 1834, the "Octavia Waltz, dedicated to Miss Walton," was published[19.] In December of the same year, it was reported in the *Tuscaloosa Register*, "The society of our town has been delighted and interested in several days past by a visit of the intelligent and highly accomplished Miss Walton, of Pensacola. -- Her departure will be a source of regret to the fashionable and gay of Tuscaloosa."[20]

Another chance meeting between Miss Walton and Dr. Henry LeVert is found in June 1835, when she arrived with her father, Col. Walton, in New York aboard the *Splendid* and Dr. LeVert also arrived in New York on the same day aboard the *Junior*, both ships from Mobile, Alabama.[21]

There is a small portrait Dr. LeVert had made of himself, dated on the back June 29th, 1835, by the artist John W. Dodge while visiting in the North, and at the same time, they both were in New York. If Dr. LeVert knew about the history of the small portrait painted of Octavia's grandfather for her grandmother, then this quiet and clever doctor might have devised a unique way of winning the heart of Miss Octavia Walton.[22]

Dr. Henry S. LeVert about the time he met Octavia Walton. Henry S. LeVert. Photograph. Pensacola, Florida, 1835. University of West Florida University Archives and West Florida History Center. Current location unknown.

While Octavia Walton LeVert told the tale of her meeting Dr. LeVert while serving the poor in Mobile, and this is a possibility, they must have known each other to some degree beforehand. Considering this and along with the Walton's recent move to Mobile and Henry already living in the city, the odds of them being around each other long enough to develop any sort of in-depth relationship is significant.

It had to be, for Dr. Henry S. LeVert was a man, unlike the ones she was customarily exposed. James Edmonds Saunders, the author of *Early Settlers of Alabama*, commented, "Mrs. LeVert, once Octavia Walton, must have had a substratum of good common sense, to have selected so solid a man as Dr. LeVert from a crowd of such frivolous suitors as contended for the hand of the Pensacola belle."[23]

Her father, Col. George Walton, and her brother, Robert, practiced law together in Mobile in 1835, but Col. Walton did not stay out of politics. The men in Octavia's life had a flair for the dramatic, possibly increasing her attraction to Henry. In *Sketches of Mobile*, they are described as notable men of the South. Robert earned the description as a remarkably handsome young man, "whose fine figure is adorned with the exquisite taste of a man of fashion. In the lineaments of his face, you will see traces of beauty mingled with intellectual excellence, for nature has stamped on his brow the seal of mental manhood."[24]

Dr. Henry S. LeVert was a vastly different type of man than Octavia's father and brother. He also must have felt he was financially secure enough to take on a person of Octavia's status and established sufficient for George Walton to release his daughter into his care.[25] T.C. DeLeon described Henry's feelings about Octavia's role in society, stating, "His profession gave him ample means, and he was complaisant enough not to balk his wife's desire to entertain all of society, including the most pronounced freaks that clung to its periphery."[26]

Octavia, now among the older belles in Society, had become dangerously close to the life of spinsterhood. She felt the pressure into marriage since, at the time, it was the aim of elite women in the antebellum South. Her status as the granddaughter of a Signer of the Declaration of Independence and the daughter of a former official from Florida freed her from the need to marry early to gain social approval and economic security. She had the luxury to hold out for romantic love, but this was coming to an end.[27]

Painting made by Thomas Sully for Octavia's introduction to Society. Leeth, Yancy. *Miss Walton of Florida.* Photograph. Mobile, Alabama, 2021. Oakleigh House Museum.

Painting made of Henry S. LeVert by T.S. Officer in 1838 to compliment Octavia's painting. Leeth, Yancy. *Henry Strachey Levert M.D. 1804-1864.* Photograph. Mobile, Alabama, 2021. Oakleigh House Museum.

On the evening of February 6th, 1836, twenty-six-year-old Miss Octavia C.V. Walton, daughter of Col. George Walton, late of Florida, married in Mobile, Henry S. LeVert, M.D. It was also noted the "bride was a celebrated belle at Saratoga last summer."[28]

A common practice during this time to be considered at this stage of Octavia's life is the issuance of enslaved to Octavia and Henry as a wedding gift. Even though this newly married couple were not members of the elite planter class, they were related to those who followed similar practices. They lived in the city, so they did not have enslaved like those on plantations. Instead, they had enough to run the household and possibly rent out some as income, a common practice for the time and something Octavia was exposed to her entire life.

It is also possible to assume the time of Octavia's marriage was the same time that she was either given the enslaved, Betsey Walton, as a wedding gift, or she might have been one of her enslaved that graduated to the position. Rumors arose later that Col. George, her father, gave Betsey to her because he saw Octavia as a better mistress than his wife, Sally.[29]

Betsey, born in 1824[30], was the perfect age at twelve to learn how to take care of the growing LeVert family. An account of an enslaved named Lucy in a similar situation at nearby Blakeley resulted in a person trained in the duties of a children's nurse, someone who had some education and worked in families of refinement and culture.[31]

According to the book, *They Were Her Property*, "Slave-owning kin gave brides-to-be enslaved people as wedding gifts, which served to augment their economic investments in slavery at a time when historians contend that married women endured "civil death" and had no other choice but to resign themselves to their fate."[32] In time, Betsey's position within the family grew more into administrative, caring for the physical and mental health of Octavia. Betsey, herself, received certain notoriety, unlike other women in her station, but still was under the bonds of slavery.[33]

Where the newly married couple first lived is unknown; it is assumed they lived within the Walton home. According to Francis Gibson Satterfield, "Dr. LeVert and Octavia must have lived with her parents for a while after their marriage for both families are listed on Government Street in the 1837 Mobile City Directory."[34]

After the wedding, the celebrated belle quickly became the expectant mother. Henry was investing his money in real estate and housekeeping since he was newly married and expecting his first child and his medical practice was slowly growing. He wrote his oldest brother, Francis, telling him, "I expect to have an heir sometime in Nov."[35]

The happy news was also tempered with concern for Robert Walton placed his practice as a lawyer on hold temporarily to serve in the Creek War. He was a major and founding member of the Mobile Rifles, becoming Colonel of that Regiment.[36]

Silver Christening cup for Henry and Octavia's first daughter. Leeth, Yancy. Octavia Walton Levert November 1836. Photograph. Mobile, Alabama, 2021. Oakleigh House Museum.

Leeth, Yancy. *Octavia Walton Levert November 1836*. Photograph. Mobile, Alabama, 2021. Oakleigh House Museum.

On November 20th, 1836, Henry, Octavia, and the Walton's welcomed their first child and grandchild into the world in Mobile, Alabama, and named her for her mother, Octavia Walton LeVert; however, the family often referred to her as "Diddie."[37] She was presented with a silver Christening cup as a gift, but from whom is unknown.[38]

Also, it seems as if marriage and a new family did not put a damper on Octavia and her mother's traveling. Henry told his brother that Octavia and Sally planned to visit Huntsville next Spring on their way to the North, where they expected to spend their Summer.[39] While marriage and the start of a family tended to end the belledom of newly married women at the various Springs of the North, making those who were introduced to

Society wallflowers and discards, Octavia Walton, now LeVert, was among the exception cases.[40]

Henry's pleasant outlook on life continued as he adjusted to a new life with his wife and child despite several unfortunate circumstances. While his new father-in-law, George Walton, was the Mayor of Mobile, this did not help anyone during the Panic of 1837; according to Weymouth T. Jordan, "Because of the panic and the drastic drop in cotton prices, the latter part of the 1830's was not a happy time for Mobile businessmen and their up-country clientele." [41]

On January 23, 1837, Dr. LeVert purchased the property located at 151 and 153 Government Street from Michael J. Kenan, W.D., for the future home for his family. In April of 1837, the framed wooden building he was constructing to house his medical practice on Government Street was blown down by a reported tornado.[42] Henry, a steady sort of man, continued to practice medicine and gain respect in his field.

On May 6, 1837, Henry Clay, an ever-present figure in the Walton's lives, made his first visit to Mobile and was invited to a public dinner held in his honor by Col. George Walton. Still, he was in town for a short time and had to leave, turning down the invitation.[43] Though not proven, it does appear Octavia and Henry Clay developed a close father-daughter relationship during her visits to Washington and the Springs in her younger years. His visit allowed Clay to see Octavia and maybe even check up on her and see if her new husband was a good match.

By September 20th, 1837, Brother Frances LeVert, received a letter from another younger brother, Eugene, informing him about Henry in Mobile, stating, "He enjoys good health as also his wife and daughter. As to pecuniary embarrassments, he does not say a word. I learned, however, from a gentleman of that city that the hospital which he was erecting has stopt, but from what cause, he could not tell me. I presume it was for want of money, as his partner Judge Hitchcock has failed."[44] Henry's struggles appear to be well known in the family but not amongst those in Society, and the focus seemed to be more upon Octavia, his new wife, than on the status of his medical practice.

Frederick Porcher, enjoying the Virginia Springs in 1838, commented on Octavia's growth into a "literary character." Having a close friendship with someone as famous as Washington Irving certainly helped Octavia in this area. Porcher further wrote, "She was now the wife of Dr. Levert of Alabama. I think I discovered the secret of her power of pleasing. She appeared to be, and I believe was, perfectly amiable, was rather small, rather under than over the middle stature, with a figure by no means good, and a face that owed more to a good-humored expression than to any power or beauty of feature for its charms; but there was a warmth and cordiality in her manner that was irresistible. She never forgot a face nor a name. I believe she never forgot one's connections, for she recognized my wife as soon as she was introduced by her new name, and inquired after her Aunts, Mrs. Wilkes and Mrs. Lightwood. Perhaps I was in an ill humor and fastidious, but it seemed to me that there was a touch of vulgarity about her, which added to her popularity."[45]

Porcher described the twenty-eight-year-old Octavia as always in motion and continuously noisy. She visited each cabin at the Sweet Springs and had a voice that could be distinctly heard all over the grounds. It was clear Octavia and Sally had a very close relationship, and when Octavia had more offers to dance at the cotillion, she suggested they dance with her mother.[46]

Octavia was gifted in making society connections was also a voracious reader. Having children and the long periods in between allowed her time to pursue her love of literature. She read books such as Ethel Churchill by Letitia Elizabeth Landon (L.E.L.) and copied phrases and quotes into her private journal, those pieces reflecting how she felt in regard to her station in life. It is also possible she collected these pieces for the salon-like gatherings she enjoyed so much.

Octavia was proud of her family, its status, and copied the statement, "talents of the high imaginative order seemed rather benefit others than their possessors." She was fully aware of her intelligence, but being a woman, could not benefit from it. Another comment she quoted from a book in her diary seems to support this idea, "The spirit within me asserts its divine rights...Can the gift of mind be given to me in vain? It were a mockery of the intellectual supremacy, did I not, believe in my own future."[47]

Octavia and M.D., her nickname for Henry, welcomed their next child on May 22, 1838, and named her Claudia Anna Eugenia, a name formed from many of their family members, including Henry's father and brother and Octavia's grandmother. She was now twenty-nine years old and had been married for three years and was the mother of two girls'.[48] Henry practiced at 45 Conti street, and her father, now Mayor of Mobile, and brother had an office at St. Anthony and Conception street.[49]

She recovered from her daughter's birth in time to travel to White Sulphur Springs in the summer of 1838, where she and her mother once again attracted attention. Delphine Weeks commented in a letter to Melanie Weeks, her sister living in Mobile, "Their manners are so Frenchified that I sometimes fancy that they are speaking in French to me."[50]

Octavia was still recovering from giving birth, but this did not stop Sally Walton, her mother, from attracting attention and earning the title of "reigning Belle of the Blue Sulphur." When they returned to White Sulphur, Octavia was better and began strumming her Spanish guitar and singing songs she learned in Florida. Normally, when a woman became married, she stopped enjoying the freedom of her belle days, but not so for Octavia. She and her mother both loved to dance and therefore continued to dance as they had before, attracting attention.[51]Miss Weeks told her sister, "The country ladies have come 16 and 20 miles, fifteen in a stage, to see the Grand Mother dance and were not a little astonished to see Grand Mother dance as light as a girl of fifteen."[52]

Octavia, as a wife and mother of two children, certainly experienced fears that her extraordinary life could change her as a person were unfounded. It seems she had married an understanding husband. Marriage, instead, enhanced her life and standing in society, and she continued to be herself, her happy self, enjoying the attention she and her mother still attracted. Sadness had yet to catch up with her and the rest of the family.

Works Cited and Notes

1. Thomas Moore, *The Poetical Works of Thomas Moore: Complete* (New York: D. Appleton & Company, 1853) Google Books.

2. Stephens, *Madame Octavia Walton LeVert*, 17.

3. Kristen Epps, *Slavery on the Periphery: The Kansas-Missouri Border in the Antebellum and Civil War Eras* (Athens: University of Georgia Press, 2016), 64.

4. Summersell, *Mobile*, 12.

5. Delaney, "Madame Octavia Walton Le Vert;" Thomas C. Fay, Fay's Mobile Directory for 1839 (R.R. Dade, 1839).

6. Summersell, *Mobile*, 21.

7. Delaney, "Madame Octavia Walton Le Vert," 20.

8. Note: Information is from LeVert descendant, Traci LeVert Foster. She stated the LeVert's came to Alabama around 1818. Eugene Verdot LeVert was the brother of Henry and there was another brother, Francis John. Francis John was a huge merchant in Huntsville, Alabama. He and Eugene Verdot were cabinet makers in Russellville when they first arrived. The mother Ann came as well. The sisters, Martha and Elizabeth Caroline, lived in and around the area of Huntsville and Tennessee.

9. Will of Claude LeVert, January 1, 1808. Will. Private Collection of Staci Plooster. Note: Will provided by Walton descendant, Staci Plooster. Digital copy of the will in the possession of the author.

10. *Gail C.S. Cantor of the University of Pennsylvania to Mrs. M.B. Satterfield*. September 15, 1976. University of Pennsylvania. Letter.

University of West Florida, *Satterfield Collection*. Note: Digital Copy in possession of the author.

11. In the U.S. School Catalogs, 1765-1935, University of Pennsylvania, Ancestry.com.

12. Satterfield, *Madame LeVert*, 36.

13. Satterfield, *Madame LeVert*, 37.

14. *Columbian Centennial*, September 29, 1832, 1, GeneologyBank; *Henry S. Levert to John Stocking Jr., September 19, 1832*. Letter. Minnie Mitchell Archives, *LeVert Collection*.

15. Satterfield, *Madame LeVert*, 38.

16. "A Toast Drunk in a Slipper," *Omaha Daily Herald*, June 10, 1879, GenealogyBank. Note: This article goes into more detail. It states she counted her offers by the hundreds. Spaniards, Italians, Frenchmen, Germans, Englishmen, Brazilians and - worst of all - Americans by the score sighed in vain at her shrine.

17. Note: Mobile Point was a small port and stopping place for steamboats between Pensacola and New Orleans.

18. Note: The poem is at the beginning of this chapter.

19. *"Daily National Intelligencer XXIL*, no. 6670, June 26, 1834, 1.

20. *Evening Star*, December 22, 1834, 2, GenealogyBank.

21. "Shipping News," *Evening Post*, no. 10225, June 5, 1835, 3, GenealogyBank.

22. *IMG_0502*. Photograph. University of West Florida Archives, *Satterfield Collection*. Note: The small painting is missing. A photo of it is located in Madame LeVert by Satterfield.

23. James Edmonds Saunders, *Early Settlers of Alabama* (Greenville: Southern Historical Historian Press, 1899), 217. Note: This book also says Dr. Henry S. Levert was a resident of Lawrence county for several years, while a student of medicine. He made his home with an uncle of mine within sight of where I pen these lines, and taught a classical school that he might perfect his professional education - and he left many dear friends behind him.

24. Bernard A. Reynolds, *Sketches of Mobile from 1814 to the Present Time*. (Mobile: B.H. Richardson, 1868), 46-47.

25. Clinton, *Plantation Mistress*.

26. T. C. DeLeon, *Belles, Beaux and Brains of the Sixties* (New York: G.W. Dillingham Co., 1907), 183.

27. Jabour, *Scarlett's Sisters*.

28. *The Pittsfield Sun*, February 8, 1836, 3. Note: From Oakleigh, On February 8, 1836 Mobile Daily Commercial Register and Patriot Monday Evening page 2, column 3. "Married, on the evening of the 6th inst. By the Rev. Dr. Kennon, Henry S. Levert, M.D., to Miss Octavia C.V. Walton, daughter of Col. Geo. Walton, all of this city.

29. Camilla Dufour Crosland, *Landmarks of a Literary Life 1820 – 1892* (London: S. Low, Marston & Company, limited, 1893), 216.

30. U.S. Census Bureau, United States Census, 1880, Betsy Lamar, Georgia, Richmond, Augusta, 096, Ancestry.com.

31. "The Fulfilled Wish of Mammy Lucy Kimball" in *Federal Writers' Project: Slave Narrative Project, Vol. 1, Alabama, Aarons-Young* to 1937, 1936. Manuscript/Mixed Material. Library of Congress, *Digital Collection*.

32. Jones, *They Were Her Property*, 27.

33. Scott, *The Southern Lady*, 29.

34. Satterfield, *Madame LeVert*.

35. *Henry LeVert to Francis LeVert*, September 9, 1836. Letter. Private Collection of Staci Plooster, *Walker Family Cemetery Collection*. Note: Author referenced copy typed by Staci Plooster.

36. *Octavia Walton LeVert (Diddie) to Mr. Leach*, October 21, 1885. Letter. University of West Florida. *Satterfield Collection.*

37. *Octavia Walton LeVert (Diddie) to Mr. Leach*, October 21, 1885. Letter. University of West Florida. *Satterfield Collection.*

38. Note: The cup is located at Oakleigh House in Mobile Alabama.

39. *Henry LeVert to Francis LeVert*, September 9, 1836. Letter. Private Collection of Staci Plooster, *Walker Family Cemetery Collection*. Note: Author referenced copy typed by Staci Plooster.

40. Perceval Reniers, *The Springs of Virginia: Life, Love and Death at the Waters, 1775-1900* (Chapel Hill: University of North Carolina Press, 1922), 87.

41. Weymouth T. Jordan, *Ante-Bellum Alabama Town and Country* (Tuscaloosa: University of Alabama Press, 1957).

42. *Boston Post*, April 10, 1837, 2, Newspapers.com.

43. *Flag of the Union*, May 6, 1837, 3. Genealogy Bank.

44. *Eugene LeVert to Francis LeVert*, September 20, 1837. Letter. Private Collection of Staci Plooster, *Walker Family Cemetery Collection*. Note: Author referenced copy typed by Staci Plooster.

45. Frederick Adolphus Porcher and Samuel Gaillard Stoney, "The Memoirs of Frederick Adolphus Porcher (Continued)," *The South*

Carolina Historical and Genealogical Magazine 47, no. 2, 1946, 83–108. JSTOR.

46. Porcher and Stoney, "The Memoirs of Frederick Adolphus Porcher," 83-108.

47. Octavia Walton LeVert, *Excerpt from Journal of Octavia Walton LeVert, 1838.* Journal/Diary. In Madame LeVert ed. by Frances Gibson Satterfield (Edisto Island: Edisto Press, 1987), 48.

48. Satterfield, *Madame LeVert.*

49. *Mobile Directory or Strangers' Guide for 1838* (Mobile: Robert R. Dade, 1838).

50. Delaney, "Madame Octavia Walton Le Vert," 36; *Delphine Weeks to Melanie Weeks, 1838.* Letter. Minnie Mitchell Archives. *LeVert Collection.*

51. Delaney, "Madame Octavia Walton Le Vert," 45; Reniers, *The Springs of Virginia*, 12.

52. Delaney, "Madame Octavia Walton Le Vert," 45; *Delphine Weeks to Melanie Weeks, 1838.* Letter. Minnie Mitchell Archives. *LeVert Collection.*

Paula Lenor Webb

Chapter 6:

All things Mostly Good in the World

What is love? It is to dwell within
A world of the fond heart's creation where
All seemed a beauteous fairyland to work
No varied season, no flight of time,
Save in the absence of the loved one.[1]

The perceptive observation of an individual sometimes provides the clearest picture of another person's life. Major Robert A. Reynolds, author of *Sketches of Mobile*, a close friend of the LeVert's and the Walton's, described how they lived in the 1840s. Regarding Octavia, whom he admired, he remarked, "There was one trait in her character, however, which pleased me more than any other, and that was the loveliness of her domestic life, for there never existed a more devoted daughter, or more attached mother, than Mrs. LeVert."[2]

George Walton, Jr. Leeth, Yancy. *George Walton, Jr.* Photograph. Mobile, Alabama, 2021. Oakleigh House Museum. Painting by C.R. Parker.

Sarah (Sally) Minge Walton. Leeth, Yancy. *Sarah Minge Walton*.
Photograph. Mobile, Alabama, 2021. Oakleigh House Museum.
Painting by C.R. Parker.

Robert Walker Walton. *Robert Walton*. Photograph. Pensacola, Florida, 2018. University of West Florida University Archives and West Florida History Center. Satterfield, Frances Gibson. Painting by C.R. Parker. Current Location of painting unknown.

Reynolds also commented on the daily lives of the Walton family. During this time, George and Sally Walton were in their fifties and settled in life. He told of how Colonel Walton always referred to Octavia as his "distinguished daughter" and how he generally greeted his son, Robert, "Good Morning, sir!" every morning despite the fact they lived in the same house and practiced at the same law firm. The LeVert girls also frequented their grandparent's home. Reynolds later recalled a sweet story, "On a certain occasion, a lady friend called on Mrs. Walton, who had two of her grandchildren visiting her, Claudia Eugenia and Sally Walker Walton...These children 'took after' their grandmother, as the following statement will show: 'What do you think? Said one of the little ladies to the visitor: 'Why just as we have come to spend the day with my dear (the grandmother) Dr. LeVert sends to us and says we must go and take dinner with him.' And the little gypsy tossed her head in high disdain."[3]

Octavia Walton LeVert. 2019. Photograph. Currently owned by Baudry Mohney. Painting by C.R. Parker.

Henry S. LeVert M.D. 2019. Photograph. Location of painting is currently unknown. Painting by C.R. Parker.

Life in the city was pleasant for the family, and Colonel Walton was re-elected Mayor of Mobile in 1839,[4] his last known year in any political office. He, Sally, and Robert moved into a nice cottage at the corner of North

Claudia Anna Eugenia LeVert and Octavia Walton LeVert (Diddie).
Parker, C.R. *Claudia Anna Eugenia LeVert and Octavia Walton LeVert*
(Diddie). Photograph. Augusta, Georgia, 1841. Morris Museum of Art.

Conception Street. George's son, Robert, was destined to
inherit the legal practice.

The Walton son-in-law was becoming well known, too. Henry's practice grew in the 1840s as he developed a good reputation as a doctor and as a true believer in the healing powers of spring waters. He and Octavia were now the parents of three daughters, Diddie who was four, her sister, Claudia Ann, was two years old, and the third girl, Sally Walker Walton LeVert, born on April 6th, 1841.[5] It was also the perfect time for the portrait painter, C.R. Parker, to capture everyone on canvas from the oldest, George Walton, Jr., to the youngest, Sally Walker LeVert.[6]

Octavia and Henry, not quite ready to buy a house but wanting to be in the center of all things society related in Mobile, moved to the Waverly House, a family-focused hotel, on Royal Street.[7] Henry planned a permanent home for his wife and three girls, but he knew the place had to be special and designed to accommodate the crowds she attracted and their growing family.

Despite her ideal circumstances, Octavia still struggled with her role in society. In a personal diary, she began around 1842; she wrote, "The triumphs of former years come over my sad heart like 'the sweet faint music of a dream.' In the gay world, I reign yet supreme, I move along the waltz like 'a thing of light and life.' Who would think ere seeking that mirthful scene I had washed away with the dew of roses the traces of bitter tears. Who would think the bright, the brilliant, the envied, the admired one sought her pillow each night with a woe-stricken heart." [8]

During these early years, Octavia and Henry both worked to support their growing family and gain standing in their community. She had to uphold a code of honor, that while her status gave her some leeway, she was still wound up in Southern social relations and the belief that a person was worth as much as others conferred upon them. Her value seems to have been determined by her inner conviction of self-worth, her claim of self-assessment before the public, and the assessment of her worth by the public.[9]

Henry also had a role to fill. He was responsible for protecting the women in his home. According to Alexis Girardin Brown, "Southern Society demanded that women remain under the protection of fathers, husbands, brothers, and even sons. Women could not even own property that was not inherited."[10]

Dr. LeVert was documented to owning four enslaved at this time, but it is noted they were not purchased but inherited from a line of slaves passed down to Octavia from mother to daughter over two hundred years.[11] There was one slave, Betsey Walton, among these four who took care of the household affairs as Octavia was a person more focused on developing her mind than managing the home. In addition, there was Colonel Walton and Robert's law practice on Royal Street was successful and her mother, Sally, was very good at handling the areas where Octavia fell short.[12]

Octavia, who loved all things French, also enjoyed a favorite French pastime, the theatre. The first theatre was inaugurated in Mobile, Alabama, in 1824.[13] She and others in her social class had both the income and the interest to support the traveling theatre groups when they came to Mobile. When the needs of the theatre community bled over into the professional practices of those who supported these groups financially, a certain degree of camaraderie was found.

Such a moment came in April of 1842 when an actress, Mrs. Charlotte Hamblin Ewing, recently married the actor Andrew W. Ewing. They had a fight following a production, and Mr. Ewing was found stabbed to death. His wife was held to blame, and according to the Mobile Advertiser, "Miss Hamblin made her escape by jumping out at a window...she left in her theatrical attire, dressed as a page." She was soon captured and held for trial. [14]

Months later, Henry, who had examined the body for the trial, determined Mr. Ewing had died of a brain aneurysm and not by the wounds inflicted by his wife. The wounds were not serious enough to produce death. It was determined Mrs. Ewing did not kill her husband, and she was set free in December.[15]

This incident reflected poorly on those associated with the theatre in Mobile, Alabama, especially women, and those who had nothing to do with the case suffered as a result. Joe Jefferson, an internationally known actor in later years, and his widowed mother were among those affected. It caused them to have to struggle to survive.

The actor, Joe Jefferson. *Jefferson, Joe (Actor)*. Photograph. Washington, D.C., 1870. Library of Congress Prints and Photographs Division Washington, D.C. 20540 USA.

On November 24th, 1842, after just arriving in Mobile, Joe's father died of yellow fever and his mother, Cornelia, suddenly had to support her family. According to Mary Crawford, "Since the acting company was composed almost entirely of the Jefferson family, the theatre was closed for two nights while the family mourned. This was all they could do for husband, father, brother. Between them, they could not scrape enough money to buy a marker for his grave. Little Joe was thirteen years old at the time of his father's death." [16]

The manager of the theatre on Royal street refused to let Cornelia act, possibly due to the upcoming scandalous trial, to help support the family, so she started a boarding house. Actors who could not pay for board and their unpaid debts made the situation dire for the Jefferson's.

Mary Crawford, of the Historical Mobile Preservation Society, wrote a version of the events, "Then something happened! Cornelia opened her door one day to the knock of a caller, and there standing before her was the most elegant and stylish lady she had ever seen or spoken to! It was Madame LeVert. Always a patron of the theatre, she had heard of the brave but failing efforts of the Jefferson widow - and had come to help. She did it in the nicest way! She rented the theatre for a night and, with the Jefferson children putting on the show, packed the house with her friends. It was a very stylish benefit. It enabled Cornelia to leave Mobile with all her debts paid and to get to Philadelphia where her son by a former husband had secured a place for them." [17]

In November of 1842, the Walton's would also experience the passing of a loved one. Eliza Walker, Sally's mother, died in Belle Vue, the home where Octavia was born. It is easy to imagine Octavia looking fondly at the copy of *Female Biography*, the book Eliza gave her when she left for Pensacola many years before, remembering their time together as a young girl. Eliza, through Sally, was the reason Octavia had the opportunities many other women during this time were denied.

In Eliza's Will, the house was left to her youngest daughter, Anna, and Sally inherited her portion of the enslaved. The administrator of the Will was specifically ordered to keep families together. It seems as though the practice of not breaking up enslaved families was shared with the Waltons and the Walkers of Augusta, Georgia, and it continued with the families that moved South. According to Frances Gibson Satterfield, "Mrs. Walker specified that at Sally's death, any of her share should go to Octavia."[18]

In 1843, while expecting her next child Octavia became involved in activities to grow her mental strengths. One of these exercises included translating poems or books from their original language into another. She wrote of this in her journal on February 12, 1843, "Yesterday for many hours I devoted myself to intense, absorbing study, in the translation of a difficult subject from one language to three others: the 'Dante's Descent into Hell' first to English, then to Spanish, then to French, and again, with the characteristic of each idiom, back into Italian. It was a delightful occupation...I was charmed with my effort. For many years I have been no idle or inactive seeker after the treasures of mind and have experienced pleasure, pride, satisfaction in the pursuit. But never had I felt more delight in my own success than now. I read it again and again...[19]

Unfortunately, the baby boy the LeVert's eagerly awaited upon died as an infant. He passed away August 12, 1843.[20] After experiencing depression, two months later Octavia wrote a poem in her journal about the loss of a loved one. It was possibly her way of coping with her son's loss, the first great loss she experienced in her thirty-three years. She wrote the poem in October of 1843:

What is love? It is to dwell within
A world of the fond heart's creation where
All seemed a beauteous fairyland to work
No varied season, no flight of time,
Save in the absence of the loved one.
To live but in the atmosphere, he breathes,
To gaze upon his eyes is in the light,
That beckons us to bless, the only sun
Of our unreal world, and in the sad hours
Of absence, to be filled with thousand thoughts
Of tenderness that to repeat we deem
Will make the hours of meeting more delicious,
Yet when the time is come...
And watch his coming at the early dawn
Of untried existence (is not love
A new existence?) Yet when he is come
To feel that deep appreciative sense of bliss
To find our joy less perfect...
This is love! [21]

This poem showed Octavia's reaction to the tragedy. She was normally full of life and engaging, but was no longer felt so positive. She resorted to reading poetry and diverting her thoughts elsewhere. She quoted the poet, Letitia Elizabeth Landon, "Wit only gains you the reputation of being hard-hearted, which is very well to be in reality, but not to have the reputation of being." [22]

Henry did not express his grief with poetry but spent focused his energy into his growing medical profession. He wrote a letter he wrote to Honorable James

Dellet, a member of the U.S. House of Representatives.[23]
He knew the current surgeon at the Marine Hospital sent
in his resignation, and he was seeking the post. He asked,
"I don't know whether or not you can have an influence
directly with Mr. Tyler, but perhaps thro' some mutual
friends this influence could be exercised. If you can be of
service, I need not say how much obliged I shall feel."[24]

Henry had good political connections, but his were
nothing compared to those of Octavia's family. They were
close friends with Congressman Henry Clay, and he
relished communicating with her on a regular basis. He
had long since noticed Octavia's intelligence during the
visits to White Sulphur Springs in Virginia, when she
debuted to Society in Washington, D.C., and even now
when she was fulfilling her role as a mother, teaching her
girls from infancy foreign languages just as she was
taught.[25] While there is an impression of some sort of
correspondence prior to 1844, possibly when Henry was
in New Orleans for his health and visiting his friend, Dr.
Mercer, it is only this year letters begin to appear.[26]

Henry Clay was running for President again, his
third try for the office. He had to meet with the Whigs of
North Carolina on April 12th, but he had time to relax
before he began campaigning, so he wrote to Octavia
about paying a visit. He and Octavia shared many of the
same views during this time, especially those relating to
slavery. According to Frances Gibson Satterfield, "He
owned slaves, yet wrote and spoke against slavery "a
curse to the master, a wrong, a grievous wrong, to the
slaves." He feared sectional controversies which would

threaten the Union and hurt his presidential hopes. He favored voluntary colonization for the freed blacks and no pressure on the slave owners - a gradual emancipation.[27]

On January 1st, 1844, Henry Clay honored Octavia with the first letter he wrote for the New Year; she had reminded him of the promise he had made to visit Mobile, and he would arrive in late February. He also wanted to meet the LeVert daughters, describing Henry and Octavia's three little girls as "the little graces."[28] He must have had concerns about his visit because he wrote her days later, warning her that he was "such a disturber of the peace that I feared you were not aware of the extent of the inconvenience which I might occasion in your home." He wanted to be sure the LeVert's could handle the crowd he naturally attracted.[29]

Henry Clay arrived in Mobile on February 25th, 1844, by steamboat on a rainy morning, but it did not stop the crowds who rushed to the docks to see the great "American Commoner." According to Matthew Powers Blue, "He delivered one of his characteristically eloquent and felicitous speeches to a vast audience in the old warehouse that stood on the southwest corner of Coosa and Water streets."[30]

While in Mobile, Henry Clay stayed at the Waverly House as an official guest of Dr. LeVert, but everyone knew it was Octavia who managed access to Mr. Clay. She had a clear interest in politics, but as a woman, she could only influence and reform the politicians she knew and might be considered a reformer. According to Beverly

Sanders, "For the most part, reformers did not have political power, although they tried to influence officeholders in Congress and in state legislatures through speeches and petitions at legislative hearings. Reformers held public meetings, conventions, lectures, and debates to promote and publicize their views, and such gatherings offered the general public not only moral uplift but entertainment in an era before mass entertainment existed. The reformers also published their ideas in their own journals and newspapers, and their activities sometimes received coverage in the popular press."[31]

After a few days in the city, Clay received visitors at the Mansion House, another fashionable hotel, an easy carriage ride or walk from the Waverly. According to *Reminiscences of Public Men in Alabama*, "Gov. Gayle and Gen. Desha officiated in the ceremony of introduction. All seemed highly pleased with the urbanity, ease, and grace with which every one was made to feel at home. There was no feeling of restraint after getting his eye or hearing a word from his lips."[32] Octavia acted as hostess and used those skills to support Clay.

It was clear Henry Clay was determined to remain a guest of the LeVert family in Mobile not long after he arrived in the city when a committee of twenty gentlemen came down from Tuscaloosa and invited him to the "Seat of Government." According to William Garrett, "Mr. Clay briefly and courteously replied, declined the invitation, as its acceptance would be a departure from the rule which he prescribed to himself not to deviate from the main route of travel, lest his journey might assume the aspect of an electioneering tour, which it was not intended to be." [33] Henry LeVert, who was ever seeking approval from his oldest brother, could not help but mention, "Mr. Clay of Kentucky is now spending his time with me. He will remain for a week yet, and then proceed on his journey north." [34]

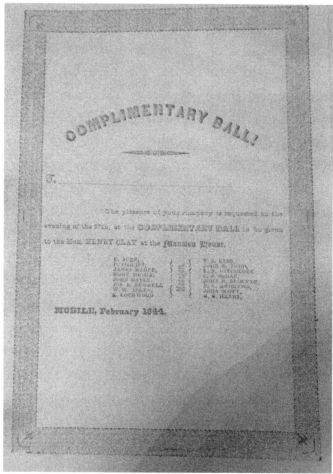

Invitation to the Clay Ball held in honor of Henry Clay. *Complimentary Ball.* Photograph. Mobile, Alabama, 1844. Historic Mobile Preservation Society.

Henry Clay stayed in Mobile, visiting the LeVert's and the Walton's until April 5th, 1844. Octavia organized a Complimentary ball that was held in his honor at the Mansion House on February 27th, 1844.[35] The *Mobile Advertiser* referenced Henry Clay at the ball, "Mr. Clay, we are pleased to add, is looking in fine health, and promises to live yet many years, the benefactor and the pride of his country."[36]

Clay left Mobile and travelled to his next stop, Montgomery, Alabama. Octavia accompanied him and was involved with arranging another ball there in his honor. Major Bernard A. Reynolds saw Octavia so attached to Clay that she appeared to be his page, or more likely his secretary. He recalled, "On the occasion of that visit, there was a 'Clay Ball' given at the hall, and at this ball, Mrs. LeVert acted, as I heard Mr. Clay call her, as his 'committee-woman.' for she led him about the room, introducing him to her acquaintances, and really she seemed to know everybody. This conduct, which in any other person would have appeared to be impertinence, was very appropriate for her. In the intervals of the dancing, she would form a circle of about thirty gentlemen. In this circle she took her position, and the band striking up a Spanish waltz, she singled out a gentleman, and having waltzed two or three times round the circle, she would disengage herself from him, and, selecting another, continue the waltzing until she had danced with every gentleman composing the ring. In all this, there was no frivolity of manners, but a certain captivating elegance, which won the admiration of the assembly."[37] Clay left for a meeting in North Carolina and courteously sent her a quick letter to let her know he made it there safely.[38]

Colonel Walton, Robert, Sally, and Octavia had frequented watering-places during the summer months for many years. However, family responsibilities and financial struggles made traveling such long distances not something they could do all the time. When Bladen Springs opened up on June 1st, 1844, it was the perfect place for the family to get away without incurring such travel expenses. The new Springs was located eight miles west of Coffeeville, and four miles from Moore's landing, on the Tombigbee River, in Washington County. The *Mobile Daily Advertiser* stated, "The proprietors assure the visiting public, whether for health or pleasure, but no expense or labor shall be spared to render Bladen Springs, every way, and agreeable retreat, during this summer and sickly season." The proprietors were also building a splendid hotel with the best accommodations.[39] In the future, their venture would be profitable.

Octavia had experienced a yellow fever epidemic as a young girl in Pensacola, having the disease herself, and it seems the fear from the event never really left her. She, with her family, regularly attended the Springs for their healing properties in addition to the developing connections to society. While she and Dr. LeVert were immune to the disease, it did not mean close friends and their children were not. When deadly fevers traveled through Mobile, taking those she cared about, she felt it deeply and wrote of it in her journal: "Why should we be

A photo of Bladon (Bladen) Springs Hotel. Gay, Ann H. *Bladen Springs Hotel.* Photograph. Butler County, Alabama, n.d. Personal collection.

exempt from the general doom? Laughter and smiles are strangers to the lips where they were once wont to dwell. In my evening drives, I always seek the graveyard. - there I wander among the tombs, or seat myself by the mounds of earth that cover what was dear to me."[40]

In a sad turn of events, Octavia and the rest of the family become no longer exempt from significant loss. Everything was soon going to change, and their perfect world was to end.

Works Cited and Notes

1. Stephens, *Madame Octavia Walton LeVert*, 71. Note: This is a poem copied by Mrs. Lucia S. Monroe from an original scrapbook of Madame LeVert found in Augusta in 1935. The only relative of Madame LeVert, Lawrence Reab, who is now in Augusta, was unable to tell where the scrapbook is. It seems it was sold away

from Augusta during the last five years. As of 03/23/2020, its location is unknown.

2. Major Bernard A. Reynolds, "Octavia Walton LeVert," *Times-Picayune*, April 8, 1877, 7, Newspapers.com.
3. Reynolds "Octavia Walton LeVert," 7.
4. "Mayors of U.S. Cities M-W," World Statesmen.
5. *Octavia Walton LeVert (Diddie) to Mr. Leach,* October 21, 1885. Letter. University of West Florida. *Satterfield Collection.*
6. Note: Artist, C.R. Parker traveled through Mobile, capturing the family in four portraits. Information located in the Fresco Frick Art Reference Library.
7. Satterfield, *Madame LeVert*, 46. Note: Also in the 1839 Directory. Note: Waverly House was the fashionable hotel existing on the same location as today's Battle House.
8. Delaney, "Madame Octavia Walton Le Vert," 51; *Octavia Walton LeVert Journal, July 28, 1842*. Journal/Diary. Ed. *Madame LeVert* ed. Frances Gibson Satterfield (Edisto Island: Edisto Press, 1987).
9. Giselle Roberts, *The Confederate Belle* (Columbia: University of Missouri Press, 2003), 3.
10. Alexis Girardin Brown, "The Women Left Behind: Transformation of the Southern Belle, 1840-1880," *The Historian* 62, no. 4 (2000): 760.
11. Alabama State Census 1850, Alabama State Census, 1820-1866, A Enumeration of the Inhabitants of Mobile County, 1850, Ancestry.com. Note: The 1860 Census also lists four slaves, but with greater description. In this census there is one female and three males. The one female is probably Betsey Walton and the three males probably helped Dr. LeVert in his medical practice among other duties. Dr. LeVert was one of the few doctors in Mobile who treated slaves.
12. *Mobile Directory or Strangers' Guide for 1842* (Mobile: Dade and Thompson, 1842).
13. Edward Devereaux Brown, "A History of Theatrical Activities at the Mobile Theatre, Mobile, Alabama from 1860 – 1875" (Masters Thesis, Michigan State College of Agriculture and Applied Science, 1952), 1.
14. "*Charleston Courier*, April 1, 1842, Newspapers.com.
15. "All Sort of Paragraphs," *Daily Atlas*, July 4, 1842, Newspapers.com.
16. *Mary Crawford Speech to Historic Mobile Preservation Society*, October 12, 1955. Manuscript. University of West Florida. *Satterfield Collection.*

17. *Mary Crawford Speech to Historic Mobile Preservation Society*, October 12, 1955. Manuscript. University of West Florida. *Satterfield Collection*.

18. Satterfield, *Madame LeVert*, 48; *Thanksgiving Day, 1980*. Letter. University of West Florida Archives, *Satterfield Collection*. Note: Octavia also wrote this information on a card in the collection.

19. *Octavia Walton LeVert Journal Excerpt*, February 12, 1843. Diary/Journal. In "Madame Octavia Walton LeVert 1810 – 1877," ed. Caldwell Delaney (Master's Thesis, University of Alabama, 1952), 53.

20. E. T. Woods, *Mobile Directory and Register for 1844: Embracing the Names of Firms* (Mobile: Dade and Thompson, 1844).

21. October 16, 1843; Stephens, *Madame Octavia Walton LeVert*, 71; Note: This is a poem copied by Mrs. Lucia S. Monroe from an original scrapbook of Madame LeVert found in Augusta in 1935. The only relative of Madame LeVert, Lawrence Reab, who is now in Augusta, was unable to tell where the scrapbook is. It seems it was sold away from Augusta during the last five years. Note: As of 03/23/2020 its location is unknown.

22. *Octavia Walton LeVert Journal Excerpt*, November 15, 1843. Diary/Journal. In "Madame Octavia Walton LeVert 1810 – 1877," ed. Caldwell Delaney (Master's Thesis, University of Alabama, 1952), 39-40. Note: As of 2020, we do not know where this diary is located Note: She also wrote: "...lips mock with sparkling words the dark and dreary world within," during this same time. (November 17, 1843, Madame Octavia Le Vert: 1810 - 1877 by Caldwell Delaney page 51.)

23. Herbert J. Lewis, "James Dellet," Encyclopedia of Alabama, last modified July 20, 2020.

24. *Dr. Henry LeVert to Hon. James Dellet*, December 23, 1843. Letter. Private Collection of Chuck Torrey.

25. Peacock, *Famous American Belles*, 112.

26. Satterfield, *Madame LeVert*, 48.

27. Satterfield, *Madame LeVert*, 48.

28. *Henry Clay to Octavia Walton LeVert*, January 1, 1844. Letter. In *Madame LeVert* ed. Frances Gibson Satterfield (Edisto Island: Edisto Press, 1987), 49. Note: The letter is also in an article published in June 2, 1907, Henry Clay and Madame LeVert from Madam LeVert's Scrap Book Published in Interesting Series of Articles in

Uncle Remus's Magazine, Augusta Chronicle page 7. Accessible through GenealogyBank.

29. *Henry Clay to Octavia Walton LeVert*, January 6, 1844. Letter. In *Madame LeVert* ed. Frances Gibson Satterfield (Edisto Island: Edisto Press, 1987), 50.

30. Matthew Powers, *The Works of Matthew Blue: Montgomery's First Historian* (Montgomery: NewSouth Books, 2010), 166.

31. Beverly Sanders, *Women in American History: A Series - Book Two, Women in the Ages of Expansion and Reform 1820 – 1860* (Washington D.C.: American Federation of Teachers), 25, ERIC.

32. William Carrett, *Reminiscences of Public Men in Alabama* (Atlanta: Plantation Publishing Press, 1872), 372, Google Books.

33. Carrett, *Reminiscences of Public Men in Alabama*, 372.

34. *Octavia Walton LeVert Journal Excerpt*, January 6, 1844. Diary/Journal. In "Madame Octavia Walton LeVert 1810 – 1877," In *Madame LeVert* ed. Frances Gibson Satterfield (Edisto Island: Edisto Press, 1987), 50.

35. Note: An original copy of the Invitation is located at the Minnie Mitchell Archives located at the Historic Mobile Preservation Society in Mobile, Alabama.

36. *Centinel of Freedom*, March 12, 1844, Newspapers.com.

37. Reynolds "Octavia Walton LeVert," 7.

38. *Henry Clay to Octavia Walton LeVert*, April 14, 1844. Letter. In *Madame LeVert* ed. Frances Gibson Satterfield (Edisto Island: Edisto Press, 1987), 51.

39. *Mobile Daily Advertiser*, June 1, 1844, Newspapers.com.

40. *Octavia Walton LeVert Journal Excerpt*, September 15, 1844. Diary/Journal. In "Madame Octavia Walton LeVert 1810 – 1877," in *Madame LeVert* ed. Frances Gibson Satterfield (Edisto Island: Edisto Press, 1987), 65. Note: This is from the missing journal.

Paula Lenor Webb

Chapter 7

Eyes that Weep

Yes, they are bending o'er her
Eyes that weep;
Forms, that to the cold grave bore her
Vigils keep
When the summer moon is shining
Soft, and fair
Friends she loved, in tears are twining
Chaplets there
Rest in Peace, thou gentle spirit
Throned above
Souls like thine, O God! Inherit
Life, and love [1]

Octavia had traveled all over the United States in her thirty-four years but not outside the country. It is certain, though, that many people she associated with went on Grand Tours of Europe and shared their stories of adventure with her. One such woman, an author, Miss Fredrika Bremer, from Stockholm, Sweden, had the resources to travel the world and did so.

Octavia was introduced to Bremer's books in late 1844 and wrote in her journal about them, "How I love her writings! She displays to you the world in a pure and radiant light, exalts every thing that is noble, good, and generous in the human heart!... Her writings have one great object - the improvement of the heart and submission to the Divine Will. Much may be learnt in her works, and in hours of affection and gloom, the mind recalls the gentle admonition to pray and be content with what so ever God shall give us."[2] Little did she know how great an influence Bremer would become.

Bremer, herself, wanted to visit the United States and affirmed, "It has long been a wish of my heart to visit America and to see with my own eyes that new, rising world. Indeed there is no foreign land in the world that I wish to know outside of North America and that especially for the peculiar turn of Mind of its people and its management of life in public as in private life, in the state, the home, in society and in Nature. In many of these spheres, Methought I see the Idea - the sun of intellectual life - clearing up, making its way to earthly reality, and transforming chaos into harmony and beauty."[3]

Octavia read Bremer's books, and she also continued her practice of translating literature from one language to another, exercising her mind. She felt the conflict of being an intelligent woman, but she was not allowed to use the mind she was blessed with. Octavia wrote, "I am a woman, and her fate is never to rise, why should I strive in the paths of learning? Who will ever appreciate them, who will ever prize them? Then came the sweet relief of tears. I felt I was like an unstrung instrument, there was entire discord in my mind."[4] Octavia was a passionate woman but writing about passion in a female voice was a risky business for her time and station.[5]

Another interest considered beyond Octavia's station during this time was politics, but she was a close friend to one of its key players, Henry Clay. The end of December 1844 found Clay's fast rise to a possible Presidential candidate ending as quickly as it started. The LeVert's received word of this, and Octavia immediately sent a letter of sympathy. She wrote, "My mind is a perfect chaos when I dwell upon the events that have occurred within the last few weeks. It seems to me I wander in a world of frightful Dreams, for which I must awake. My heart refuses to credit the sad reality."[6] Clay later explained the reason his campaign failed so quickly because he felt she deserved the truth. So he told her his son, Henry Clay Jr., had incurred a large debt, but circumstances appeared as if he had mismanaged the money.[7]

Even though Octavia was now in the role of wife and mother, she remained in contact with people she knew when she was the Belle of Saratoga. One such friend, General Edmund Gaines, asked her in a letter, "Wouldest thou contribute to the happiness and prosperity of thy friends and country? Then devote a portion of thy leisure moments to the subject of national defense - the theory of which is as completely within thy comprehension as is the routine of fashionable amusements for a single winter, if not of the music and dancing of a single evening."[8] She chose to remain in the South, focused on her family and not society.

It is not known exactly when Octavia began traveling with a servant, but the first mention is on January 27th, 1846, when she and Henry traveled to New Orleans and arrived at the St. Charles Hotel with one "servant." In all likelihood, this was Betsey Walton, who was around twenty-four years old and Octavia's helpmate.[9]

Octavia's travels became less frequent towards the end of 1846 because she was expecting another child. Much like in the past, when she could not physically travel as she so loved to do, she focused on reading and developing her mind. In one of her journals, a sudden increase in poems, notes, and quotes she enjoyed, reflected, she spent more time focusing on these passions. She wrote on August 13th, 1846, "I sit in the midst of my books! Those unchanging friends - those magicians which close the mighty charm, that separates the Past from the Present, so gently, that our spirits are unconscious of the effort, while we yield to its power."[10]

During this time, she wrote many things. She quoted a favorite poetess, Letitia Elizabeth Landon, and local poet, A.B. Meek. She practiced phrases she could use in letters to loved ones, unique ways to make readers feel valued. She wrote, "I welcomed your letter with delight, and have treasured it among my most precious tokens of the loved and absent ones."[11] Octavia was developing her writing style and possibly reading her collection of phrases during various Salon meetings held in her hotel or at other locations in Mobile. Pregnancy made her rest her body, but her mind flourished as a result.

Henry had borrowed money from his brother, Francis, to set up his medical practice. Finally, he had resolved his debts. When this happened, their mother passed away, and Francis offered to take Henry's portion of the inheritance in exchange for a settlement for all debt. He agreed and was finally free of family debt.[12] The arrangements were finalized in January of 1847.[13]

Meanwhile, Octavia pursued her interests. She was mistress at keeping her mind busy when she did not control the situation around her. To ease some of the stress, she sent her oldest daughter, Diddie, to visit her Aunt Anne, who now lived at Belle Vue, but Octavia missed her terribly. Unaware of her pregnancy, Henry Clay wrote her of the loss of his oldest son, the Mexican American War, and asked if she would be in New Orleans in December.[14]

The closer her due date, the more challenging the task Octavia tackled. Amazingly, in October 1846, she began to translate from French to English chapters of the book, *Twenty Years After, the Sequel to the Three Musketeers by Alexander Dumas*.[15] According to *Women of the South*, "she translated in the most faithful and spirited manner, Dumas' "Musketeers;" and a few months since, there appeared in the columns of the "Mobile Register" a translation by her of the pamphlet, "The Pope and the

Congress." This is pronounced by French scholars the most admirable rendering which has yet appeared."[16]

In her current state, she also might have missed the traveling she was so fond. To keep busy, she copied a poem titled, *The Alabama*, by Samuel Lover in her journal about the Alabama River,

I thought of thee, as down the stream,
I floated, in a wand'rer's dream,
As sunset cast its glowing beam,
On the banks of the Alabama.
The waters calm reflected bright,
The golden glories of the light
While stealing on, the shades of night
Came o'er the Alabama.

The evening star came peeping through,
The misty veil of evening's dew,
Like Love thro' tears, its brightness grew
Like thee - on the Alabama.
And sparkling there, as Beauty's Queen,
Resided o'er the tranquil scene,
I wished that thou hadst with me been
On the lovely Alabama.

An then the Moon, with silver beam!
Shed brighter lustre o'er the stream,
But brighter was the Poet's dream,
Of thee, - on the Alabama.
The sunset bright - the moonlight fair-
The spring-tide balm of evening's air

With thought of thee, could not compare
On the lovely Alabama.

However far - however near -
To me, alike, thourt with me here
On the winding Alabama.
The watch-dog's bark, on shore I hear-
It tells me that some home is near-
And Memory wakes affection's tear,
On the distant Alabama.[17]

The time for the newest LeVert to enter the world approached in late November of 1846, with Octavia confined to the Waverly Hotel. She was now thirty-six years old. Henry, concerned for his wife, expected trouble with the delivery. He shared with his brother, Francis, "I am apprehensive that she will be ill for many months, to say the least of it." A second letter to his brother on December 8th indicated things went better than expected, "Octavia was confined on the 6th. She has another daughter. Both herself and the child are doing well so far."[18]

Into the world came Henrietta Caroline LeVert on December 6th, 1846. This little girl was their last child and their last hope to have a son. Octavia decided to partially name this new baby for Henry's sister, giving her the middle name of Carolina.

Henrietta Caroline LeVert's Christening cup, a gift from Henry Clay.
Leeth, Yancy. *Henrietta Caroline Levert's Christening cup*. Photograph.
Mobile, Alabama, 2021. Oakleigh House Museum.

Henry Clay, now in New Orleans, learned that Octavia had given birth to a daughter. He commented, "You are too good a Christian not to submit to the will of Providence, and be resigned to the sex of your infant; although I dare say, if it had been HIS pleasure, you would have preferred a son."[19] Octavia wrote Clay and informed him she named her daughter, Henrietta, in his honor. He sent her a silver Christening cup with "Henrietta Carolina LeVert" engraved on the side as a gift.[20]

The LeVert home in Mobile, Alabama. *Madame LeVert House & Office, 151 & 153 Government Street, Mobile, Mobile County, AL*. Photograph. Washington, D.C. , n.d. Library of Congress Prints and Photographs Division Washington, D.C. 20540 USA http://hdl.loc.gov/loc.pnp/pp.print.

The settlement of debts in the LeVert family offered Henry the opportunity to provide a home suitable for his family. The house was constructed in 1847 by Thomas S. James, Lewis Judson, and William H. Pratt. It was located on Government Street, a couple of blocks from the Mobile Riverfront, and in the center of all activity within the city. From the house, one could easily walk to the market, the United Episcopal Church, and the local theatre. It was also an easy walk to Walton's, allowing Octavia to visit Sally and her brother and the four lovely little girls in their home.[21]

In addition, this home became a symbol of their status, reflecting the LeVert's elite life. According to Roberts, "A family's ownership of slaves, their ability to stage and attend lavish social occasions, their acceptance of other elite families, their clothing, manners, and leisure activities, all influenced their overall social standing."[22] Henry did his part by being an excellent doctor. Octavia did her part by being the ideal wife, mistress, and mother to their children.

In this Federal style home was the beginning of one of the most well-known and fashionable salons in the South, a salon that became known throughout the world. Octavia, a member of Mobile's elite, had a salon dedicated to the discussion of the virtues and vices of the latest newspaper articles, journals, fiction, and non-fiction books, despite its possible dangers to the sensibilities of Southern women.[23] According to Wells, "Despite the difficulty that parents faced in finding time to read, women in the South balanced their reading of fiction with works on history, politics, and travel. Although women were generally barred from participating actively in politics or government, they still kept abreast of contemporary issues."[24]

Mary Forrest described Octavia's home best, "Her residence is on Government Street, in the most convenient and central part of Mobile. It is a plain, substantial mansion, combining taste, elegance, and comfort. She has an immense library and rare works of art. A genuine republican in her feelings, she respects and cherishes all genius and merit; however, humble its condition or origin. Whoever has talent and moral worth has a claim upon her. She is kind and hospitable simply for the pleasure of doing good because it is her nature to be so. No human being has ever been pained by an unkind or ungenerous act of hers. In conversation, she never flags, yet never utters a commonplace."[25]

Years later, Major Bernard A. Reynolds recalled how both Sally Walton and Octavia LeVert influenced Mobile society, "Mrs. Walton was occasionally very fantastic in her dress, but it was confined to dress, for she had her full share of strong common sense, with which was mingled with a good deal of spice. Mrs. LeVert occasionally dressed herself in the extreme of the fashion, but her dress was generally within proper bounds, and always neat and elegant. Her home was the resort of most persons of distinction who visited Mobile, who had or had not letters of introduction. By dint of perseverance, she had made her name a household word, not merely at the South, but at the North, and she was, perhaps, flattered and caressed more at the North than at the South."[26]

The LeVert's and the Walton's were in the prime of their lives and comfortable in Mobile, Alabama. The LeVert's traveled back and forth between Mobile and New

Orleans, attending various balls, musicals, and theatre productions.[27] They mingled with the best of society. Life was good.

A longtime friend asked Octavia about her life and family, and she wrote her reply in her journal, "I am sure you will forgive a Mother's vanity, while I describe them. The Eldest, "Octavia Walton," is a Brunette, with glorious large dark eyes, like those of a Circassion Maid, soft brown hair, and a radiant intellect. The second, "Claudia Eugenia," is a lovely Blonde, bright rosy-lipped, and sparkling as Hebe. The third, "Sally Walker," is the Beauty of the whole South. Neither the Painter or the Sculptor could detect one fault in face or form. Her eyes are as black as night and yet as soft as the first blush of dawn. Her hair is golden, as rather like sunbeams. T'would seem the sunlight was imprisoned in every bright curl, which hung around her oval face like a halo of light. Her brow is high, her nose completes the classic profile so rarely seen save in antique gems. Her mouth is small, her lips like twin-cherries or wet coral. Her form is worthy of the beautiful face. The fourth was a Boy, but Death robbed me of him. The fifth, "Cara Netta," is a rose-bud of six months growth with her sweetest leaves, of course, yet unfolded, but giving an earnest of decided loveliness. I fancy I hear you murmur, "Good Heavens, what a family!" Now you will doubtless picture me in your mind as a round, fat Matron! But you shall not rest in error, for I am none of these, neither are wrinkles or grey hairs as yet my companions. Time's wing in passing over me, has not brushed away my freshness of feeling, or stilled the merriness of heart which animated me in other days."[28]

Octavia had done her womanly duty and was the mother of four beautiful daughters. She worked with each one, teaching them foreign languages, educating them within the home just as her mother and grandmother taught her, and she enjoyed being involved with their daily lives. Octavia, who was now reaching a matronly age of thirty-eight, did not embrace this role readily. She still had so much to do.

Since Henrietta was so young, the family decided not to travel very far during the summer months in 1847. Instead, they visited a new resort, Bladen Springs, located just north of Mobile. Octavia wrote in her journal, "I have recently visited a Watering Place in Western Alabama, called Bladen Springs. I found it a perfect "Balm in Gilead." The waters are wonderful for their health-giving qualities. They resemble greatly the far-famed waters of Germany, "The Seltzer and the Spa." The country around is highly romantic. Tall Pines, with their mysterious whisperings, encircle a spot, like an Oasis, filled with verdant Elms, Walnut and Hickory. The sparkling Fountain bubbles up! Neath the soft shadow of its guardian trees, and it needed but one wave of the wand of Imagination for people to see the green swarm with Fairies. The tranquil scene appeared to be fitted for their haunts and gambols."[29] Obviously, she appreciated the beauty of nature.

Monument in honor of the Georgia signers of the Declaration of
Independence. 2019. Photograph.

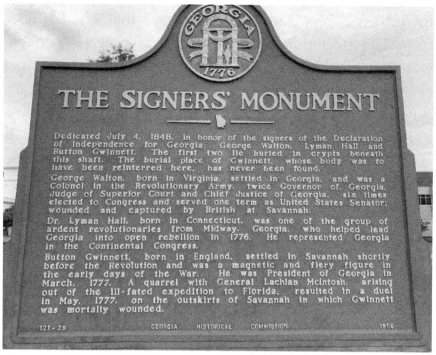

Historical Marker for the Signers' Monument. 2019..

In early 1848, the City of Augusta, Georgia held a large ceremony and moved the remains of two of the three Georgia signers of the Declaration of Independence, George Walton, Sr. and Lyman Hall, from their resting places to a large monument in the Center of Greene Street, in Augusta. In this place, they constructed a large shaft of granite to commemorate their valor and their patriotism.[30]

In May of 1848, Henry and Octavia traveled together up to the Springs of the North, where she used to be the "Belle of Florida." She was going back, but no longer as the young woman she once was. Now she was almost forty years old, but this didn't matter. She was there for one of the grandest parties of the season. A great fete was happening in Newport, and it was the talk of

161

town, it was reported, "We hear, says the N.Y. Express, from Newport that there are now at that fashionable watering-place nearly 2000 visitors, many of whom have been attracted by the great fancy ball to take place on Wednesday evening of next week. The managers have already been chosen and costumers are present in abundance, though many visitors have already come prepared with very rich costumes for the occasion."[31]

While Octavia revived her role in fashionable society, Henry went to Liverpool, England, to handle financial matters to benefit the city of Mobile. He left for Europe on August 30th, 1848, from New York, certainly seen off by Octavia.[32] In this case, it seems that they both were fully aware of their goal, to bring positive attention to their home city, Mobile.

Octavia used the skills she had developed over a lifetime, how to work with those with power and influence in society circles. When she attended the fete the next day, she was immediately recognized. According to a reporter at the event, "As my eyes were wandering over the fair flowers of the land, I noted a stir at the doorway when I turned and beheld the beautiful and celebrated Madame Le. V., of Mobile, floating along like a bright vision of loveliness. On one side walked the brave and gallant Gen. Worth, who has won immortal honor in Mexico, and whose name will live through all time; on the other side was the distinguished Col Bragg, the hero of Buena Vista, the chivalric soldier of many battles. This entree was the great feature of the evening. It was a glorious trio. Madame Le V. is of the noblest blood of

America. Her brave grandsire, George Walton, was one of the signers of the Declaration of Independence, which made us what we are - the greatest people on earth. This accomplished granddaughter is worthy of his name. The heroes of Mexico seemed to have forgotten their perils and trials as they listened with delight to the eloquent language and caught radiant smiles of this enchantress of the South. I must tell you her toilet - it was in perfect taste. A robe of rich lace, superbly embroidered; a bird of Paradise in her dark and glossy hair; a sprig of diamonds on her bosom, and her exquisitely beautiful arms encircled with armlets. I wonder if more ladies do not adopt this fashion. It is peculiarly becoming. In ancient days they were considered the most delicious ornament of beauty."[33]

Her success at this ball was immediately known, written about in all society papers, and talked about in all the best circles. Even her dearest friend and confidant, Henry Clay, received word of her reception at the fete. He wrote, letting her know he received an account of her appearance at the fancy ball and rejoicing with her in the distinguished reception she received. However, he did give her a word of caution, saying, "You do not appreciate these flattering testimonies beyond their actual worth, and that you are not likely to be intoxicated by them."[34]

One of the most opportune connections she made on this trip was that of Henry Wadsworth Longfellow, and she sent her first letter to him on October 4th, 1848, expressing her condolences for the death of his infant, Fanny. Octavia, who had lost her son as an infant, sympathized with him and his wife. However, Octavia

163

was seeking something more in their relationship. No one in Mobile understood her drive to write and create. She needed someone like him as a guide.

Octavia meets Henry Wadsworth Longfellow. Brayer, Geo. H. *Longfellow*. Photograph. Washington, D.C., 1882. Library of Congress Prints and Photographs Division
Washington, D.C. 20540 USA.

Somehow Octavia felt a connection to Longfellow, unlike any of the other poets and writers she knew. She asked him, "I depart tomorrow for my home in the South, by the shores of the Mexican Sea. I am almost tempted to ask you to become my correspondent. Would you? Will you? Oh! How happy I should be to hear from you. My direction will be "Madame Walton LeVert", Mobile, Alabama."[35] This was her first reference to herself as Madame LeVert.

Dr. LeVert returned from Europe aboard the steamship, *United States*, with grand news. He and S.G. Fisher had gone to London to sign a contract with the R.M. Steamer Co., which agreed to purchase $300,000 worth of Alabama coal annually from the depot at Mobile Point, increasing international business at the growing port.[36]

While many of the wealthy and affluent citizens in Mobile tended to leave the area in the summer of 1848 to avoid yellow fever and others like it, no one expected the scarlet fever epidemic, according to the *Mobile Advertiser*, "During the whole of this year, says the Advertiser, there has not at any time been so much sickness in the city as exists at this moment, especially among children. The scarlet fever is very prevalent, though less fatal than usual."[37]

Octavia's eight-year-old daughter, Sally, was the first to contract scarlet fever, and it is certain Henry did all he could do to treat his daughter. It appears her health was improving, for a letter from Henry Clay in February indicated that he knew she was sick, but she was recovering.[38]

The grave of Robert Watkins Walton in Magnolia Cemetery, Mobile, Alabama. 2021.

Scarlet fever was not the only virus traveling through the community, and while Sally was recovering, the family received an unexpected blow. Octavia's

The grave of Sally Walker Walton LeVert, Magnolia Cemetery, Mobile, Alabama. 2021.

brother, who had been her life-long companion and was only thirty-six years old, had died of inflammation of the brain on March 22nd, 1849.[39] She wrote to Longfellow in desperation, "You must have deemed my silence strange, and you will forgive it when I tell you that for four long months I have been a close prisoner in the sick chamber of my suffering child. She still lingers. But oh! My heart is crushed now by affliction deep, deep, and bitter. My only Brother is dead. There were, but two of us bound together by more than the usual affection of brother and sister. He was almost my idol. He is gone. He was buried yesterday with military honors. I send you an Obituary. It is not the language of praise. It is simply the truth."[40]

Unfortunately, the death of her brother was only the beginning of the sorrows she soon experienced. On May 3rd, 1849, Sally Walker Walton LeVert [41], at eight years old, lost her fight with scarlet fever and her sister, Claudia Anna Eugenia LeVert, who was eleven years old, passed away on May 8th, 1949.[42] Octavia kept Henry Clay and Longfellow aware of the health of her children. They had stayed in contact, inquiring about the children's health frequently.

She wrote Longfellow on May 23, 1849, "Oh! My dear friend, pity me and pray for me, for I am indeed bereft. In five days, I have buried my two beautiful children. They died in my arms. Both the victims of Scarlet Fever. I have no words to shadow forth the deep utterable agony of my soul. I feel I shall soon follow them…Will you not embalm my children's memory in some lines from your gifted pen? They would be most grateful to me. Sally died May 3rd Claudia hung near her dying sister until her pure spirit left its earthy tenement, then followed her to the grave on May 5th. Claudia sickened and died 8th of

The grave of Claudia Anna Eugenia LeVert, Magnolia Cemetery, Mobile, Alabama. 2021.

May. she called for her sister as she died, 'Sally, Sally.' Oh! My Kind friend, no wretchedness was ever so great as mine. I admired my children. They were so perfect, so loving, so beautiful. I cannot be comforted."[43]

It was quickly announced in newspapers all over the North and South that the LeVert's had such a great loss in their family. Henry LeVert, who was greatly distressed at such a great loss, still had to focus on supporting his family. Finally, relief came on August 11th, 1849, he received the appointment by the Secretary of the Treasury as the surgeon and Physician to the Marine Hospital in Mobile, in place of Dr. P.H. Lewis.[44]

Octavia's grief over her terrible loss was all-consuming. Dr. LeVert, worried about his wife, wrote to a nephew, "I fear that Octavia will never recover from the death of the children."[45] No one could return Octavia to the joyous, carefree person they knew before. She wrote to one friend, "Night has closed around me. As soon might one expect the rose to blossom neath the shadow of the glacier as for one ray of sparkling wit to emanate from the woe stricken soul of your blighted friend. For me, the world is hung in a funeral crape, and all that was bright in my nature lies buried in my children's tomb."[46] The depth of her sorrow was evident.

The Octavia Walton LeVert, known by everyone as a vibrant person, died inside when these three lives, the closest family to her, passed away. Hope and recovery seemed unreachable. She had long since had the ability to deal with hard things in life by immersing herself into developing her mind. Knowledge had always been her saving grace, and in this sadness, things would be no different.

Works Cited and Notes

1. Satterfield, *Madame LeVert*, 80.
2. *Octavia Walton LeVert Journal Excerpt,* Late 1844. Journal/Diary. In *Madame LeVert* ed. Frances Gibson Satterfield (Edisto Island: Edisto Press, 1987), 64-65.
3. Signe A. Rooth, *Seeress of the Northland: Fredericka Bremer's American Journey, 1849-1851* (Chicago: American Swedish Historical Foundation, 1955), 2.
4. *Octavia Walton LeVert Journal Excerpt*, Late 1844. Journal/Diary. In *Madame LeVert* ed. Frances Gibson Satterfield (Edisto Island: Edisto Press, 1987), 64-65.
5. Lucasta Miller, *L.E.L. The Lost Life and Scandalous Death of Letitia Elizabeth Landon, the Celebrate "Female Byron"* (New York: Alfred A. Knopf, 2019), 9.
6. *Octavia Walton LeVert to Henry Clay*, December 6, 1844. Letter. In *The Papers of Henry Clay Vol. 10. Candidate, Compromiser, Elder Statesman. January 1, 1944 - June 29, 1852*, ed. Melba Porter and Carol Reardon (Lexington: University of Kentucky, 1991).
7. *Henry Clay to Octavia Walton LeVert, May 20, 1845*. Letter. In *The Papers of Henry Clay Vol. 10. Candidate, Compromiser, Elder Statesman. January 1, 1944 - June 29, 1852*, ed. Melba Porter and Carol Reardon (Lexington: University of Kentucky, 1991).
8. *Edmund Pendleton Gaines to Madame LeVert*. Manuscript. In "Madame Octavia Walton LeVert 1810 – 1877," ed. Caldwell Delaney (Master's Thesis, University of Alabama, 1952). Note: Cited as Edmund Pendleton Gaines to Madame LeVert, quoted in the Augusta Herald, November 22, 1901. The article is missing as of 2020.
9. *Times-Picayune*, January 27, 1846, 2, GenealogyBank.
10. LeVert, *Octavia Walton Le Vert Journal 1846-1860*, August 13, 1846.
11. LeVert, *Octavia Walton Le Vert Journal 1846-1860*, August 22, 1846 - 96.
12. *F. J. LeVert to H. S. LeVert*, October 22, 1846. Letter. Louis Round Wilson Library Special Collections, *LeVert Papers*. Note: F.J. LeVert to H.S. LeVert proposing settlement of debt on general terms.
13. *F. J. LeVert to H. S. LeVert*, January 1, 1847. Letter. Louis Round Wilson Library Special Collections, *LeVert Papers*. Note: Letter discusses the final settlement H.S. LeVert and F.J. LeVert.

14. *Henry Clay to Octavia Walton LeVert*, November 6, 1846. Letter. In *The Papers of Henry Clay Vol. 10. Candidate, Compromiser, Elder Statesman. January 1, 1944 - June 29, 1852*, ed. Melba Porter and Carol Reardon (Lexington: University of Kentucky, 1991), 284.

15. LeVert, *Octavia Walton Le Vert Journal 1846-1860*, November 1, 1846 – November 10, 1846.

16. Forrest, *Women of the South Distinguished in Literature*, 26. Note: I have not been able to find the translation in the Mobile Register as of 05/10/2020.

17. LeVert, *Octavia Walton Le Vert Journal 1846-1860*, November 10, 1846 - 15.

18. Satterfield, *Madame LeVert*, 60.

19. *Henry Clay to Octavia Walton LeVert*, December 6, 1846. Letter. In *The Papers of Henry Clay Vol. 10. Candidate, Compromiser, Elder Statesman. January 1, 1944 - June 29, 1852*, ed. Melba Porter and Carol Reardon (Lexington: University of Kentucky, 1991), 298.

20. *Octavia Walton LeVert Journal Excerpt*, February 28, 1847. Journal/Diary. In *Madame LeVert* ed. Frances Gibson Satterfield (Edisto Island: Edisto Press, 1987), 61. Note: The Christening cup is now located in Mobile, Alabama at Oakleigh Place.

21. Robert Gamble, *The Alabama Catalog: Historic Alabama Buildings Survey: A Guide to the Early Architecture of the State* (Tuscaloosa: University of Alabama Press, 1987), 304-305. Note: The address for the house was 151 Government Street.

22. Roberts, *Confederate Belle*, 16.

23. Mary Kelly, *Learning to Stand and Speak: Women, Education, and Public Life in America's Republic* (Chapel Hill: University of North Carolina Press, 2006), 8.

24. Jonathan Daniels Wells, *Women Writers and Journalist in the Nineteenth-Century South* (Cambridge: Cambridge University Press, 2011), 61.

25. Forrest, *Women of the South Distinguished in Literature*, 26.

26. Reynolds "Octavia Walton LeVert," 7.

27. LeVert, *Octavia Walton Le Vert Journal 1846-1860*, March 11, 1847; LeVert, *Octavia Walton Le Vert Journal 1846-1860*, July 2, 1847.

28. *Octavia Walton LeVert Journal Excerpt, July 1, 1847*. Journal/Diary. In *Madame LeVert* ed. Frances Gibson Satterfield (Edisto Island: Edisto Press, 1987), 71.

29. LeVert, *Octavia Walton Le Vert Journal 1846-1860*, August 29, 1847.

30. *Vermont Gazette*, February 1, 1848, 2, Newspapers.com.

31. *Newport*, August 26, 1848, GeneologyBank.com.

32. "New York, New York, Passengers in the steamship Cambria," *The Evening Post*, August, 30, 1848, Newspapers.com.

33. *Times-Picayune*, September 3, 1848, Newspapers.com.

34. *Henry Clay to Octavia Walton LeVert*, September 16, 1848. Letter. In *The Papers of Henry Clay Vol. 10. Candidate, Compromiser, Elder Statesman. January 1, 1944 - June 29, 1852*, ed. Melba Porter and Carol Reardon (Lexington: University of Kentucky, 1991), 541.

35. *Octavia Walton LeVert to Henry Wadsworth Longfellow*, October 4, 1848. Letter. University of West Florida, *Satterfield Collection*.

36. *Octavia Walton LeVert Journal Excerpt*, November 1848. Journal/Diary. In *Madame LeVert* ed. Frances Gibson Satterfield (Edisto Island: Edisto Press, 1987), 75.

37. *New Orleans Crescent*, December 14, 1848, Newspapers.com.

38. *Henry Clay to Octavia Walton LeVert*, February 6, 1849. Letter. In *The Papers of Henry Clay Vol. 10. Candidate, Compromiser, Elder Statesman. January 1, 1944 - June 29, 1852*, ed. Melba Porter and Carol Reardon (Lexington: University of Kentucky, 1991).

39. Forrest, *Women of the South Distinguished in Literature*, 22.

40. *Octavia Walton LeVert to Henry Wadsworth Longfellow*, March 24, 1849. Letter. Harvard University, *Longfellow Papers*.

41. "Sally Walker Walton LeVert," Ancestry.com.

42. "Claudia Ann Eugenia LeVert," Ancestry.com.

43. *Octavia Walton LeVert to Henry Wadsworth Longfellow*, May 23, 1849. Letter. Harvard University, *Longfellow Papers*.

44. *New Orleans Crescent*, August 11, 1849, Newspapers.com.

45. *Henry LeVert to Claudius Mastin*, October 8, 1849. Letter. In "Madame Octavia Walton LeVert 1810 – 1877," ed. Caldwell Delaney (Master's Thesis, University of Alabama, 1952). Note: This letter is now missing. Delaney found this letter at the Minnie Mitchell Archives.

46. Delaney, "Madame Octavia Walton Le Vert," 57.

Paula Lenor Webb

Chapter 8

A New Literary Star Emerges

Bright, lovely Beings! One each imaged face,
More of the Seraph, than the child we trace,
Sweet Mother! - check thy deeply mournful sighs,
Weep not to spare, those Seraphs to the skies!
Oh! Not for them, need flow the bitter tear,
How blest their sunny fate, both there and here -
Though swift the stroke - Tho' short the warning given,
Twas but a step from such a Home - to Heaven.[1]

People continued to stream into Mobile in the 1850s, expanding its borders beyond Broad Street. Roads tentacled out to the unusual white-hued Spring Hill toll road, formerly known as the "Shell Road," constructed of oyster shells dredged up from the Bay. To avoid confusion, locals called it "Old Shell Road."[2]

The LeVert home, a horse and buggy ride from Mobile Bay or other parts of the expanding city, made it convenient to visitors. It was easy for its well-known hostess to entertain the fashionable elite. Nonetheless, it

175

once had been a loving home full of four giggling girls. Two of those "Graces," as Henry Clay fondly named them, had died of scarlet fever. The house on Government street used to stay candle-lit all night locked its large double doors, and snuffed out its silver candles. Octavia exiled herself from society for the next three years.[3]

Henry LeVert, a level-headed man, was concerned about his wife and remaining family. He supported Octavia, Diddie, Cara Netta, and the enslaved in the home. When the family experienced significant loss, Henry was appointed by the United States Secretary of the Treasury, William M. Meredith, to the position of Surgeon and Physician of the Marine Hospital in Mobile, replacing the recently deceased, Dr. P.H. Lewis.[4] This diversion helped take his mind off the situation.

As Henry's practice grew, so did Mobile's multicultural population. In the 1850s, the city contained about nine thousand blacks with a thousand, possibly creole, were free. They were employed in all walks of city life. House servants played a significant role. Many blacks were hired out, and widows and families were dependent upon the earnings of enslaved they seldom saw. They included barbers, cooks on river steamboats to New Orleans, or people who served in a variety of other capacities.[5]

The LeVert home contained four known enslaved at the time. One of them was Betsey, whose care focused on the grieving Octavia. Typically, while Octavia traveled, the children were left with Betsey, who also had a close relationship with the lost children. She was present when the two children died and, no doubt, also experienced the grief of their loss.[6]

The Walton household was also grieving due to the loss of their son, Robert Walton. He was a partner in his father's law firm and groomed to take over the practice as George Walton, Jr., sixty-four years old, and drew closer to retirement. One family friend remarked, "By all our community the death of Major Walton will be lamented; but to his immediate family circle, his loss will be irreparable."[7]

George, Sally, and their son Robert had shared the same home when he died. George and Sally always had their differences, but they could no longer live in the same residence at the loss of their son. Colonel George Walton left Mobile; Sally retained twelve senlaved, most likely using their rent as income. According to the 1850 U.S. Census, she was in her own residence, not shared with Henry and Octavia.[8] While no actual documentation to support this idea exists, research has shown that moneyed white women, lacking a husband or son, relied on income earned by renting out their slaves.[9]

Despite having her own residence, Sally was not entirely alone. She had a close relationship with her daughter, Octavia. According to the writer, Mary Forrest, "In enumerating the ruling characteristics of Madame LeVert, we must not forget one which stands out perhaps more prominently than any other - her devotion to her mother. We do not remember ever to have seen the filial relation more fully realized. The mother is worthy of the daughter; a through gentlewoman of large heart, and brilliant, versatile gifts; indeed, we have heard it said that when the two have appeared together in society, the former has sometimes been obliged to 'look to her laurels.' It is frequently the case that mother, daughter, and grand-daughter attend the same party, dance in the same quadrille, and attract their own separate corner-coteries."[10]

Octavia had other support. Many shared her grief when her two little girls, Sally Walker and Claudia Anna, died in 1849. A friend and noted poet, Caroline Lee Hentz, wrote a poem on the children's death. It was widely circulated in the newspapers throughout the North and the South.[11] As she wrote:

They sleep in death - the summer gales
Sigh o'er their grassy bed;
Where murmuring Nature softly wails,
Above the early dead.

E'er sin could mar their spotless charms,
With Heaven's own seal impressed,
The Savior ope'd his sheltering arms,
And clasped them to his breast.
They sleep in death - the dews of night,
That weep upon their tomb,
Ne'er moistened flowers more sweet and bright,
More transient in their bloom.

Alas! The dews of night still fall,
The flowers of autumn glow,

While they, the loveliest flowers of all,
Blighted and pale, lie low.

And in each youthful hand, they hold
A sweet and golden lyre -
Rejoice-two Cherubs are enrolled
In Heaven's eternal Choir.

They live in Heaven - a kinder breast
Than fondest Mothers bear,
Cradles them to their Eden rest,
With never a slumbering care.

That Savior, whose divine embrace
Once blest the lambs of earth,
Now crowns them with his Father's grace,
And owns their Heavenly birth.

Columbus, Ga, November 1849

Great tragedy can result in life-changing moments where dreams and directions shift. Octavia always wrote in her journal and studied other authors' writings, especially material written by other women. Many friends encouraged her to write on a larger scale, but she was busy filling her role as a mother. She seemed happy to instruct her children, develop their minds, and read in her library.

The death of the two girls and her brother seems to have sparked a change in her mindset. This change came about most unexpectedly; little did the grieving family in Mobile know an international travel writer and a friend of

Lady Emmeline Stuart-Wortley visited Octavia in Mobile. Lewis, Frederick Christian. *Lady Emmeline Stuart-Wortley-Mackenzie (1806-1855)*. Photograph. London, n.d. United Kingdom

the Queen of England, Victoria, would pay them a visit in a matter of months.

Lady E. Stuart Wortley, her daughter, Victoria, and two maidservants arrived in New York aboard the steamship, Canada, from Liverpool on May 17th, 1849.[12] While exploring New York and the surrounding areas, she spent time with many of Octavia's close connections, including poet and politician, Edward Everett, and writer, Daniel Webster.[13] When Lady Wortley was invited to spend the winter season with a family in Georgia but turned it down in favor of a trip down the Mississippi River to New Orleans. She learned a fellow international travel writer, Fredrika Bremer, soon planned to pay a visit to the United States as well.[14]

The explorers, Lady Emmeline and Victoria, arrived in New Orleans on December 20th, 1849, and stayed at the Veranda Hotel, exploring the city and planning the next part of their trip to Mexico. She found a British steamer destined for Mobile before it traveled to Vera Cruz and made arrangements.[15] However, when the steamer reached Mobile, she ran into many problems. Lady Wortley and her daughter could not find a steamer out of Mobile. So she stayed with Octavia's mother, Sally, as a guest. According to the book *Queens of American Society*, "Lady Emmeline remained some weeks the guest of Madame LeVert; and the friendship thus formed continued unchanged till Lady Emmeline's death."[16]

It allowed Lady Wortley to spend time exploring the city of Mobile, which she did not originally intend to visit and spend time with Octavia and her family. Despite her deep depression, Octavia escorted the Lady to various locations in Mobile. She must have arrived with a letter of introduction from one of her friends to force Octavia out of mourning her lost brother and daughters. According to Elizabeth Ellet, "It was shortly after these afflictions that Lady Emmeline Stuart Wortley, the daughter of the Duke of Rutland, came to Mobile. She, too, was a mourner for her noble husband and child; and at the very commencement of her acquaintance with Madame LeVert, a tender and holy sympathy bound together the hearts of two stricken mothers."[17]

Octavia guided Lady Wortley to the Choctaw Native American tribes in the city and the Magnolia groves nearby. Octavia's oldest daughter, Diddie, became a companion to Lady Wortley's daughter, Victoria, whose godmother was the Queen of England, Victoria.[18]

During this time, Diddie was growing into a young adult, and at fourteen-years-old, Henry and Octavia started introducing her to a greater social circle, paying close attention to people she was around. For Diddie, it was time to start abandoning her braids and short skirts of youth and begin wearing long dresses and placing her hair up like her mother and grandmother.[19] Also, Octavia devoted herself to educating Diddie in French, Spanish, German, and Latin.[20]

It was time for Diddie to start experiencing the same social foundations as her mother. She could be a part of greater social groups and help develop allegiances, much like Octavia did for Henry and her family. Octavia was training her to fulfill the role of wife and mother. According to the *Confederate Belle*, "There were few alternatives to marriage and children. The life of an "old maid" was hardly the crowning achievement of a successful belle hood, and some young women worried that they would fail to attract a suitor who would ensure them financial security and social respectability."[21]

Lady Wortley arrived in time to see one of Mobile's oldest traditions, Mardi Gras. In the early years of the celebration, it was practiced during the New Year. She witnessed one of the parades with a myth theme, "Pig-tailed Mandarins, pagodas, and colored lanterns on poles, clashed with tridents, chariots, and mythological divinities."[22]

Octavia took Lady Wortley to the grave of her daughters, who noted, "Two other lovely children Madame LeVert had the misfortune to lose, and she has not recovered the severe shock of their death. We went with her to the cemetery, where she reposed her darlings."[23] Octavia later wrote Edward Everett, friend, and aid to Daniel Webster,[24] "Lady Emmeline, like myself, is the Mother of children in Heaven who were taken from us by the same fell disease. The similarity of our fate linked the chain of friendship between us, and we felt at our first interview, 'There is no tie of sympathy more strong, then that which united the afflicted.'"[25]

One of the most interesting accounts during her visit was of meeting an elderly slave in Octavia's household. At this time, Octavia's home had document four slaves in residence.[26] Since slaves were passed down through the women in this family and they specified that family groups be kept together in their wills, this enslaved woman was probably the daughter of one of Dorothy's slaves and Betsey's grandmother. Lady Wortley was fascinated with the oldest of them and shared her impression. She placed the black woman's age at around a hundred and enjoyed her recollection of witnessing George Washington with George Walton, Sr., Octavia's grandfather, in Augusta, Georgia. Lady Wortley wrote, "She gave us all this information in the most elevated tones, a speaking trumpet voice."[27]

While in Mobile, Lady Wortley tried to make plans for her next journey to Mexico, but she ran into endless travel complications. Finally, possibly at Octavia's salon, she met the United States Representative to Mexico and managed to arrange passage on his ship.[28] According to Caldwell Delaney, "Lady Emmeline remained with Madame LeVert while awaiting a ship to Mexico, the next point on her tour. During that time, she met at the LeVert home Robert Letcher, the New United States minister to Mexico, and Lord Mark Kerr, aide to Lord Elgin, governor-general of Canada. When the regular mail steamer did not arrive, Letcher summoned a warship from Pensacola and took Lady Emmeline and Lord Mark to Vera Cruz with him as his guests."[29]

Lady Wortley's visit seems to have revived Octavia and what remained of the family. She wrote Longfellow again, sharing with him the poem written by Caroline Hentz. She also seemed to be enamored with Longfellow, who had extensive connections in literary circles, an area she aspired to achieve. Octavia wrote, "I hope, dear Mr.

Longfellow, you will welcome this greeting from your far away Southern friend, and excuse me for trespassing upon your valuable time. But I cannot resist the impulse I feel of writing to you and recalling myself to your memory. I am persuaded your kind heart will pardon me. To our acquaintance was so brief, it was sufficiently long to find 'Open Sesame' to my friendship, and I can never forget you."[30]

Octavia told him how she read his latest book, *Seaside and Fireside*, and how she used his books with others to help distract her by educating herself to get through her grief. She continued saying, "Nine long months have winged their flight to the unreturning Past since my precious Angels were gathered, and transplanted to the Garden of their God. Oh! My kind friend, would I could tell you that I am resigned. But, Time the great Soother of wounded souls, has had no power over mine. Still fresh is my anguish, as in the first 'Iron days" which blighted the fairest hopes of existence. You must not suppose I yield myself to despair. Ah! No, I struggle against the bitter waters of sorrow's dark sea, which threaten to engulf my life. I implore resignation from on High, and I trust in God's good time I may view my affliction in a different light, and my say, 'Thy will, not mine, be done.'" Octavia cleverly interjected in her letter about the famous author, Miss Fredrika Bremer, who was currently traveling in the United States. Lady Wortley must have shared the news with her, and Octavia knew she must have spent time with Longfellow. She wrote, "I look with delight an acquaintance with her. I have written

185

to invite her to become my Guest during her sojourn in our city. Tho I have secluded myself entirely from society, I would make an exception for her. I have not the happiness of knowing Mrs. Longfellow, but I pray you present me to her in a kind manner." She closed the letter with her admiration of him, once again exhibiting her ability to charm.[31]

What was so special about Fredrika Bremer that the result was Octavia writing to Longfellow and seeking an audience? According to Adolph Benson, "The success of her domestic novels was as immediate on this side of the Atlantic as in England, and her English translator was not far wrong when she declared in 1852, in a preface to the collected edition of her translations, that the works of Fredrika Bremer had become familiar to every household where the English language was spoken."[32]

Though Octavia was starting to write to friends again, she continued to exclude herself from society, not ready to manage a room like she once did.[33] She documented the gradual process of her recovery from such great grief in the journal she began in 1849. On February third, she wrote, "There is healing in the bitter cup. God takes away those we love as hostages of our faith. Faith is that precious Alchemy which transmutes Grief into Joy. Grief is the memory of widowed affection. The more intense the delight in the presence of the object, the more poignant must be the impression of the absence."[34]

Her close friends advised her to seek a change of scenery to get her mind off her loss, but she felt that all those things she loved before no longer mattered. She lamented in her journal, "What effect can change of scene have upon me? I bear with me ever those wounds of the heart, fresh and bleeding. Wherever I could go, Grief would still be my companion. Hence the isolation of my own home with its mournful associations is most congenial to me.[35]

She found comfort in old friends during this challenging time of her life. While she sought to remain away from society, they kept reaching out to her. One person was her tutor from her days as a young girl in Pensacola, Florida, Henry Marie Brackenridge. Her letter to him showed how close she felt to him despite the distance of time.

In this special letter, she shared how thrilled she was that he remembered her. She remarked, "Ah! How the happy days of the 'Sweet old Time,' cluster around my heart, as I write to you! And gently does Memory span the Chasm, which separates the past, from the Present. Then, all was bright, as the Peri's first glance of Paradise, but now, the Sirocco of Sorrow has blighted all the fairest hopes of my existence."

Octavia further shared her intense grief, a common and understandable theme in the letters to close friends as she worked through it and slowly moved forward, seeking solace in literature and teaching her daughter, Diddie, she said, "Oh! My friend, how often, then, has my memory dwelt upon you, and I have blessed you, for the love of learning, you instilled into my young mind when as a little child I sat at your feet and listened to the eloquent words, which made instruction, from your lips so enchanting, and awakened a pride in my heart to be learned like you. Often have I said to my Octavia, 'Thus did my friend Judge B. teach me, when I Was only ten, and I can never fancy any other method as good.' 'The good, men do, live after them,' some wise man has said, but the good you have done, my beloved friend exists now, while health & intellect are still yours."

Octavia continued, "I educate my child, entirely myself. She has wonderful talent and acquires every science as tho' by intuition. She is but 12 and is far advanced in all the branches of English Education. Is a good French scholar. Learns Spanish, German & Latin. Octavia was charmed with "Paul et Virginie," - she read it immediately and is now re-reading it aloud to me. I never speak to her, save in French or in Spanish, and by this means, she is compelled to understand them perfectly."[36]

Octavia was also relieved to know Judge Brackenridge was with her father, Colonel George Walton, who was still grieving Robert and his granddaughters' loss. It appeared her father, after leaving her mother and the life in Mobile, moved to a residence in Washington D.C., and Judge Breckenridge visited with him often. After so many years, it seemed the two old gentlemen were once again on friendly terms.

Octavia, in favor of the Union, a person who was a part of exploring and expanding the United States as a young girl and one who followed national politics, struggled with the possibility that the country could be broken up. She wrote to Breckenridge, "You would scarcely believe, I read all the speeches made in Congress. Tho' they breath of War, and Disunion, I cannot imagine it within the circle of, the Possible, that this mighty fabric, whose foundation, was cemented with the blood of my brave Grand-Sire, can crumble and dissolve way, by the diastard blows of traitors, fit companions for Arnold. Avert in Heaven? I was delighted with Mr. Clay's speech and have town written to him to express my admiration of it - Mr. Clay is a valued friend of happier days. He has most kindly snatched a few moments from his many duties to write to me."[37] Henry Clay's great speech she referred to was his last. He left Washington before the close of the session due to illness.[38]

While Sally Walton and the LeVert's were not up to handling the stresses of large society life, they could handle something simple with those at home. Growth comes in small steps. On June 1, 1850, Bladen Springs, just north of Mobile by steamer, opened for business in Choctaw County. "At all of these places the best accommodations may be enjoyed, and everybody who can get away should visit one or other of them for recreation and improvement of health."[39]

Fredrika Bremer visited Octavia and helped to focus on writing. 2021. Photograph. *The Homes of the New World; Impressions of America.* By Fredrika Bremer.

Another person who visited Octavia and fostered her transformation after her great loss was the famous author and abolitionist Miss Fredrika Bremer. Despite Bremer's stance on slavery, her fame as an author did not affect her travels through the South. According to Johnathan Daniel Wells, "Southern reviewers, editors, and literary critics grew accustomed in the late antebellum period to northern authors who opposed slavery, and some southerners did not hold such opinions against the authors and were able to assess literary quality based on the merits."[40]

Octavia had invited Fredrika to her home years before after reading one of her books, and she came. According to Caldwell Delaney, "In January 1851, Madame LeVert was visited by Fredrika Bremer, the Swedish Novelist. Miss Bremer was at that time at the height of her fame. As the author of five well-known books, which had been translated and circulated throughout Europe and America, she was greatly lionized in the United States."[41]

Miss Bremer, who was exploring the United States without a dedicated escort, arrived in Mobile on January 7, 1851, in the company of two of Octavia's good friends, Robert Geddes, and his wife.[42] Family friend, Major Bernard A. Reynolds, accompanied Octavia to the steamer that brought Bremer to Mobile. His role was to help play host to the famous author, escorting her to visiting the city and the theatre. Although Octavia was still not ready to go into society, she did not want her situation to affect her visitor.[43]

Bremer, who had already met many of Octavia's friends, did not know what type of woman to expect. Octavia was described as a "belle" and "the most splendid ornament of society," but these were lofty descriptions for a forty-one-year-old developed Southern woman. In addition, in her book, Bremer later reported she was exposed to the darkest areas of slavery during her journey down the Mississippi River to New Orleans. She knew Octavia was a slave-owner and curious as to how she treated them.

Bremer wrote of her first observations of Octavia, noticing since Lady Emeline Stuart Wortley's visit drew her out of her deep depression, and she was slowly recovering. Bremer commented, "But all is still a burden to her, and she is, as it were, dead to the pleasures of the world. She believes that she can never overcome that sense of sorrow which seemed to have crushed her. Nevertheless, she is cheerful, and even sometimes laughs heartily - but her eyes show that they have shed many tears."[44]

As it turns out, Miss Bremer flourished in Mobile. She stayed at Sally Walton's home, describing her as the widow of George Walton, Jr., even though he was very much alive and living in Virginia. She described the home as sunny and peaceful. While Bremer was against slavery, she saw the enslaved in the home as happy and in good health. Despite the egregious lack of freedom, this perspective was a welcome change from the other versions of slavery she saw while traveling.[45]

It seems that Fredrika Bremer found a kindred soul in Octavia during her visit to Mobile. She described Octavia as being close to her as a young sister. She commented, "But she has become so from being so very excellent, because she has suffered much, and because under a worldly exterior there is an unusually sound and pure intellect, and a heart full of affection, which can cast aside all the vanities of the world for the power of gratifying those whom she loves. And with this young lady have I conversed of Transcendentalists and practical Christians, of Mormonism and Christianity, and have found it a pleasure to converse with her, a pleasure to her also, which I little expected...She says that I have given to her that spiritual food of which she stood in need, and she has given to me a pleasure, a gratification which is nourishing to my heart."[46]

While Bremer was an abolitionist and Octavia a Southern slave owner, it was clear Octavia was strongly influenced by what she read and Northern ideals. Yes, these two educated ladies had their differences, but these rough edges were smoothed over by their mutual literary interests that bridged the gap caused by sectionalism.[47]

Bremer was also pleasantly surprised at how close Octavia and Betsey were despite their slave and owner relationship. According to Bremer, "Betsy seems really not to live for anything else than for her Mistress Octavia; to dress her hair every day at la Mary Stuart, and to see her handsome, gay, and admired, that is Betsy's life and happiness."

According to Bremer, despite seeing well treated and happy slaves in both Octavia's home and in the home of Sally Walton, she "still belongs to those whose excellent hearts and understandings do not confuse good and evil. Whenever an opportunity occurs, she simply and earnestly expressed her conviction that slavery is a curse, and on this subject, we are perfectly harmonious." It seems as though Octavia did not approve of slavery, but since she inherited the slaves she currently owned, and they had long been a part of the family, she did not know how to separate the two.[48]

Octavia was not the only educated woman who encountered the struggle with slavery. According to Wells, "Georgia's Ella Gertrude Thomas, for example, was a sensitive reader who thought carefully about the political implications of her reading. As she put down in her diary: "But as the to doctrine of slavery although I have read very few abolition books (Uncle Tom's Cabin making the most impression) nor have I read many pro slavery books - yet the idea has gradually become more and more fixed in my mind that the institution of slavery is not right."[49]

While Octavia and Betsey's relationship appears close with strong emotional ties, Octavia acting on Betsey's behalf and giving more privileges, there is a question of what difficulties resided in the situation. According to *Scarlett Doesn't Live Here Anymore*, "Mistresses usually saw the relationships in extremely one-sided terms. They expected their favorite slaves to identify completely with their own concerns and desires and refused to acknowledge that slaves had separate lives and desires and interests. Disappointment was inevitable. When it came, mistresses felt not just inconvenienced but personally betrayed."[50]

Clearly, Bremer had to be aware of Octavia's musical ability, but after she got to see her personal journals, she guided Octavia to write. Octavia had already developed her pseudonym, "Madame Walton LeVert," and planned to carry it over to her writings.[51] Octavia now planned to join Fredrika Bremer in her journey to Cuba and start working on her dream of becoming a writer.

According to Satterfield, Octavia had brightened up, "She was now for the first time after her sorrow about to leave home with a delightful friend. Miss Bremer reported that "the good Dr. LeVert had given his wife a handsome sum of money" so that she could enjoy herself in Cuba. Mrs. Walton and the two little LeVert girls, Diddie and Cara Netta, were on hand to give their mother an affectionate farewell in the hope of seeing her return happy. Betsey, who spoke Spanish fluently by then, was traveling with them, for Octavia could not dispense with her, and Betsey felt no one else could take care of her mistress. She managed all of the details of the journey. A friend of Octavia later wrote, "North, South, East, West - through twisting ranks of Abolitionists, up the Rhine, over the Alps - everywhere goes Betsey."[52]

When they finally made it to New Orleans and the St. Charles Hotel on January 15th, 1851, there was a problem.[53] Bremer found Betsey standing in the middle of

Octavia's room, frowning. Betsey told Bremer, "It was here in this very room," she whispered to Miss Bremer, "that she lived two years ago with those two little girls, and here she dressed them for a children's ball!" Miss Bremer went to Octavia and lifted her head. Still weeping, she asked Miss Bremer if she could change rooms with her. Even that did not erase the memories, and it was difficult to get Octavia to go downstairs the next morning to one of the elegant drawing rooms to greet old friends. According to Bremer, "Pale, and with eyes still red from weeping, she was still charming in a back satin dress with its many points and adornments."[54]

Miss Bremer invited Octavia and Mrs. Geddes to come to her rooms to begin the sketches of them in her album. "I enjoyed the contemplation and the drawing of these two amiable ladies," Miss Bremer wrote, "the noble, earnest, regular profile of Mrs. G. And the round, childlike, piquant, countenance of Octavia LeVert, with its little turned-up nose, which I imagine resembles Cleopatra's, and the fantastic arrangement of the hair, the artistic labor of Betsy's hands."[55] Also, Miss Bremer drew Octavia's servant, Betsey.[56]

Picture of Octavia drawn by Fredrika Bremer. 2021. Photograph.
Madame LeVert A Biography of Octavia Walton LeVert, by Frances Gibson
Satterfield.

Picture of Betsey drawn by Fredrika Bremer. 2021. Photograph. *A Mobile Sextet*, by Caldwell Delaney.

Octavia's perspective of life had changed a bit since the visits from Lady Wortley and Miss Bremer. She was still the grieving mother, but the visits had revitalized her. She wanted to explore; now she was in a position to see the world, much like the ladies who'd visited her. These visits fed the silent wish Octavia to write professionally and encouraging her to make the leap.

When their trip to Cuba was delayed, the ladies decided to make the best of the situation and seek things to write about in New Orleans. They went to the theatre and visited local cemeteries, including Greenwood and Mount Auburn's Egyptian Marble Entryway.[57]

They also visited the famous songstress Jenny Lind, Fredrika Bremer's countrywoman, from Sweden. She seems to have touched her because Octavia wrote an account in her journal, "I have heard more than once the divine songstress Jenny Lind. Words can never do justice to that sweet & matchless voice! The melody seems to gush from her soul in rills of song, and it flows over you till you feel lost, drowned in waves of harmony. To call her a Nightingale gives but a faint idea of her surpassing powers. You feel the soul in her accents, that never breathed from the sweetest of birds. In the Trio of the Flute, in which her voice mingles with those sweet instruments, sweeter and clearer than their most exquisite notes, this divine soul still exercises its magic influence over you. But it is not only as the Queen of Song, one must regard this Swedish Maiden. I look upon her, as the most simple-hearted, generous & unselfish of human beings. Her spotless purity - her guileless symplicity - her splendid charities places her over-shadow the charms of the singer."[58]

Jenny Lind, famous songstress. *Jenny Lind*. Photograph. Washington, D.C.,
1850. Library of Congress Prints and Photographs Division Washington,
D.C. 20540 USA.

This review of Jenny Lind resulted in Octavia's first
serialized review in newspapers throughout the North

and the South. It became a good place for Octavia's literary career to begin. According to Wells, "The diverse character of magazines and newspapers, in which recipes and housekeeping hints appeared alongside essays on Shakespeare or commentary on political issues, fit well with the emphasis on the breadth of learning expected of the "Renaissance woman."[59]

Little did Octavia or Fredrika realize they both experience one of the most dramatic events in New Orleans history, the fire at the St. Charles Hotel. Octavia shared the event in her journal, and Fredrika's account ended up in her book, *Homes in the New World*. Equally, their encounters resulted in a rather dramatic story.

January 31, 1851, started nicely for Octavia and Fredrika. They were at Mrs. Geddes.' home, talking about love and enjoying a warm fire. Fredrika was also working on her drawing of Octavia.[60] Suddenly, a messenger came to Mrs. Geddes', requesting her keys to their rooms at the St. Charles Hotel because it was on fire.[61]

Despair washed over Octavia because before leaving the St. Charles Hotel, she had locked her room and given Betsey leave to go out. There was no one to send into the hotel to rescue her clothes, the cash she brought for the trip, or her effects. Everything she had would be lost to the flames. Bremer remarked, "Ah! It is quite certain everything will be destroyed," said Octavia, and sat tranquilly before me, an image of unexampled equanimity. The heart which had bled with the deepest sorrow could not agitate itself by the loss of earthly possessions; the eyes which had wept so long over a beloved brother and those dear children had no tears for worldly adversity. I saw this evidently, while Octavia calmly reckoned up everything which her room contained, and which would now be consumed. She said that early that morning, she had seen a volume of black smoke issue from under her bed. She gave the alarm and went a message to the master of the hotel, who replied that here was no danger; that the smoke had merely found its way thither through a defect in one of the chimney flues, and that all would soon be put to rights. An hour afterward, smoke was again in the room; but it seemed perfectly to have subsided when she left the hotel."[62]

Bremer, who had placed as much faith in Betsey as Octavia, tried to comfort Octavia by mentioning Betsey would hear of the fire and rush back to the hotel, but Octavia told her that Betsey had traveled a long way outside the city and the hotel was made of wood and would be consumed in a matter of hours. Determined to see the destruction, Octavia went to a friend's house, not too far from the hotel.[63]

Octavia shared the experience in her journal, "When we were within six squares of the Hotel, we were compelled to leave the Carriage. Mrs. W. endeavoured to persuade me, to return home with her. But I said, no, no, if the St. Charles, is doomed to ashes, I am resolved to be in at "The Death." We winded our way slowly through the crowd. Thousands & tens of thousands per persons filled the streets. When we neared the noble Edifice, I looked at the magnificent Dome, a deep black mass, like a funeral

Pall rested upon it. Soon, a bright serpent-like flame, sprang through the Cupola, high into the Heavens. The cloud parted, and rolled away. The sun shone forth, and its beams lingered lovingly upon the glittering Dome. As I gazed upon it, there came a crash such as ears have rarely heard. The Dome had fallen! Then arose a wild wail of sorrow, from the multitude, (numbering more than 50,000 person.) Above, the terrific crash was heard this cry of despair. Thus in early day, was destroyed this graceful Dome! By making a long detour, I reached the Balcony of the Verandah, a Hotel vis a vis. From thence, I watched the entire destruction of this Pearl - this Gem of Hotels.

'Take it for all and all,'

'We ne'er shall look upon its like again.'

It was, in truth, a National ornament. It was the Pantheon of American Structures! Never did I realize so perfectly the truthfulness of the oft repeated quotation, 'Blessings brighten as they take their flight.' Never to my eyes had the splendid Edifice appeared so beautiful, as when all its admirable proportions were cased in fire, relieved by an intensely black sky. It was the most wildly grand & awfully magnificent spectacle, imagination can picture. It combined all the grandeur of a Conflagration with the horrors of an Earthquake. As the Portico with its graceful columns, and exquisite statuary fell to earth, the houses around trembled & rocked. Four hours I watched the progress of the flames. Every portion of the Building was destroyed e'er the 'Parlour' was touched. Ah! No language can describe the years of Memory, that crowded into that brief space. All the happy scenes of by gone years passed before my mental vision, arrayed in the brightness of their first enjoyment. I likened it to my own Destiny. There was a time when Life was bright as a dream of 'Fairy Land,' and, now, mid crushing Hopes, and blighted feelings I stand wrecked in happiness, with no visions of future joy to gladden my soul. Alas! Thus pass away all that is dearest, truest & brightest. ----the wail for the lost St. Charles, finds an Echo throughout the country. How many have spent their most joyous days within its walls."[64]

Meanwhile, Betsey arrived at Mrs. Geddes's home, where Bremer waited to learn more about the fire. Betsey, out of breath, searched for Octavia to tell her that all her things were safe and she had all of Octavia's money with her. When Betsey received word the hotel was burning, she'd rushed back to the hotel. A friend of Octavia's broke down the door to her room, and they managed to save all of Octavia's property.

While they rushed to the hotel to find Octavia, Betsey shared her personal story and exposed a portion of her own life history so rarely recognized during this time. Bremer reported, "Betsy told me still more as we went along, of how much she loved her mistress; of how she might have been married more than once, and how there was still a free man in the North who would gladly have her, but she would not think of leaving Mrs. Le V..."[65]

They later learned a few people were injured by the fire, and some lost much of their property. The most frightening of all was that the fire broke out by Octavia's room. It was fortunate that the fire did not start that first night.[66] The excitement was too much for Octavia and Betsey. Concerned their families would be worried about them after hearing about the massive fire, they decided not to go to Cuba with Fredrika but, instead, return to Mobile.

Octavia continued to correspond with Lady Emmeline Wortley and was invited to contribute to a sketch of her friend, Mrs. Caroline Lee Hentz for the book, *Female Prose Writers of America*, by John S. Hart.[67] It was clear she was becoming more confident as a writer, and her reputation for hospitality at her home in Mobile was growing beyond the confines of the South.[68]

Octavia's new venture into writing changed from a fancy of a well-to-do woman in high society to something of substance. People noticed, and she had their attention. The *Brattleboro Eagle* reported, "Mrs. LeVert who for several years has been a reigning belle, at Newport and Saratoga, has turned her attention of late to literary pursuits. She is a lady of brilliant conversation, elegant manners, and fine education. She makes her debut as an authoress, with a finely written account of Mrs. Caroline Lee Hentz, the novelist, whom she describes as tall, graceful, dignified, and in all respects a most fascinating person, and reminding one of Frederica Bremer in the elevating tone and tendency of her works.[69]

The LeVert family slowly worked into their new normal life, the children and Robert always resting in the back of their minds. Octavia wrote in her journal more about events around her, practicing her descriptions and use of words. She seemed to be preparing for a much larger project. Octavia realized her beauty had faded and felt she needed to do something to garnish the attention she loved. Writing appears to have filled the void.

Despite her advancing age, she was still the focus of many portraitures. While it is unknown exactly where the sitting for the Louis Lang portrait of Octavia took place, she did have one made in 1852. In this painting, she is clearly older, now forty-two years old. Her hair is still as dark as ever, but now she was showing the signs of age, and her dress was black as if still in the mourning the loss of her children.[70]

Octavia also wrote of the stormy winter in the same year and was rather focused on the death of four giant orange trees that grew in her garden. She commented, "The bright green leaves, encased in ice glittered like so many enormous Emeralds. The golden Fruit, half covered by the snow, seemed like gloves of virgin Gold, enwrapt in a delicate chasing of purest silver. The clouds departed, and the sun came forth. But there was no warmth in his beams. For days the snow lingered, and when it melted, the emerald leaves, and golden orange with its silver net work fell to the earth, and the noble Tree yielded up their life. The Snow Spirit had laid its icy hands upon them, and they passed away like all else, must die, that is bright and beautiful. You will believe me, when I tell you I wept their loss. I had cherished them and petted them, but they have left me, as many I adored have done before."[71]

A letter in October 1851 to Octavia from Lady Emmeline Wortley indicates a plan afoot for Octavia to travel to Europe. It also seems as if everyone knew of the failing health of their mutual friend, Henry Clay. Octavia wrote, "I cannot tell you how deeply I sympathize in your regrets, for save on the cherished point of reciprocal friendship I claim an equal interest in the great statesman. A mind like that of Henry Clay belongs not to a country, but the century - not to a people, but to mankind." Bold thoughts strongly expressed. But the feelings of these ladies are as strongly knit as is their friendship, and both look forward with delight to a happy reunion next summer at Belvoir Castle, the Duke's seat."[72]

A letter from her lifelong friend, Henry Clay, confirmed her fears about his failing health. His mind was still acute, but he admitted to delicate health. He was still determined to go to Washington to make his final speech to Congress. He was pleased Octavia was established in her beautiful home and eagerly sought to read the book recently published by Lady Emmeline Wortley. She wrote of her visit to the United States. He spoke of his affection for Dr. LeVert, George Walton, Jr., Sally, and the remaining children, but he did not know George was no longer living in Mobile.[73]

The year 1852 would be another one full of significant change and growth. Octavia, ever a great reader and lover of books, was exposed to Harriet Beecher Stowe's installments of her work, *Uncle Tom's Cabin*, when it first appeared as a serial in a newspaper and was later to be published by John P. Jewett in 1853.[74] There seemed to be developing a struggle with Octavia in her correspondence with Fredrika Bremer, both educated ladies who seemed to have found a kindred spirit and the freedom to express concepts normally not discussed in polite society.

In a letter to Miss Bremer on May 10th, 1852, it was clear Octavia was struggling again with depression. She was slow to return correspondence to her dear friend, but with reason. She wrote to Bremer, "I have passed a most sad and careless winter. Ill health has often confined me to the house, and when I left it, so many painful associations hung around each object I was vain to hurry back, to the seclusion of my own library, where among my books, I am always more content and calm. Death, has again been busy in our family. Last week, dear mama lost two of her servants, a woman and a man, (brother and sister). You can well appreciate and understand this sorrow we feel for their loss. Next to our own kindred it is the greatest grief. Their ancestors belong to ours, near 200 years ago, and our attachment to the slaves, is far different from the usual relation between mistress and servant. A northern woman, making me a visit a few days since, remarking the traces of tears upon my cheek exclaimed: 'Ah! Madame, where I to tell an Abolitionist, I had seen you weep for the death of a Slave, he would not believe me.'"[75]

In addition, Octavia was coming to terms with the failing health of her lifelong friend and mentor, Henry Clay. She shared with Bremer, "I have recently received a letter from Mr. Clay, in which he tells me, he is better, but still the final issue of his melody is doubtful, although the physicians think him improving. I am sure you mourn with me the shadow that is drawing over his brightness. But it is the cloud that gathers around the setting sun, and is dipped in the gold of its departing beams. The friendship and affection of such a man our gifts I have made a prize. Like diamonds they are indestructible like gold imperishable."[76]

Octavia, Sally, Diddie, and Cara Netta had planned to travel through the summer of 1852, venturing first to Bladen Springs, north of Mobile, but this was to become their only trip. They could not make it to the watering places of Virginia. Her youngest daughter, Cara Netta, now six years old, had developed a fever. Fearful of losing her remaining children, Octavia refused to take any chances with their health. The entire family rushed back from Bladen Springs to Mobile on the steamship, *Octavia*. Diddie, now sixteen years old and developing into a typical southern lady, grieved at fading her plans for enjoying the summer. Octavia called it her "debut in disappointment."[77] Cara Netta recovered from her illness, but the challenges of this year continued.

Octavia's dear, lifelong friend, Henry Clay, died on June 29th, 1852.[78] Can a person who loves so profoundly accustom themselves to a method of handling grief? It seems Octavia had determined a path. She wrote Bremer on September 4th, 1852, "As long as no mention is made of my griefs, I can control my anguish. But let any circumstance, or chance touch but the Stone which is as the Barrier to Recollection, and forth rushes a wild stream of bitterest sorrow, and wave after wave of wild agony sweep over my soul bearing away all the Resignation of earnest prayer. The flood lasts for a time, until the waters have spent their force, and my indomitable will replaces the Rock over the Sepulchre of buried hopes and Joys, and I am calm once more. Hence, never to be human being, dare I speak of my afflictions, between the Good God and myself they rest."[79]

On August 30th, 1852, another event affected the LeVert family. Octavia wrote in her journal about the most terrific Hurricane of the nineteenth century. It started on August 24th and increased to a gale during the night. The following day the violence of the hurricane intensified steadily through the day. The wind sounded like the shock of cannon fire that struck their house with extreme force.

Octavia continued, "No sleep came to my eyes, & by the window I watched for the coming day. Ah! How terror multiplies Time! The night seemed endless, the minutes dragged on as tho' they were hours. At last came the Daylight and I thanked the Good God, I was permitted to look upon it once more. The black heavy clouds, gradually rolled up, as the light came on, and revealed the unchecked horrors of the Tempest. Great trees were up rooted as tho' they were Spring flowers. Houses were un-roofed, and one Square below us, rushed in the mad billowy waves of the Gulf, bearing on their tide, every variety of merchandise, which their fury had torn from the various stores. All Front, Commerce & Water, the three business streets of the town. Never did I behold such a scene of Desolation & Ruin. It was a sight to remember forever! The sky had in inky darkness, unrelieved by one gleam of Lightening. It was like a grand Funeral Pall over those who had perished in the Tempest - Tender children were swept away from their Parents arms, and old age, struggled with the waters o'er the weet cup of life, was exhausted. Strong men battled with the flood nobly e'er they perished, and young women were engulfed like the Autumn leaves, in the mad seething Waters. At mid Day the Hurricane abated and the waves, as tho' wearied with the Devastation they had wrought, quietly retired to their usual channels. Then did the Merchants perceive the intensity of their losses! Thousands and hundreds of thousands, even unit millions of dollars were destroyed in the flood. All descriptions of provision - all kinds of fabrics - of beautiful jewelry - of gorgeous carpetings where in one mass of terrible ruin. The wharf's all gone, and their places supplied by thousands of trees, torn from their native soil, and wildly dashed upon the shore. The hopes of years - the labour of months in a few short hours all gone, all despair where "Expectation yester night sat smiling."[80]

Yet, despite this great hurricane, Octavia continued to host guests from all over the world. One was Louis Kossuth, an Hungarian patriot, who visited Mobile in 1852. According to Mrs. Sarah DeBois, "On arrival he was met by Madame LeVert with her carriage, who yielded her seat to him and walked beside the same in the procession to her home on southwest Government and St. Emanuel Streets, where the Hungarian was highly entertained."[81]

Octavia and her salon gained both fame and prominence in the South. She single-handedly turned

Mobile into a destination for refinement and taste. She was able to move beyond the tragedies in her life, but her efforts to distance herself from the grief were to also lead to a cataclysm unlike anyone had ever seen.

Works Cited and Notes

1. Emmeline Stuart Wortley, "Thursday Night," in *Octavia Walton Le Vert Journal 1846-1860*, ed. Octavia Walton LeVert. Journal/Diary. SPR638, Closed Stacks, Alabama Department of Archive, January 3, 1850.

2. Francis Ludgere Diard, *WPA Report, Chronology of Mobile Years and Events*. S-201, University of West Florida Archives, *Satterfield Collection*. Note: Report for Week Ending August 5, 1938.

3. Forrest, *Women of the South Distinguished in Literature*, 22.

4. *The Daily Crescent*, August 11, 1849, Chronicling America.

5. Peter J. Hamilton, *Mobile of the Five Flags: The Story of the River Basin and Coast About Mobile from the Earliest Times to the Present* (Mobile: The Gill Printing Company, 1913), 283.

6. Alabama State Census 1850, Alabama State Census, 1820-1866, A Enumeration of the Inhabitants of Mobile County, 1850, Ancestry.com.

7. "Obituary," *Times-Picayune*, March 29, 1849, 1, *America's Historical Newspapers Database*; "Obituary," *Mobile Advertiser*, March 29, 1849, 1, *America's Historical Newspapers Database*.

8. Alabama State Census 1850, Alabama State Census, 1820-1866, A Enumeration of the Inhabitants of Mobile County, 1850, Ancestry.com.

9. Jonathan Martin, *Divided Mastery* (Cambridge: Harvard University Press, 2004), 83.

10. Forrest, *Women of the South Distinguished in Literature*, 28.

11. "Lines," *The Daily Crescent*, January 2, 1850, Chronicling America.

12. "Passengers Arrived," *Spectator*, May 17, 1849, GenealogyBank.

13. Note: Edward Everett was Daniel Webster's assistant till he died in 1852. President Millard Fillmore appointed Everett to Secretary of State, a position he held till 1853. U.S. Department of State Website. Archive.

14. Lady Emmeline Stuart Wortley, *Travels in the United States, etc., during 1849 and 1850,* (New York: Harper & Brothers, 1851), 74-77, Google Books.

15. "Lady Emeline Stuart Wortley," *Times-Picayune,* December 22, 1849, GenealogyBank.

16. Ellet, *Queens of American Society,* 404.

17. Ellet, *Queens of American Society,* 404.

18. Wortley, *Travels in the United States,* 135.

19. Edwards, *Scarlett Doesn't Live Here Anymore,* 20.

20. *Octavia Walton LeVert Journal Excerpt,* January 19, 1850. Journal/Diary. In *Madame LeVert* ed. Frances Gibson Satterfield (Edisto Island: Edisto Press, 1987), 84.

21. Roberts, Confederate Belle, 17.

22. Wortley, *Travels in the United States,* 132.

23. Wortley, *Travels in the United States,* 135.

24. "Madame Le Vert's Diary," *Alabama Historical Quarterly* 3, No. 1 (Spring 1941): University of West Florida Archives.

25. *Octavia Walton LeVert Journal Excerpt,* January 1850. Journal/Diary. In *Madame LeVert* ed. Frances Gibson Satterfield (Edisto Island: Edisto Press, 1987), 91.

26. Henry S LeVert, Alabama State Census, 1820-1866, Ancestry.com.

27. Wortley, *Travels in the United States,* 136.

28. Wortley, *Travels in the United States,* 137.

29. Delaney, "Madame Octavia Walton Le Vert," 63.

30. *Octavia Walton LeVert to Henry Wadsworth Longfellow,* January 19, 1850. Letter. Harvard University, *Longfellow Papers.*

31. *Octavia Walton LeVert to Henry Wadsworth Longfellow,* January 19, 1850. Letter. Harvard University, *Longfellow Papers.*

32. Adolph B. Benson, "American Appreciation of Fredrika Bremer," *Scandinavian Studies and Notes* 8, no. 1 (February 1, 1924): 14-33.

33. *Octavia Walton LeVert to Henry Clay, February 3, 1850.* Letter. In *Madame LeVert* ed. Frances Gibson Satterfield (Edisto Island: Edisto Press, 1987), 87.

34. LeVert, *Octavia Walton Le Vert Journal 1846-1860,* February 3, 1850 – 41.

35. Delaney, "Madame Octavia Walton Le Vert," 58.

36. *Octavia Walton LeVert to Henry Marie Brackenridge,* March 11, 1850. Letter. University of Pittsburgh, *Henry Marie Brackenridge and Family Papers.*

37. *Octavia Walton LeVert to Henry Marie Brackenridge,* March 11, 1850. Letter. University of Pittsburgh, *Henry Marie Brackenridge and Family Papers.*

38. *Octavia Walton LeVert Journal Excerpt, March 31, 1850.* Journal/Diary. In *Madame LeVert* ed. Frances Gibson Satterfield (Edisto Island: Edisto Press, 1987), 58.

39. *Times-Picayune,* May 11, 1850, Newspapers.com.

40. Wells, *Women Writers and Journalist in the Nineteenth-Century South,* 30.

41. Delaney, "Madame Octavia Walton Le Vert," 64.

42. Note: In Fredrika Bremer's book, she only describes the family in New Orleans as "Mr. and Mrs. G." They were in fact, Robert Geddes and his wife. This was discovered with the help of Heather Szafran, Reference Associate, Williams Research Center, The Historic New Orleans Collection, 410 Chartres Street, New Orleans, LA 701300.

43. Reynolds "Octavia Walton LeVert," 7.

44. Fredricka Bremer, *Homes in the New World Impressions of America. Vol. III* (Hardpress, 2018), 18.

45. Bremer, *Homes in the New World Impressions of* America, 19-23.

46. Bremer, *Homes in the New World Impressions of* America, 22-23.

47. Wells, *Women Writers and Journalist in the Nineteenth-Century South,* 58.

48. *Octavia Walton LeVert Journal Excerpt,* January 7, 1851. Journal/Diary. In *Madame LeVert* ed. Frances Gibson Satterfield (Edisto Island: Edisto Press, 1987), 101-103.

49. Wells, *Women Writers and Journalist in the Nineteenth-Century South,* 62.

50. Edwards, *Scarlett Doesn't Live Here Anymore,* 22.

51. Wells, *Women Writers and Journalist in the Nineteenth-Century South,* 76.

52. *Octavia Walton LeVert Journal Excerpt,* January 13, 1851. Journal/Diary. In *Madame LeVert* ed. Frances Gibson Satterfield (Edisto Island: Edisto Press, 1987), 103.

53. *Times-Picayune,* January 15, 1851, 1, Newspapers.com.

54. *Octavia Walton LeVert Journal Excerpt,* January 13, 1851. Journal/Diary. In *Madame LeVert* ed. Frances Gibson Satterfield (Edisto Island: Edisto Press, 1987), 104.

55. *Octavia Walton LeVert Journal Excerpt,* January 13, 1851. Journal/Diary. In *Madame LeVert* ed. Frances Gibson Satterfield (Edisto Island: Edisto Press, 1987), 104.

56. Note: In Caldwell Delaney's book Mobile Sextet on page 16, there are the drawings of Fredrika Bremer of Betsey and of Octavia.

57. LeVert, *Octavia Walton Le Vert Journal 1846-1860,* January 1851 – 49.

58. LeVert, *Octavia Walton Le Vert Journal 1846-1860,* January 1851 – 49.

59. Wells, *Women Writers and Journalist in the Nineteenth-Century South,* 57.

60. LeVert, *Octavia Walton Le Vert Journal 1846-1860,* January 31, 1851 – 50-53.

61. Satterfield, *Madame LeVert,* 104-105.

62. Satterfield, *Madame LeVert,* 104-105; LeVert, *Octavia Walton Le Vert Journal 1846-1860,* January 31, 1851 – 50-53.

63. Satterfield, *Madame LeVert,* 104-105.

64. LeVert, *Octavia Walton Le Vert Journal 1846-1860,* January 31, 1851 – 50-53.

65. Satterfield, *Madame LeVert,* 104-105.

66. Satterfield, *Madame LeVert,* 104-105.

67. John S. Hart, *Female Prose Writers of America* (Philadelphia: Butler, 1855), 153, Google Books.

68. LeVert, *Octavia Walton Le Vert Journal 1846-1860,* March 8, 1851 – 56-59; *Republic,* April 7, 1851, Chronicling America.

69. *Brattleboro Eagle,* February 23, 1852, 3, Newspapers.com.

70. Louis Lang, "Mrs. Henry Strachey LeVert," Painting. Fresco Frick Art Reference Library: 1852.

71. LeVert, *Octavia Walton Le Vert Journal 1846-1860,* Winter, 1851 – 66.

72. "Mobile Correspondence," *Times-Picayune,* October 7, 1851, 4, Newspapers.com.

73. *Henry Clay to Octavia Walton LeVert,* November 14, 1851. Letter. In *The Papers of Henry Clay Vol. 10. Candidate, Compromiser, Elder Statesman. January 1, 1944 - June 29, 1852,* ed. Melba Porter and Carol Reardon (Lexington: University of Kentucky, 1991).

74. Mary Kelly, *Learning to Stand and Speak,* 59.

75. LeVert, *Octavia Walton Le Vert Journal 1846-1860,* March 10, 1852 - 67-68.

76. LeVert, *Octavia Walton Le Vert Journal 1846-1860,* March 10, 1852 - 67-68.

77. *Octavia Walton LeVert to Daniel Fowler Prout,* July 31, 1852. Letter. University of West Florida, *Satterfield Collection.*

78. Satterfield, *Madame LeVert*, 113.
79. LeVert, *Octavia Walton Le Vert Journal 1846-1860*, September 4, 1852 - 77.
80. LeVert, *Octavia Walton Le Vert Journal 1846-1860*, August 30, 1852.
81. Diard, *WPA Report*.

Chapter 9

To See the World

Bright flag, at yonder tapering mast,
Fling out your field of azure blue!
Let star and stripe be westward cast,
And point as freedom's eagle flew!
Strain home, oh! Lithe and quivering spars!
Point home, my country's flag of stars.
~ N.P. Willis[1]

When the Franklin Hotel burned in 1829 and the Waverly Hotel, the home of the LeVert's before they built a new one, burned in 1850, many wondered how long the space along Royal street would remain vacant. Not long, it seems, for the Battle brothers, John and Samuel, this led to the purchased of the property and built a hotel unlike any other in the area.

The Battle House, named for its proprietors, opened on November 15, 1852. It was a four-story brick building, wrapped in a two-story gallery of cast iron, unlike the former wood structures. A location perfect for cooling off in the Gulf heat and observing activities in the city. According to the *Mobile Press Register*, "The newspaper described it then as a 'grand imposing edifice, (which) seemed like some fairy palace which had sprung up'."[2]

This new hotel enticed visitors. It made Mobile, Alabama, an exciting place to visit. With Octavia Walton LeVert, a long time staple of National Society in a local setting, and other noted writers and actors it indicated the increased wealth to the city and the developments in theatre, literacy, and art. Octavia, surrounded by this growing culture, was emboldened by the support of Lady Wortley and Fredrika Bremer, prepared for a Grand Tour of Europe.

Three miniature portraits also appear about this time, they are of Madame Octavia Walton LeVert, Octavia Walton LeVert, also known as "Diddie," and the youngest daughter, Henrietta Charlotte LeVert, known as "Cara Netta." While unknown, the artist was able to capture a moment in the lives of those who remained in Mobile after a massive loss.

Octavia, sad after losing her brother and two daughters, at age forty-three still retained the beauty of her youth. In a small portrait from this time, her hair is piled on her head in a fashionable wreath, almost like a crown, but she is draped in black and the sadness in her eyes is quite visible. Her small portrait was encased in a jewelry setting designed to be worn around the neck.[3]

Small paintings of Octavia, Diddie, and Cara Netta (Henrietta) LeVert.
Leeth, Yancy. *Octavia, Diddie, and Cara Netta LeVert*. Photograph.
Mobile, Alabama, 2021.
Oakleigh House Museum.

Her oldest daughter, Diddie's is a smaller portrait incased in a pin. It was painted when she was around fifteen years old, it shows the early signs of adulthood and the features she was noted for during her life: the darker hair, compared to her mother's, and her strong resemblance to her father, Dr. LeVert.[4]

The youngest daughter, Cara Netta, was in the same fastening as the oldest daughter, but she was a young child, around five-years-old. They were mementos of loved ones to be carried around. More than likely, they were a gift from Dr. LeVert to Sally Walton, Octavia's mother, to keep her family close during the upcoming years of extensive travel, significantly since her advanced age prevented her from traveling as she had in the past.

This became yet another year of change for the LeVert's, the letter Henry wrote Judge James Dellet to help him get the position of Surgeon at the Marine Hospital at Mobile was suddenly removed. He was replaced by Dr. Lopez. To dissuade negative press, local newspapers quickly remarked about his good reputation, and he stood in the first rank among the physicians and surgeons of the South.[5]

In regards to Octavia, her writings in newspapers and magazines were garnishing quite a bit of activity. Since she was a well-known personality for most of her life and exposed to higher levels of Society, her writings were a natural fit for her development into a literary celebrity, an important feature in Victorian popular culture. According to Rory Michelle Moore, "They did this through cultivating a mediated intimacy between star authors and admirers by reporting on events that feted them in their gossip columns as well as by offering space for celebrities to rebuff erroneous reports, other forms of print publicity including portraits, biographies, and memoirs."[6]

It was time for Octavia to expand her writing experience and tackle something much larger, something much like what Lady Wortley and Fredrika Bremer wrote, only for Octavia, it would turn into her Grand Tour. Octavia focused on writing a memoir, and it seems a journalist for the New Orleans paper, *The Daily Delta*, thought she was very capable. It shared the following, "Few ladies have gone to represent us abroad, possessing as many attractive qualifications as Mrs. LeVert. She has half the languages of Europe at 'her tongue's end' - conversing with equal fluency and correctness in the French, Italian, Spanish and German. No American lady possesses greater advantages for receiving or imparting enjoyment during her tour, and no one will have more welcome access to the interior life of the highest circles in Europe. She visits England with her father and daughter, and the special guest of Lady Emmeline Wortley, and at the feudal residence of her father, the Duke of Rutland, called 'Belvoir' or familiarly Belvoir castle. Few such structures of the olden times remain in old England; and few such daughters of the new have visited the parent lead as our own Mrs. Octavia LeVert."[7]

Octavia intended to write up a description of her travels abroad, and she must have mentioned it enough for a journalist for the Daily Delta to state, "Madame LeVert is eminently qualified to produce on her return a most acceptable book of travels, for she will have the opportunity which few travelers possess, of giving us a true and reliable picture of the manners and habits of a class of people we have all a curiosity to know and understand, and we trust she will be sufficiently regardful of those she had left behind her to give us the benefit of her observations."[8]

Such a unique trip, especially compared to the sort of traveling Octavia had taken in the past, most certainly had to come with the support of Henry. She could not make the trip in this era without a man to escort this group of ladies. It was determined that her father, Colonel Walton, was to fill the position. Henry, Sally, and their youngest daughter, Cara Netta, remained at home. It was a good time for Dr. LeVert stayed behind while the family went to Europe. Eighteen fifty-three turned out to be the greatest yellow fever epidemic Mobile ever experienced.[9]

Octavia, Diddie, and their servant, Betsey, traveled from Mobile to New Orleans and left on May 9th, 1853, for New York on the steamship, *Black Warrior*.[10] Packed in their luggage were letters of introduction from Lady Emmeline Wortley and Fredrika Bremer. Those would be most useful.

Octavia, Diddie, Colonel Walton, and Betsey left the United States on the steamship, *Atlantic*, on June 11th, 1853.[11] They bid farewell to friends who saw them off as the ship left its moorings. It was a lifetime dream of

Octavia's to visit Europe, and now, at forty-three years old, it became a reality. She commented, "My emotions were full of radiant delight, as bright and sparkling as the myriad diamond drops which fell in showers from the swift-moving wheels of the glorious steamer."[12]

The travel desk she used while traveling through Europe and a small purse she purchased in Paris. Leeth, Yancy. *Octavia's Travel Desk and Purse.* Photograph. Mobile, Alabama, 2021. Oakleigh House Museum.

However, this well-traveled lady, who had spent her life on boats, trains, in carriages, and on foot, was surprised to become seasick the third day on the ship. She was kept in bed and laid still for several days, but not wanting to miss anything she forced herself go up to the deck and experience the ice and wind as they neared the icebergs.

When she set foot on British land, her sickness subsided, and she remarked, "At last I was in England! Even the most unenthusiastic must feel a wild bounding of the heart when they first touch the shores of Mother-Land. As for me, joy, radiant joy, filled my soul, and I could have thrown myself on my knees and kissed the earth - the home of my ancestors - the glorious land which holds forth its hands in love and sympathy to its children, far over the vast Atlantic."[13]

After they rested from their journey in Liverpool, the wandering Waltons traveled by train to London. From the hotel's entrance, Octavia observed the ladies elegant dresses on their way to meet Queen Victoria, but she also noticed the poor's shoddy attire. She watched an elderly woman sweeping the crossing and putting out her hand for charity, and she remarked, "Thank God, I have never seen this in my own country!" Yet, in the struggle that ensued in the next ten years of her life, did she return to this memory?

Letters of Introduction, written on behalf of many of Octavia's friends in America, such as Lady Wortley and Fredrika Bremer, opened the doors to the highest levels of European Society. Their days became filled with theatre, church visits, and answering invitations. Once a guest at Octavia's home in 1850 when she visited America, Lady Emmeline Wortley was making arrangements for the family even though she had already left for another trip abroad. Lady Wortley's father, the Duke of Rutland, stepped in to fill in his daughter's role as a guide.

Queen Victoria. *Queen Victoria*. Photograph. Washington, D.C., 1866. Library of Congress Prints and Photographs Division Washington, D.C. 20540 USA.

Madame Octavia Walton LeVert had been popular her entire life. Admired as a child, sought after when a belle, treasured as a wife, but nothing compared to the

Prince Albert. *Prince Albert.* Photograph. Washington, D.C., 1866.
Library of Congress Prints and Photographs Division Washington,
D.C. 20540 USA http://hdl.loc.gov/loc.pnp/pp.print.

fame that followed her after meeting the English Queen,
Victoria, at the State Ball. It all started earlier that morning
when she visited Buckingham Palace. Mr. Ingersoll, the
American Minister, met her at nine a.m. They were
welcomed into the palace and taken to the yellow

drawing-room where they waited until ten o'clock. Then Queen Victoria entered the room with "God save the Queen" played by a band. Soon to follow was Prince Albert and his entourage. The room was filled with more than two thousand guests, all elegantly dressed. Looking around, Octavia observed, "every lady in magnificent toilette, and every gentleman in court-dress, or in uniform."[14]

Octavia later described the Queen for her mother, "Queen Victoria is much handsomer than painters have represented her. She is not tall, but her form is of graceful symmetry; and her bust, arms, and feet are beautiful. A bright and beaming smile lights up her face. Then there is such an air of honest, earnest goodness about her - a genial manner, so lovely and loveable – 'my heart was quickly won,' and sincerely could I have exclaimed, like her own loyal subjects, 'God save the Queen.'"[15]

The letter Octavia wrote to her mother reached their Mobile residence by the end of July and was soon published in the local newspaper. Other newspapers in the South and then the rest of the country shared her written encounter with Queen Victoria, causing a sensation among those who knew Octavia and those who learned of her for the first time. She wrote of the Court Ball, "The whispers around me were amusing. Who is she? Why this unusual presentation? Is she a celebrity? - and these were replied to as vaguely as was to be expected...The Chamberlain then rejoined me, saying: Her Majesty commands me to welcome you heartily to England - and trusts that what you have seen and have yet to see, may greatly please you. And I begged him to 'assure the Queen that I am enchanted with her country, and with her people.' Her majesty looked on me so smilingly, I felt like rushing forward to salute her: which it is contrary to etiquette to speak to the Queen on State occasions, nor does she address any one, save the personages of her Court. Yet, there is no pretension about her. Her looks are kind - are honest: she is, indeed, great enough to be, and appear, perfectly natural. I was introduced to a great many of the notabilities and enjoyed their conversation much; while many addressed me who were not so made known, yet with that perfect air of good breeding that dispelled all reserve - for my special introduction to the Queen gave me that high stamp which all acknowledged."[16]

On July 5th, 1853, they visited Westminster Palace and heard a debate in the House of Peers. While she enjoyed the debate, she could not help but point out a shortcoming, "At one end of the room is a gallery enclosed with a gilded lattice-work, or grating, where women are permitted to hear, but not be seen. It reminded me of the golden screens placed in the palaces of the Turkish Sultans, behind which their slave-wives are allowed to listen to the music intended to delight their masters' ears. I inquired why there was such a lack of courtesy towards the fairer portion of creation, and was answered, that their presence was deemed by the ancient legislators of England, as of too absorbing an interest; hence they were wisely kept out of sight."[17]

Two days later, they visited the Duchess of Sutherland's splendid mansion, *Stafford House*. Octavia commented, "The stairs are covered with scarlet cloth, and many fine works of art adorn this wonderful hall. Among them I saw an exquisite marble bust of Lady Constance Grosvenor, by the Baron Marochetti, and a bust in plaster of Mrs. Beecher Stowe, the authoress of *Uncle Tom's Cabin*." While reporters constantly commented on how Octavia got to meet the Queen, Harriet Beecher Stowe did not. It is noted she did not make any sort of remark in her book or in public.[18]

Octavia's first visit to Europe was documented by a London writer, Mrs. Camellia Dufour Crosland, and her observations are very interesting. She was aware of Octavia's status back in the United States; she noted, "She was spoken of as the Queen of Mobile, and was, I believe, considered the leader of fashion and the first personage there. Her entertainments, often in the nature of garden parties, sometimes numbered a thousand guests, and, by all accounts, lavish hospitality in various directions was the order of the day."[19]

It appears Camilla Crosland was comfortable with asking Octavia questions regarding many different issues, especially that of slavery, "Appreciating all sorts of talent, and eager for all sorts of information, she was ready to discuss any subject, not shirking even the "domestic institution," as slavery was called. She defended it to a certain degree, but assuredly not wildly and enthusiastically. I remember her saying that many of her "servants" were descended from those who had been in the Walton family two hundred years ago, but that she did not desire to possess any more of "that description of property." She insisted on the slaves being generally attached to their owners, and being happy, and cited her own maid - Betsy, I think she called her - who at that moment was left at the hotel with the key of her dressing-case in which were four hundred pounds in notes and gold."[20]

While Mrs. Crosland showed her approval of Octavia, she did not share the same feelings for her father, Colonel Walton, "Our American friends accompanied us, and I took the arm of Colonel Walton, as we moved about, looking out for friends and acquaintances. Rarely, however, have I felt so humiliated as I was by the deportment of this sometime governor of a state - this haughty, self-sufficient slave-owner, who thought himself the equal of any peer in the room, but who from time to time relieved his cough in that American mode which Mrs. Trollope is characterized as disgusting. Nearly forty years have passed since then, and I do not suppose such filthy vulgarity could be perpetuated; but I felt pained and ashamed beyond description at our having been the introducer of one who seemed to disgrace us, as well as himself. The better class, in a country that is really civilized, have a certain respect for the servants who wait upon them and clean after them, the want of which is always taken as a sign of gross vulgarity; but slavery was a vice that tainted the whole nature, and corrupt manners as well as morals, after all, interlace each other rather closely."[21]

Mrs. Crosland further mentioned that some years later she'd heard from an excellent authority that Betsey was Octavia's half-sister, a gift to her by her father, because he thought Octavia would be a better mistress than his wife, Sally, had been.[22] Clearly, Betsey belonged to Sally Walton before she was Octavia's, which caused Sally and Betsey's relationship to be strained.

In a surprising turn, Lady Emmeline Wortley was able to spend time with Octavia, after all. The steamer she was to take to Dover was delayed, and she used the opportunity to go to London to see Octavia, who remarked, "Ah! What a joy it was to meet her! Kind, Affectionate, and precious friend that she has been to me for long, long years. Once more to see her had been the greatest inducement to visit England. I gave up every engagement, that we might pass all the hours of her sojourn together."[23]

On July 19th, the LeVert family group left London and took the train to Paris, which strongly reminded Octavia of New Orleans. They then ventured to Brussels, Cologne, and boarded the steamer, *Konig*, on the Rhine River. A train took them to Heidelberg, Germany where they went to Carlsruhe. Octavia commented, "Throughout France, Belgium, and Germany, I have remarked the hard lot of female peasants. The men go as soldiers in the legions of foreign lands, or serve in the armies at home; but upon the women falls all the labor of cultivating the soil. In Belgium I have seen a woman ploughing the field, fastened to the same plough with an ox, and often an aged female reaping the grain. It was always a sad spectacle to me, and I thanked the good God my destiny was cast in a land where woman was cherished as the 'better portion of creation,' loved and cared for in old age as well as youth."[24]

On to Como, Verona, and Padua they traveled. When Octavia's party ventured to the Austrian border, they met the most stringent of questions and inspections by the guard. They were asked, 'What was her name?' 'Was this her only daughter,' when they were referring to Diddie. Next Octavia noted the most interesting exchange, "Then came the same questions to all the others, until their reached Betsey, whom he styled a Moor; whereupon she implored I would inform him she had nothing but pure American blood in her veins, and was a slave from the South. However, he insisted (as she was a mulatto) in writing her down 'una Moretta.' They were soon permitted to depart.

The family returned to America on October 20th, 1853 aboard the steamship, *Atlantic*, with a host of other distinguished travelers, including the Honorable Mr. Ingersoll, the late minister to England; the Honorable Mr. Bayard and wife, who was charge de Affairs to Belgium; J.W. Gerald, of New York; the Honorable Mr. Chandler of Philadelphia; and Lieutenant Maury, of Washington, whose adopted son, Dabney Herndon Maury, became a vital connection to the LeVerts and Mobile in the years to come.[25]

Before heading home, the family spent time with Colonel Walton and then returned to Mobile by train.

While on a passenger train between Wilmington and Charleston, a man with a child rushed through the rear car, shouting the train cars were on fire. Everyone panicked and hastened for the door of the car. It was later discovered instead of a fire, someone left a camphene lamp burning, and it exploded, but the fire was quickly extinguished.

Octavia, Diddie, and Betsey were in that car, but they realized Betsey was missing when things settled down. Octavia hurried to the conductor and requested the train go back for Betsey, who had a measure of fame from the story told in Miss Bremer's book, *Homes in the New World*. According to the Washington Sentinel, "On resuming their seats, "Betsy" was missing. The conductor was sent for and requested by the passengers to reverse the engine and go back a mile or two to look for the poor slave who had probably leaped from the car when the alarm was sounded. This he refused to do, giving as a reason that he would be too late to connect at the Camden junction. He was then offered one thousand dollars to comply with the humane request of the passengers. This also he refused. On arriving at the station a gentleman promptly chartered an engine and returned to the spot where the alarm occurred; and there he found the poor woman lying beside the track, in a state of insensibility, with her body so bruised and swollen that the physician could not decide whether her bones were broken or dislocated."[26]

Octavia took Betsey to Augusta, Georgia, immediately after the incident; they were afraid she might not recover. The conductor who refused to return to get Betsey received a fair amount of negative press. It was reported in the *Daily Journal*, "Great blame is attached to the conductor for his apparent indifference to the life of the poor slave. Betsy has been frequently in the North and in England, France, Germany, and Italy with her mistress. Many times the abolitionists urged her escape, but never with success. Such attachments are by no means uncommon, and they speak well for the care, affection, and attachment of those who hold the two relations of master and slave."[27]

The family finally made it back home to Mobile, Alabama. Octavia and the family returned successfully from their trip abroad. Meanwhile, Fredrika Bremer's book, *Homes in the New World*, grew in popularity throughout the United States. The LeVert family's fame also grew because they were a part of the book.

In December of 1853 began another endevior Octavia was destined to join in the near future. Ann Pamela Cunningham, a person in Octavia's social circle and the daughter of Colonel Robert Cunningham, received a letter from her mother. The letter was about her visit to Mount Vernon and the condition of George Washington's home, "I was painfully distressed at the ruin and desolation of the home of Washington, and the thought passed through my mind: Why was it that the women of his country did not try to keep it in repair, if the men could not do it? It does seem such a blot on our country!"[28]

Miss Cunningham, stirred by the letter, announced she would take up the cause and save Washington's home. She wrote a letter published in the newspaper, *Mercury*, first to the ladies of the South, asking for help. She sent a second letter in April 1854, this time in the *Washington Union*, under the guise of "Southern Matron," and started to solidify her plans to save the historic property. She soon recruited Edward Everett, a well-connected man who graduated from Harvard, became a famous pastor, and briefly succeeded Daniel Webster as Secretary of State.[29] Everett, a good friend of Octavia's, used his influence to convince her to join the cause.

Octavia spent 1854 at home but decided to revisit Europe in 1855 to represent Alabama at the Exposition Universelle in Paris, France. On December 21, she wrote a letter to her acquaintance, Stephen A. Douglas. After his wife and daughter died in 1853, Douglas decided to take an extended tour of Europe. During his visit, his travels took him to London, Constantinople, Moscow, St. Petersburg, and Paris, and he secured many diplomatic audiences.[30] Octavia knew of his trip and asked for letters of Introduction to United States Ministers abroad. She remarked, "I do not know any of them, and I am sure a commendation from you will have great weight and influence."[31]

Only the LeVert family went on the second tour of Europe: Henry, Octavia, and their oldest daughter, Diddie.[32] Possibly Betsey was still recovering at home from the train incident and could not join the family this second time.

Besides, Dr. LeVert, a man long devoted to his medical profession, welcomed a new partner into his practice. His nephew, Dr. Claudis Mastin, was the son of Henry's sister Caroline and Captain France T. Martin of Huntsville, Alabama. Claudius attended the University of Virginia and spent time in the Medical Department of the University of Pennsylvania. He married Mary McDowell, of Huntsville, in 1848 and spent time in Europe visiting the University of France and the Royal College of Surgeons in England.[33] The partnership allowed Henry to travel and spend time with his family. It gave him the freedom to go to Europe and be assured things were in good hands back home.

When the LeVert family shared their intent to take a European Tour, Letters of Introduction poured in.[34] They arrived in New Orleans on January 24th, 1855, and stayed at the St. Charles Hotel.[35] While at the hotel, they attended a dance with Mrs. General Gaines, a good friend. Octavia appeared at this event in the same dress she wore on her presentation to Queen Victoria during her last visit to England.[36]

The LeVerts left New Orleans on the steamer, *Black Warrior*, and Octavia was again seasick for two days while they traveled to Havana, Cuba. She spent most of her time on the ship deck instead of in her cabin. During Octavia's first trip to Europe, she was very descriptive in her writing of all things around her. She wrote from the perspective of a very excited woman on her first tour of Europe. Octavia's second trip was from a more experienced perspective. Instead of writing for the sake of writing, she wrote with more control of her intentions. Her study of the palm tree is an example. She mused, "It seems to me that no tree in the world is so suggestive of poetry as the palm tree. The trunk rises smooth as a marble column, to about the height of seventy or eighty feet. Then branch out the great leaves, falling one over the other like plumes of feathers in a field-marshal's hat. The sea breeze, sighing through them, calls forth a sound as soft as the tone of an Aeolian harp, thrilling the soul with sweet joy."[37]

First, the LeVerts went to Cuba and stayed in Havana until February 12th, 1855, receiving letters from Sally, Colonel Walton, and the youngest daughter, Cara Netta. Octavia, with a flair for the dramatic, stated, "Should this be the last line my hand ever traces, may the memory of me never awaken a pang in a human heart, but linger around it like the aroma of precious flowers. In peace and good feeling to the whole world, I venture upon the perils of the vast ocean, with a firm assurance of the protection of that mighty Power 'who ruleth over earth and sea.'[38]

They arrived in Cadiz on March 3rd, 1855, and she was quick to write of her journey. She was again seasick, and this time Henry carried her up to the deck into the saloon where she remained during the voyage. When she felt better, she took the time to reconnect with Henry. She shared enchanted moonlight walks with Henry and commented, "We frequently walked the upper deck for hours, gazing upon them, and watching the long line of phosphoric radiance which followed our steamer. Our last look was always to the western stars, shining over our home, and our last thought was of the dear ones there." When the crowds left the saloon, the steward, Luigi, placed two sofas together, and Octavia and M.D. talked of home till they fell asleep.[39]

They arrived in Cadiz, Spain, and soon traveled to Seville, Madrid, and Escorial. April 1855 found them in Rome, Italy. They were going to St. Peter's Cathedral to attend the *Washing of the Feet,* so they were required to dress in all black, and they draped lac mantillas over their heads. Octavia was engrossed in all the beauty, but the repeated entreaties of Diddie induced her to the Chapel of St. Michael, where the ceremony of washing feet took place. She remarked, "The crowds I had often encountered at Washington, 'long years ago,' in the Senate-chamber, to hear the immortal Clay, or the majestic Webster, were but shadows of the substantial throngs in this chapel."[40]

While Octavia's first trip to Europe was full of discovery and excitement, this second trip leaned toward writing for the intent to publish, either in newspapers or later a book. All situations she experienced had significant moments, remembered forever, and repeated in American salons and publications.

When Henry, Octavia, and Diddie were presented to the Pope, Pius IX was one such moment. A letter from Mobile's Bishop Portier introduced them to Monsignore Barnado, giving them that rare opportunity. Dressed in deep black with long black veils thrown over their heads, they were led to the Vatican. There they met the Pope in the reception room. Octavia recalled, 'As we approached him, he held out his hands, and in a sweet voice said, 'Welcome to Rome, my friends.'"[41]

Octavia continued to recall, "We conversed at first in French and Spanish (English, the Pope said, he could never learn); but fearing it might be some effort to his Holiness to speak them, I begged he would address me in Italian, which, although not so familiar to me as the other languages, I could understand exceedingly well. How glad I was afterwards this thought came to me, for his utterance of the Italian was as soft and melodious as the trains of music, so rich, full, and sonorous."[42]

A momentous moment came when the Pope asked the name of Octavia's daughter. She replied, "She bears my name, your Holiness, and I was called after the Roman Octavia, whose character my mother greatly admired." The Pope then told them they should be proud of that name, for the Roman Octavia possessed every virtue and grace which should adorn a woman. Octavia wrote to her mother, "Thank you a thousand times, Mamma, for giving me the name Octavia."[43]

After the Pope blessed Diddie, the weary LeVerts returned to the hotel where Octavia wrote, "I have faithfully given my darling Mamma a picture of the scene, and a true history of the incidents of our interview; and I will now knock at the 'golden gate of dreams,' first asking the good God to bless Mamma, and dear little Netta, for the sake of their loving."[44]

They left Rome and traveled to Naples and found a hotel facing Mount Vesuvius. They explored the area and the mountain, seeing the sights, but the most memorable was Mount Vesuvius's eruption. They then traveled to Naples, Capri, and Florence, Italy.

Octavia's energy was endless. When she visited Galileo's house, she went to his tower where he studied the stars. She wrote to her mother, "In my youth, you recollect, Mamma, how passionate was my love for the study of astronomy, and how often during long hours of the night I watched the heavenly bodies." She was thrilled to stand exactly where Galileo stood so many years ago.[45]

While in Florence, the LeVerts had a unique treat arranged by mutual friends. They spent the evening with the poet, Robert Browning, and his wife, the great poetess, Elizabeth Barrett Browning. The Brownings moved to Italy after they married to improve Elizabeth's health, and it seemed to work. She was becoming stronger and had given birth to a son. Octavia commented, "What a visit of joy… in their love-sanctified and at-beautified home. Their union seems perfect in happiness, the mind as well as the heart having met its own affinity."[46]

The family continued to roam all over Europe. Octavia intended to go to Stockholm to see Fredrika Bremer, but a recent letter told her that Fredrika's mother had passed away and was in great sorrow. She left for the island of Gothland to pass the summer months and would not be back till September when she implored Octavia to make her visit. She said she would if she could get away from Paris.[47]

In July 1855, the family was in Paris for the Great Exposition. Unlike before, she had more time to stay and explore. It was Paris, after all. They stayed at the Hotel de Castile during this visit. Octavia remarked, "It appears a continued gala-time, for the Exposition has summoned people of all climes and nations. To welcome and enchant them, the city is superbly embellished; and by way of rendering the fascination more secure, cordial words and smiling glances greet the strangers at every turn."[48]

The Palace of Industry. *Palais De L'industrie*. Photograph. Washington, D.C. , 1855. Library of Congress Prints and Photographs Division Washington, D.C. 20540 USA http://hdl.loc.gov/loc.pnp/pp.print.

On July 11th, 1855, Octavia told her mother of their first visit to the Paris Exposition. They went at ten in the morning and did not leave until six in the evening. She told her, "The "Palace of Industry" is still in a most unfinished state; therefore we can scarcely decide upon its merits or attractions. It is a vast building of light-colored stone, roofed over with glass, and presenting a noble facade."[49]

Octavia continued, "Our own flag floats over a great space, devoted to Good Year's India Rubber articles, from big boots to small combs. Then comes Paine's Vermifuge, and Swaim's Panacea, similar medicines, and a few Daguerreotypes. We are so sorry we did not bring Mark's last picture of Octavia; it is immeasurably superior to any specimens of the kind here, and would certainly have taken first prize if it had been placed in our department."[50]

Octavia also filled an interesting role during the Exposition; she was given a unique position at the World's Fair. She wrote to her mother, "Apropos to the Exposition, I have never yet informed you that I am the only "lady-commissioner" duly accredited to the World's Fair. Our Governor comes in for a large amount of compliment for his selection, and for his gallantry. But what think you? Alabama has not a single article in the "Palace of Industry!" If there were only a few cotton seed, it would "serve to swear by." When I meet the commissioners of other nations, and they inquire, "Pray, Madame, what products of Alabama have you in your department?" I am obliged to point to Octavia as the only one we have. Whereupon many flattering words are uttered, and Alabama is not so much in the shade as might be supposed."[51]

Octavia continued to send letters home to her family in the United States by steamship, again indicating the plan to use the notes for a book shortly.[52] There was much material for the book for she was introduced to many people, probably due to the Letters of Introduction provided by Stephen Douglas. According to the *Library of Southern Literature*, "On this journey were met such interesting people as the Brownings, Napoleon III, and the Empress Eugenie, the Countess de Montijo, the Count and Countess of Alba, Pope Pius IX, with whom the party had private audience; besides Powers, Buchanan Read, Crawford, Ives, Gibson, and Harriet Hosmer among artists and litterateurs. Everyone of note in diplomatic life did them honor, and all Americans of charm and position gathered around them. So many persons, indeed, from every nation made their party a center that a wit described Madame LeVert's salon in Paris as the "Tower of Babel." On a visit to Lamartine he said to her: "You have in your power to fill with pleasure the hearts of your nation. Promise me to write a few souvenirs of European travel." Such was the inspiration, and thence the name of *Souvenirs of Travel*, which is made up entirely of the journal and letters of these two journeys."[53]

The family remained in Paris, but moved to apartments on the Boulevard des Italiens, just over the Passage de l'Opera. Octavia also sought to meet with the famous French writer and poet, Alphonse de Lamartine. She tried to meet him during her first trip in 1853, but was unsuccessful. This time they visited his home and left their calling cards, resulting in the parties invitation to spend an evening with Lamartine and his wife.

Octavia wrote about the meeting, "De Lamartine turned to me and said, 'Your country, Madame, has the most precious manuscript in the world - the signed Declaration of Independence! Do not your people make pilgrimages to look upon it?' Think how my heart swelled with joy as I answered him, 'yes, it is sacred to all our citizens, but most precious to me, since my grandfather's name, which I proudly yet retain, is thereon inscribed, as one who gave his blood and his fortune to perpetuate our free institutions.' De Lamartine rose up and bowed to me profoundly, exclaiming, 'Madame, in that name you have a noble heritage. It is the true patent of nobility, and you rightly cherish your descent from such a brave and heroic patriot with honest pride!'"[54]

The family remained in Paris in August 1855, attending plays, visiting the Beaux-Arts Exposition during the same time as Queen Victoria[55], and attended the Grand Ball with invitations provided by the Secretary of the American Embassy.[56] She once more tried to join Fredrika Bremer in Stockholm, Sweden, but the lateness of the season, it was now September, and the fears of the autumn storms on the Baltic canceled the plans.[57]

The LeVerts also attempted to contact Lady Emmeline Wortley and her daughter, Victoria, while they were in Europe, but arrangements could not be made.[58] They left Paris on September 21, 1855, and headed for the next part of their trip. Octavia remarked, "Leaving Paris is like another separation from home. We have found such charming and excellent friends here, that my heart is overflowing with good feeling towards the whole world." They traveled to England and Scotland and then embarked upon the Atlantic, but she did not write of this trip.[59]

The family returned to the United States by the steamer, *Arago*, and with Octavia's new respect for her role as State Commissioner during the Grand Industrial Exposition at Paris.[60] Dr. LeVert, Octavia, and Diddie were welcomed back home with great fanfare. People noticed how happy she was compared to her sorrow of recent years and how Dr. LeVert was looking robust and comfortable. The LeVerts were welcomed home with hundreds of warm hands and with warm hearts in them; they were stretched out to welcome them home.[61]

The LeVerts entered a new phase of their lives and making changes to their normal daily activities. The salon in Paris resulted in Octavia starting her official 'Mondays.' According to the *Library of Southern Literature*, "The nearest approach to a salon which America has known was afforded by Madame LeVert's 'Mondays.' On these days during the season, her large and elegant home on Government Street was crowded from eleven in the morning until eleven at night, with not only the elite of Mobile and of the South, but the elect of every clime."[62]

In the past, the Waltons and LeVert's had to travel all over the country and the world for exposure to the upper class of society, but things had changed. Anyone who came to Mobile, Alabama, visited Octavia, or to be more specific, Madame LeVert, and to attend one of her 'Mondays.' She quickly rose in fame and notoriety in the United States, and her association with Mount Vernon carried her a step further.

Works Cited and Notes

1. N. P. Willis, "Lines on Leaving Europe," *Army and Navy Chronicle* 4-5 (1837): 39.
2. Paul Cloos, "Battle House a Symbol of Hospitality," *Press Register*, March 29, 2019.
3. Louis Lang, "Mrs. Henry Strachey LeVert." Painting. Fresco Frick Art Reference Library: 1852.
4. Louis Lang, "Octavia Walton LeVert (Diddie)." Painting. Fresco Frick Art Reference Library: 1852. Note: Cara Netta LeVert image was not located in this collection.
5. *Daily Delta*, April 28, 1853, 3, Newspapers.com.
6. Rory Michelle Moore, "Literary Sensations: Victorian Women Writers and Celebrity Culture" (PhD diss., University of California Riverside, 2013), 12.
7. *Daily Delta*, June 22, 1853, 4, Newspapers.com.
8. *Daily Delta*, July 13, 1853, Newspapers.com.
9. Diard, *WPA Report*.
10. *Times-Picayune*, May 11, 1853, 1, Newspapers.com.
11. *Southern Standard*, June 25, 1853, 3, Newspapers.com.
12. Le Vert, *Souvenirs of Travel*, 1:1.
13. Le Vert, *Souvenirs of Travel*, 1:3.
14. Le Vert, *Souvenirs of Travel*, 1:31. Note: Octavia is describing the events of July 2, 1853.
15. Le Vert, *Souvenirs of Travel*, 1:33. Note: Octavia is describing the events of July 2, 1853.
16. "Letter from the First Private, Mrs. LeVert - Her Reception," *Daily Delta*, July 31, 1853, 1, Newspapers.com.

17. Le Vert, *Souvenirs of Travel*, 1:47. Note: Octavia is describing the events of July 2, 1853.

18. Le Vert, *Souvenirs of Travel*, 1:55. Note: Octavia is describing the events of July 2, 1853.

19. Crosland, *Landmarks of a Literary Life 1820 – 1892*, 216-217.

20. Crosland, *Landmarks of a Literary Life 1820 – 1892*, 217.

21. Crosland, *Landmarks of a Literary Life 1820 – 1892*, 219.

22. Crosland, *Landmarks of a Literary Life 1820 – 1892*, 218.

23. Le Vert, *Souvenirs of Travel*, 1:62. Note: Octavia is describing the events of July 12, 1853.

24. Le Vert, *Souvenirs of Travel*, 1:142. Note: Octavia is describing the events of July 1853.

25. "The Richmond Mail," *Virginia Chronicle* 1, no. 166, October 20, 1853, Newspapers.com.

26. *Washington Sentinel*, November 9, 1853, Chronicling America.

27. *Daily Journal*, November 18, 1853, GenealogyBank.

28. Grace E. King, *Mount Vernon of the Potomac: History of the Mount Vernon Ladies' Association of the Union* (New York: The Macmillian Company, 1929), 18.

29. . King, *Mount Vernon of the Potomac*, 33.

30. "Guide to the Stephen A. Douglas Papers 1764-1908," University of Chicago Library, Biographical Note.

31. *Octavia Walton LeVert to Stephen A. Douglas, December 21, 1854.* Letter. Special Collections Research Center, University of Chicago Library, *Stephen A. Douglas Papers*.

32. Forrest, *Women of the South Distinguished in Literature*, 23.

33. Satterfield, *Madame LeVert*, 205.

34. Satterfield, *Madame LeVert*, 135.

35. *Times-Picayune*, January 18, 1855, 4, Newspapers.com.

36. *Times-Picayune*, January 24, 1855, Newspapers.com.

37. *Times-Picayune*, January 25, 1855, 5, Newspapers.com.

38. Le Vert, *Souvenirs of Travel*, 1:318. Note: Octavia is describing the events of 29 July, 1856.

39. Le Vert, *Souvenirs of Travel*, 1:322. Note: Octavia is describing the events of 12 February, 1855.

40. Le Vert, *Souvenirs of Travel*, 2:80. Note: Octavia is describing the events of 3 March, 1855.

41. Le Vert, *Souvenirs of Travel*, 2:164.

42. Le Vert, *Souvenirs of Travel*, 2:165

43. Le Vert, *Souvenirs of Travel*, 2:167.

44. Le Vert, *Souvenirs of Travel*, 2:168.

45. Le Vert, *Souvenirs of Travel*, 2:225.

46. Le Vert, *Souvenirs of Travel*, 2:229.

47. Le Vert, *Souvenirs of Travel*, 2:276.

48. Le Vert, *Souvenirs of Travel*, 2:283.

49. Le Vert, *Souvenirs of Travel*, 2:287.

50. Le Vert, *Souvenirs of Travel*, 2:289.

51. Le Vert, *Souvenirs of Travel*, 2:295.

52. *Times-Picayune*, January 29, 1855, Newspapers.com.

53. Edwin Anderson Alderman, Joel Chandler Harris, and Charles W. Kent, *Library of Southern Literature: Biography* (Martin & Hoyt Company, 1909), 3223, Google Books.

54. Le Vert, *Souvenirs of Travel*, 2:302.

55. Le Vert, *Souvenirs of Travel*, 2:320.

56. Le Vert, *Souvenirs of Travel*, 2:324.

57. Le Vert, *Souvenirs of Travel*, 2:336.

58. Le Vert, *Souvenirs of Travel*, 2:343.

59. Le Vert, *Souvenirs of Travel*, 2:346.

60. *Times-Picayune*, November 12, 1855, Newspapers.com.

61. *Times-Picayune*, November 25, 1855, Newspapers.com.

62. Alderman, Harris, Kent, *Library of Southern Literature*, 3223.

Chapter 10

Among the Stars

In the flood of congratulations swelling around you,
Allow me to cast my faithful tribute of delight.
Thank the Good God! You have succeeded.
It was your due,
And well merited are the honours you have received.[1]

After returning from becoming well-known in Europe, Dr. Henry LeVert's ever-popular wife, Octavia, and oldest daughter, Diddie, were considered among the most distinguished and accomplished Mobile citizens. The result was an endless number of visitors and parties at their elegant home. The increase in activity was a drastic change from the situation after tragic loss five years before. Octavia's natural energy had always drawn attention, it resurfaced, and she now became a queen of Mobile's Society and a growing literary star.

Mobile was also developing fast, and the famous Battle House Hotel, the views of Mobile Bay, and the notable actors and actresses who appeared in its theatres offered a higher standard of living rivaled only by New Orleans. Cultured newcomers flocking to the Port City resulted in LeVert's home opened to an endless number of visitors. According to DeLeon, "Mrs. Le Vert's evenings were eagerly sought by all classes in the amusement hungry city."[2]

Madame Octavia Walton LeVert had more choices than many women of her age had in this era. She also had the freedom to set up her Salon anywhere, but she chose to keep it in Mobile. It provided a way to be a part of society and remain connected to her family, mainly her mother, Sally, at sixty-three years old, could no longer travel as she had in the past.

Octavia wanted to be near her mother, so she stayed in Mobile. Prior to the Civil War, mothers were customary to maintain a close relationship with their children, and this family was no exception.[3] The deep bond between Sally Walton and Octavia couldn't be denied. When husband and father, George Walton, Jr., left after at the death of a son and brother, Robert, Sally chose to remain close to Henry and Octavia in Mobile. This pattern of female dedication is repeated amongst the LeVert daughters but especially for the oldest, Diddie. At the age of twenty, Diddie was available for marriage, but her focus seemed more on assisting her mother than seeking a husband.

Octavia's social career climbed in the mid-1850s, and it promised to grow further when she completed her book, *Souvenirs of Travel*.[4] Her home on Government Street had always been a place people gathered to discuss literature or politics, but when she returned from Europe, it started to attract both national and international figures. Octavia had to figure out a way to keep her Salon's popularity without letting it intrude on her family's daily lives.

The only photo known to exist of Octavia's Salon. Taken many years after she left the city. 2021. Photograph. Originally taken by Mariam Acker Macpherson. Use allowed by her daughter, Paula Watkins.

Around this time, she reopened her Salon and made it more like those she held in Europe, and this turned out to be the start of her "Mondays." According to Corinne Chadwick Stephens, "Every Monday from eleven in the morning until eleven at night, she kept 'open house,' and invited her friends to come. Madame LeVert was the first woman in America to hold salon in the true French fashion."[5]

Local society was not quite prepared for the European flair Octavia had added to her Salon. In one case, she sent out invitations with an "R.S.V.P." which caused quite a stir and jokes in Mobile. The Cox family received one such invitation, and Mr. Cox answered, "W.S.C.C." When Octavia asked the meaning, he wrote, "Wife Sick, Can't Come!"[6] His reply amused Octavia.

Another interesting story about Octavia's Salon involved Henry Maury, Marshal for the City of Mobile.[7] When he refused eggnog at her home, without a smile, he stated, "Thank you, none for me! I prefer eggs poached, I take my cream and sugar in my coffee, and I'm man enough to drink my whisky straight."[8]

At the age of forty-six, Octavia's popularity did not dampen or the flattering descriptions of her. A writer for the *New Orleans Delta* commented, "What sculpted beauty in that form! She is not tall, but of such perfect symmetry, such undulating grace, such decorous dignity, such cordial courtesy, such infinite adaptiveness of manner, you have never seen before."[9]

Octavia also continued to venture into the risqué for the time and wore Turkish-style costumes to events, wearing trousers in the true harem style. According to Corinne Chadwick Stephens, "With her natural fondness for display and elegance, her costume seems an understandable one, and, because her pride in her shapely

An example of the Turkish-style costume Octavia liked to wear. *The Bloomer Costume*. Photograph. Washington, D.C., 1851.
Library of Congress.

feet - said by a wit to be the smallest in the world - she simply could not resist the desire to show them off. By wearing 'gold and scarlet' slippers, with the baggy harem pants caught in at the ankles, Madame LeVert accomplished her designs perfectly."[10]

This woman could think independently and push societal norms, but not too much. When professionally published women only used pen names on their works, Octavia used a name very close to her own. She also utilized her higher station to create a dialogue about gender equality and women's roles in the political realm. She presented herself as an intelligent being. Her actions helped open the door to women's rights.[11]

Octavia's extravagance was a perfect balance to Henry's quiet ways. He was a man who kept to himself and respected the role his wife played in society, but he needed space of his own and had to have an escape. The solution came when Dr. LeVert bought a property in 1856 and built an office and dwelling at 153 Government street.[12] This provided a place for Henry to get away from the business in the house.

Life continued for Octavia as it had before. Her long-time friend and fellow writer, Mary Forrest, worked on the book *Women of the South Distinguished in Literature*. Forrest featured Octavia as one of the subjects. Simultaneously, Octavia shared parts of her book, *Souvenirs of Travel*, with Forrest. The preview Forrest wrote stirred up the excitement of what was to come. She said, "Made up of familiar letters to her mother, the book has all the freshness and vivacity of the author's own effluent presence. It is like nothing we ever read, unless we accept a description (which it contains) of the play of

Historical Marker for the Office of Dr. Henry S. LeVert. 2020.
Photograph.

the "Fountains of Versailles." Over and around all, like an atmosphere, floats the couleur de rose, which belongs not

The Office of Dr. Henry S. LeVert on Government Street in Mobile,
Alabama. 2020. Photograph.

to the belle of many seasons, not to the cool and cautious world woman, but to the simple-hearted and impressionable child." [13]

Sad news motivated Octavia to complete her book when she learned Lady Emmeline Stuart Wortley, one of its characters, had died. In the Syrian Desert, a horse ridden by her daughter, Victoria, rushed the Lady and crushed her leg, resulting in her death. Octavia shared the news with Mary Forrest, who then published the account. Forrest wrote, "A letter from my dear friend Madame LeVert, has just come to me, burdened with grief for the death of the noble and gifted Lady Emmeline Stuart Wortley - and rich in interesting details of her life, and the sad event which terminated it." [14]

Time passed, and in February 1856, Octavia traveled to the rebuilt St. Charles hotel in New Orleans and attended the Mardi Gras Eve Masquerade.[15] She also participated in the inauguration of the Andrew Jackson statue in Cathedral Square and wrote about the event for the *New York Mirror*. She commented, "… I have never beheld such a splendid spectacle in America. The unveiling of the statue was perfectly dramatic and electrical." [16]

Following in Octavia's footsteps, the LeVert household women developed new roles in the societies in which they existed. Diddie, Octavia's oldest daughter, attended events with her mother and was trained to embody the idea of Southern gentility and enhance the family honor by marrying well like her mother. They worked to develop her intellect, exposure to notable people in Society, and her worldly knowledge by taking her on a European tour twice. They were investing much time into developing her status in Society.[17]

It may seem the youngest daughter, Cara Netta, lacked the attention her older sister received so readily from the family, but this was not the case. She was still a very young child, only ten years old, and not ready to travel with family as her older sister. She remained home in the care of her grandmother, Sally, and in the care of Betsey.[18]

Meanwhile, Octavia was changing and growing her role as author, Madame LeVert, and wrote about events within her social sphere. She was a woman who experienced Society at its highest level and shared her experiences with the public. Her articles were published all over the United States because there was such a great interest in that lifestyle.

When she wrote the dedication to the cornerstone of the statue honoring her longtime friend, Henry Clay, in New Orleans, she was excited to participate. She told Virginia Governor Henry A. Wise what an honor it was, stating, "The Committee of the Association knowing the great affection and reverence I felt for Mr. Clay, and the faithful and paternal kindness with which he regarded me, since my early girlhood, wrote and asked me to prepare a brief address." [19]

The celebrated event of the laying of the Clay Monument's cornerstone occurred on April 12th, 1856. According to Corinne Chadwick Stephens, "This address, since no lady of that period would dream of reading a speech in that kind of public appearance, was read by Captain Charles D. Draux at the dedication, April 12th, 1856. In this paper, Madame wrote that while Mr. Clay was great in "the forums of the nation," his character showed at its best "in the home circle, by the domestic fireside." [20]

After the dedication, the S.H. Goetzel Publishing Company in Mobile produced a leaflet of the speech to honor the event. Octavia used it to promote her writing. She sent copies to various friends and connections she maintained during her life and those she acquired during her European trips. She had a natural sense of what was needed to increase awareness of her writings. Getting her name known for speaking at the Clay dedication could develop an interest in the book she was now working on.

One such connection was to her longtime friend Washington Irving who wrote her a personal letter, remembering when they met while wayfaring together in Alabama in 1833. He closed the correspondence with these words, "Your eulogium of Henry Clay touches a sympathetic shard in my being. When I was a young man, I entertained a romantic admiration for him and formed a friendship with him which continued through life: though we met very rarely and at long intervals." [21]

Octavia also quickly informed the publishing world of her upcoming book, as stated in the *Daily National Intelligencer*, "We are glad to hear that there is some probability that Madame Levert will shortly give to the world her sketches of European travel, and sincerely trust the report will prove correct. No more interesting volume will have appeared from the press in many a day; none that will command more readers or call forth more praise. Few travelers, probably, had opportunities of seeing Europe similarly fortunate to those enjoyed by this Lady; and she saw it from hamlet to capital, from prince to peasant, with an eye to all that was presented of thought, suggestion, or interest." [22]

Towards the end of 1856, word continued to spread about Octavia's upcoming publication in Mobile. William Gilmore Simms, an American writer and South Carolinian politician, advised her to publish the book elsewhere, "I learn with great surprise that you propose to publish in Mobile. This, according to my experience, will seriously prejudice your claims and impair the success of your performance. If you are not too deeply committed to any local publisher, I beg leave most earnestly to counsel you to get it issued either in New York, Boston or Philadelphia." [23]

It appears Octavia was seeking advice from friends on how to layout her book and where to get it published. Simms continued to advise her to publish the book in two slender volumes if the material was more massive than she calculated. He also advised her to publish her book in the North since the South did not have a large city and regular publisher. He told her, "I have no doubt that Redfield, my publisher, will be glad to entertain the proposals of your agent, & will deal with him as liberally, and, I am sure, as honestly, as any of the trade. I believe I wrote to you this effect from N.Y. He authorized me, in fact, to do so." [24]

Another notable American during this time was Edward Everett. He was a well-known politician and orator and was recently on tour promoting his address on George Washington's character. It was part of his efforts to fundraise for the Mount Vernon Fund and preserve George Washington's home and tomb in Virginia.[25] Seeking to increase her literary connections, Octavia mailed him a copy of her dedication to the Clay Monument in New Orleans and invited Everett to visit her in New Orleans or Mobile.[26] Everett shared his efforts to raise funds for Mount Vernon Fund with Octavia, and soon she focused her powers of persuasion towards this noble cause.

In early 1857, Octavia expressed her excitement about the Mount Vernon Fund and shared it with her friend and popular actress, Anna Cora Ogden Mowatt. She commented, "There is a charming feeling awakened here, and I am proud and glad that I have been the means of arousing the patriotic feeling of the people." [27]

Fundraising was a new venture for this lady who grew up in a wealthy society, with most of her needs fulfilled. It seemed Octavia wanted to try to bring in funding for Mount Vernon on her merit, and when she received the first donation of a thousand dollars, she was thrilled. Octavia continued her efforts by holding various balls and parties at her Salon and by selling a professional

Mount Vernon, the home of George Washington. *Mount Vernon. Front of Mount Vernon Mansion.* Photograph. Library of Congress Prints and Photographs Division Washington, D.C. 20540 USA, 1920.

photograph of her mother, herself, and her daughter, Diddie.[28]

During this time, Octavia continued to work on *Souvenirs of Travel,* and her friends eagerly awaited its release. Former President Millard Fillmore, who she met while she traveled through Europe, wrote her on February 16th, 1857, inquiring about Miss Octavia and wishing they visited Washington. He commented, "I am looking anxiously for your travels. When will the book be out? I perceive that they honor you wherever you go, and I sincerely rejoice in your property." [29]

Though Octavia was busy working on her book, she still attended events with her family. In February of 1857, she traveled with her mother, Sally, who was now sixty-five years old, her oldest daughter, Diddie, and the youngest daughter, Cara Netta, now eleven years old, and her servant, Betsey Walton, to New Orleans to attend the St. Charles Hotel Dress Ball.[30] A few days later, the family attended the Continentals Anniversary Ball where it was reported, "Among the gay and evidently grand crowd we were happy to see many fair and gallant representatives of our sister city of Mobile. In one quadrille, M' me Walton, her daughter, Mrs. Levert, and her granddaughter, Miss Octavia LeVert, had places, and it would be difficult to say which of these representatives of three generations acquitted herself more gracefully, or seemed to be enjoying the occasion with the highest zest." [31]

In April 1857, a Continentals group formed in Mobile in honor of the Battle of Lexington; held their first parade. As the granddaughter of a signer of the Declaration of Independence, Octavia wrote the dedication and hosted the group in her Salon. The *Mobile Advertiser* reported, "Early in the afternoon the streets, particularly in the vicinity of the New Armory and of Temperance Hall, began to fill with men, women, and children, and when the march commenced, the crowd on every side was tremendous. Mrs. LeVert, robed exquisitely in "red, white, and blue," gracefully represented the fair donors. Captain Ketchum briefly responded, and Corporal Chandler, on the part of the

Continentals, made a very chaste and appropriate

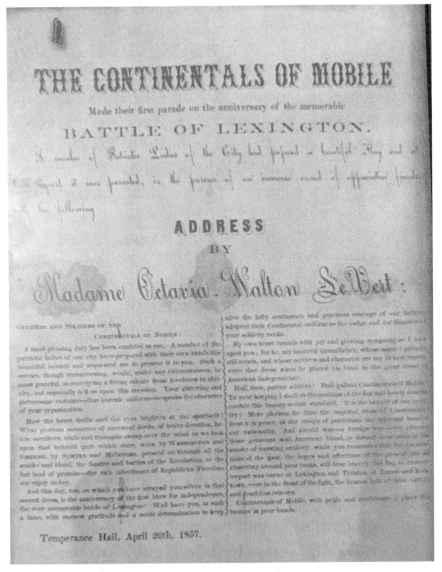

Octavia's address to the Continentals. 2019. Photograph. Item owned by
Reab Barry.

address, all of which was received with great satisfaction
by the auditors."[32]

Continentals dressed in three-cornered hats, with particolored feathers, knee-breeches, and boots, a group of eighty-six members who counted among the best citizens of Mobile paraded through the city's streets. In her role as "Madame LeVert," Octavia presented them with a flag made by patriotic ladies of Mobile. Her speech was printed on a leaflet, much like her speech at the Clay monument in New Orleans, and shared with friends and family.[33]

Octavia was close to completing her book and preparing for publication when her attention shifted more towards fundraising for Mount Vernon. Her efforts grew in her role as the Mount Vernon representative for Alabama. Octavia continued to reach out to her friend, Edward Everett, inviting him to repeat his address about Washington in Mobile and visit her Salon.[34]

In August of 1857, as her book's release became closer, she traveled to Boston with her oldest daughter, Diddie, who was eager to meet Henry Wadsworth Longfellow.[35] It also appears they could see her father, George Walton, Jr. He was seventy-one years old and still dabbling in politics, but his life was not anywhere near the one he had before. He was renting rooms in Salem, Virginia, and was attended by someone by the name of Andrew.[36] Nonetheless, he looked forward to word of his daughter's upcoming book about their 1853 trip through Europe.[37]

Octavia's book, *Souvenirs of Travel*. Leeth, Yancy. *Souvenirs of Travel*.
Photograph. Mobile, Alabama, 2021. Oakleigh House Museum.

In early September 1857, the *Mobile Register* announced the book by Madame Octavia Walton LeVert was now available from the new publishing house of S.H. Goetzel & Co. on Fulton Street, New York, and Dauphin Street, Mobile. Octavia had found a way to make her book available to both her Northern and Southern friends, pleasing everyone. The *Charleston Daily Courier*, who copied the story, reported, "The first edition, composed of five thousand copies, is already appropriated by the orders received from various sections of the country, and a second edition is in preparation even while the first is yet being distributed. Such a demand for the 'travels history' of any lady is without precedent, we learn, and is highly complementary alike to the heart and head of our charming towns-woman." [38]

The article continued, "To the ladies, in particular, the work will be of particular interest, as no previous work is so replete with all those matters of Society, fashion and anecdote, in which they so much rejoice; indeed when we contemplate the authoress herself, the peculiar time and nature of her European visit, and the sources of information so unlimitedly opened to her, her book must possess all the elements of sure success. In a very a few days now, the volumes will be on hand, and it is scarcely necessary to bespeak for them an extensive perusal, for there will be scarcely a dwelling in Mobile without them."[39]

Mary Forrest,[40,] whom she wrote to repeatedly while she was writing *Souvenirs of Travel*, commented, "In entering the field of authorship, Madame LeVert would seem, at last, to have tested the ore of every vein of her versatile genius. ... Now she has written a book; and to do this requires solitude which brings one face to face with one's self-the introversion which deepens-the reserve which fortifies; while a book that contains, in any sort, the soul and sinew of the writer, is something lucked from the hurrying tide; something to be taken tenderly down from its nook in the old library, through many generations. In this light, especially these "Souvenirs" are invaluable." [41]

In the simplest terms, but not to underrate the significance of the publication of *Souvenirs of Travel*, when the first edition of Octavia's book was released in the latter part of 1857, it was an immediate sensation. As a result, her already popular and lofty status in American Society took on a completely different form. Octavia and her publisher, Goetzel, utilized their connections to promote *Souvenirs of Travel* to the public. The more reviews from Octavia's relationships, the more copies of the book would sell. She also reached out to G.M. Dallas, a member of the American Legislation in London, assigning him the duty to present her book to Queen Victoria.[42]

In the United States, Octavia made the arrangements to have Goetzel provide copies of her book to some of her most famous friends: the writer, Henry W. Longfellow, world-renown actor Edwin Booth, and former United States President, Millard Fillmore. Her book was also successfully circulated in the North's esteemed literary circles and among her close friends in Mobile and New Orleans.

In addition, word of Octavia's book spread to other female writers, and by September 15th, 1857; Mary Forrest received a copy and shared it with poet Sarah Helen Whitman.[43]

Octavia also sent a copy to her lifelong friend, Washington Irving, who learned of her intellect when he'd met her in a carriage ride in Alabama many years before. He wrote to her, "Souvenirs has made me once more your fellow traveler; but through must more civilized and brilliant scenes than we once witness together in Alabama. A veteran cosmopolitan as I am, I have well been able to keep company with you in your European travels; but as I read your bright and sparkling narrative and see what a continual fairyland your buoyant spirits and happy temper spread around you, I feel how greatly you have the advantage of me in catching the most favorable view of every picture." [44]

On October 16th, 1857, Octavia was riding on the success of her book. She traveled back up North to Boston. While there, she continued to promote her new book and raise money for the Mount Vernon Fund. For more help, Octavia reached out to her friend, Edward Everett, inviting him to many of her fundraising events.[45]

While Octavia's popularity was increasing, her father was struggling. She received correspondence from him. He was now living a meager existence and had to leave the mountain region, the hot springs the family had visited for years, White Sulphur Springs in Virginia. He needed funds for room and board for himself and Andrew. He asked his daughter for $50.00 to cover their expenses.[46] There is no proof she helped him, but it is most likely she did.

In 1858, Octavia gleamed over her book's success while focusing her efforts on raising money for the Mount Vernon Fund. Now officially appointed as the Vice-Regent for Alabama, she collected funds by utilizing her connections and popularity.[47] By the end of February, she wrote to Mrs. S.L. Pellet, the Secretary for Mount Vernon Appropriations, that she was responsible for collecting over $5000 in donations. She shared with Mrs. Pellet, "Ah! Dear Mrs. Pellet. I have no words to tell you how I have labored and toiled night and day in the noble cause. I have done all myself unaided and alone. Women to whom I appealed had no time from dressing and visiting to give me help. They deal me a wild, enthusiast, but surely and resolutely I continued on and success has rewarded me."[48]

Octavia continued filling her role with the Mount Vernon Association while still promoting her book well into the following year. A reference to her success was published in the *Charleston Daily Courier*, "The *Souvenirs* have indeed been wondrously fortunate. Even the critics, 'the hyenas of the Press,' have treated the book tenderly and lovingly. God has really blessed the work of my hands and my mind, for the sake of the pure and unselfish motive which prompted me to write it. To you, a good and earnest friend, I will say candidly, not for fame did I write the book, but that I might have the pecuniary means to aid persons who are poor, suffering, and afflicted. Not one cent shall I ever appropriate to my own use." [49] She worked towards the impression of generosity.

Octavia took her dedication to heart and set aside a portion of her income from *Souvenirs of Travel* for the Mount Vernon Fund.[50] According to the *Daily Constitutionalist and Republic*, "This most zealous patriot has just sent to the Secretary of the Mount Vernon Association one hundred dollars as the percentage upon the sales of the first edition of her Souvenirs of Travel. This offering is the very first remuneration that she has yet received for her literary labors, and she devotes it as once to the cause she has so warmly espoused. This noble, large hearted woman, who has proved herself so worthy of her great ancestors, is toiling incessantly to swell applications in every social avenue, she has addressed glowing appeals to societies, and to the men of influence; has gone to the stores of merchants, to the offices of cotton brokers, and asked them in the name of their great father, to give something from the store of wealth to secure his home and grave." [51]

Octavia continued raising money for Mount Vernon into the Summer months of 1858 as she, Henry, and Diddie traveled to White Sulphur Springs, and she kept luring her friends and connections to her cause.[52] She then traveled to Niagara Falls, where she met up again with former President Millard Fillmore and his wife.[53] She wrote to a friend, "Our dear friend Mr. Fillmore claimed our long promised visit, and we have been his guests for some days. We are received by himself and his agreeable wife in the most cordial manner. Instead of days, they wish our visit lengthened to weeks." [54]

The family then traveled to Boston, staying at the St. Nicholas Hotel. Her father, George Walton, Jr., also stayed with the family while they were there. George greeted a journalist waiting on Octavia. They wrote about her father, reporting, "Col. Walton, who adores his illustrious daughter, entertained me for an hour, with anecdotes of her. Among others, he mentioned an incident in her first winter in Washington, which has never been in print. At the age of sixteen, Madame LeVert made her debut in Washington. Beautiful, rich, and accomplished as she was, she was nevertheless introduced into Society as the daughter of Gov. Walton. 'Now,' said the courtly old gentleman, 'that is reversed, and I am introduced as the father of Madame LeVert.'" [55]

A report in the *N.Y. Daybook,* shared throughout the South details a brilliant ball with the focus on the LeVert women: "The ladies were mostly en grand tense and looking well; or the information of the curious we may state that Mrs. Levert wore pink and white, very becoming colours for her blonde charms; and those lucky enough to approach close, discovered that she adopted the Parisian mode of powdering with a substance resembling gold dust; her beautiful daughter, with her Spanish style and ejos bonita divided the honors of the evening with Madame Mere." [56]

Some of her time in Boston at the St. Nicholas Hotel was reflected in an interview for *Life Illustrated.* The reporter, a lady who described herself as Mrs. George Washington Wyllys, noted, "Who has not heard of Madame Octavia Walton LeVert - in her girlhood the brilliant belle of Washington, winter after winter, and now in the bloom of womanhood the loveliest and most distinguished daughter of the South - the beautiful American who was the idol of the English aristocracy and literati, on her recent absence in Europe, and the talented author of "Souvenirs of Travel," whose simple winning details have earned it a place in every American home?" [57]

Indeed, Wyllys' words appear very glowing and even pretentious, but the sentiment for Madame LeVert was still the same. Octavia had become a household name, and many were star-struck to be in her presence. Even as she approached her fiftieth birthday, one reporter who was quite enamored with Octavia said, "But all these apprehensions were dispersed like a cloud of night phantoms the instant Madame LeVert glided in… She was attired with that picturesque richness which is so characteristic of southern costume - everything seemed perfect, from the small, exquisitely shaped ear, from which descended a tri-foil of diamond fire, to the beautiful arms, full of nestling dimples, and the tiny foot which seemed formed to test only on banks of roses." [58]

In addition to this discussion, talk circulated of her now-famous home in Mobile, Alabama, where all distinguished strangers made a point to pay their respects to her as they visited the city. In one interview, Octavia first mentioned the next book she planned to provide to the literary world, titled *Souvenirs of Distinguished Americans.* She said she intended to write about her acquaintances with those well-known people she knew. Considering the caliber of talent Octavia was exposed to during her life, Wyllys acknowledged that it was very interesting.[59]

In October 1858, the family traveled to Richmond, Virginia, where they stayed at the Exchange Hotel.[60] Octavia then took passage on a boat on the Potomac River to see for herself the state of Washington's Mount Vernon residence. She wrote to Mary Morris Hamilton of the encounter, "I have been recently to Mt. Vernon and have knelt with entire devotion before the tomb of the patriot and hero. Even with the adoration of the Catholic before a holy shrine. Deeply was I grieved to behold the state of neglect into which this sacred spot has fallen. There is no excuse for Mr. Washington for this utter neglect of the house and grounds. He was absent or I should have told him so. The view from the front terrace is admirable." [61]

Octavia returned to Mobile by the end of November 1858.[62] A letter from her friend, Edward Everett, reached her when she arrived home, declining her request to visit Mobile due to family issues.[63] After spending a few months in Mobile, Octavia, and Diddie once more traveled to various locations, attended social functions, and spent time with notable people. They went to New Orleans and participated at the Continental's Ball, escorted by the city's mayor. It was another fundraiser for the Mount Vernon Fund; the theme for the event was George Washington.[64] It was a bonus that she finally was able to meet and spend two weeks in New Orleans with the famous actor, Edwin Booth,[65] and attend the St. Charles Ball.[66]

In April 1859, Octavia was back in Mobile. The New Orleans firemen were soon to follow. They accepted an invitation from the Mobile Fire Department in celebration of their 21st anniversary. The *New Orleans Daily Crescent* described the group marching down Government Street in ranks of ten and twelve, with arms hooked as they marched to the home of Madame LeVert. It was reported, "The thing was very pretty, and was much admired. Arriving at Madame LeVert's mansion, the scene which followed was one of the highest gratification to all. The firemen filled the hall and parlors; and if they found pleasure in the overflowing bowls which awaited them after their hot and fatiguing march, they found still greater pleasure - especially the New Orleans delegation, most of whom had never seen the Madame - in experiencing that Lady's cordial greeting, and charming hospitality. She was assisted in doing the honors by her mother, Mrs. Walton, and her daughter the pretty Miss Octavia. The New Orleans men were perfectly captivated by this reception, and the Mobile men were delighted with the pleasure of their guests." [67]

Despite the almost constant attention and fame as a notable literary, Octavia could not forget her children and brother's significant loss ten years before. In her journal, she wrote, "The past week was the anniversary of those "Iron Days" of my life. Oh! Like a boiling flood poured dark memories over my soul of that bitter past. I could not check the torrent in its mighty force, though brave were my struggles! Long seemed the hours of the pitiless night. It was a torture, they alone can measure, who have drank from the grief cup, like our desolated hearts. Never! Nevermore can I be glad & merry. The pall of anguish does not crush me 'neath its heavy folds now as formerly, but its shadow rests upon me, and still blights the real earnest joy the world once gave me. But I must learn to "labour & to wait." God knoweth best & against his decrees it availeth not to repine." [68]

May 1859 was the dedication of Henry Clay's statue, her lifelong friend, in New Orleans, and it was an event Octavia would not miss. She wrote, "I have no words to portray the sublime emotions which swept over my soul, as the flags fell away, and the statue of our honoured and beloved friend was revealed to my eyes. Tears fell in torrents - tears of joy, messengers from the

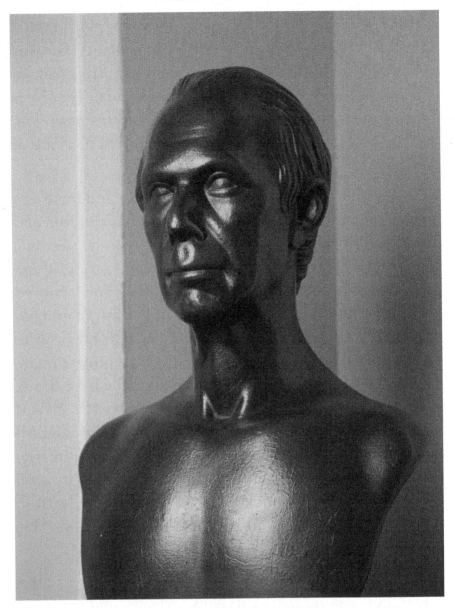

A bust of Henry Clay believed to be owned by Octavia. Leeth, Yancy. *Bust of Henry Clay*. Photograph. Mobile, Alabama, 2021. Oakleigh House Museum.

heart of its full delight. Far above the roar of the cannon - the pealing of bells and the music of military bands swelled loudly the enthusiastic shouts and cheers of 50,000 voices. Involuntarily I looked up to the bright heavens. I felt the spirit of our noble friend must be hovering near, and that even in his celestial home, joy must thrill his soul - joy to witness this scene. Glorious are the memories of that pageant. Like a beautiful picture, it will hang forever on the walls of memory."[69]

By June of that same year, Octavia's efforts as the Vice-Regent of Alabama for the Mount Vernon Fund resulted in having only $30,000 needed to purchase Mount Vernon to be complete. The Washington family's payment was significant in that these ladies had acquired the home they worked so hard to possess. It was reported in the *Independent Monitor*, "Upon the payment of thirty thousand dollars, Mount Vernon becomes the property of the Women of America. To ensure the speedy possession of the Home and Grave of Washington, all the Vice Regents of the Association have determined to solicit contributions on the approaching Anniversary of American Independence. Madame Octavia Walton LeVert, Vice Regent for Alabama, therefore appeals to the patriotic and generous women and men of her own state to give a small tribute, on our sacred National Fete day, to aid in the accomplishment of this noble purpose. Contributions, enclosed and addressed to "Madame LeVert, Mobile, Ala.," will be quickly forwarded to the Treasurer at Washington." [70]

The LeVert family ended the decade with no less flare than when it started. Henry LeVert continued his practice but was gradually transferring duties to his nephew, Dr. Claudius Mastin. Octavia continued fundraising for the Mount Vernon Fund[71] and working on her next book. The *Daily Confederation* remarked, "Her genius finds a scope this time in a home field, from which it will gather no less a harvest of reputation than it did from a foreign one. In her forthcoming volume (now in press) she will hold sparkling discourse of her travels and adventures in the United States, and spice it with the most delighted chit chat about the political, literary, and fashionable circles which she has constantly moved." [72]

Madame Octavia Walton LeVert's glorious year concluded with the honor of hosting a former United States President, Millard Fillmore, who came south specifically to visit her Salon during the winter of 1859.[73] At the apex of her fame, Octavia showed great promise in her literary career. Little did anyone know how drastic things were to change in only a few years.

Works Cited and Notes

1. LeVert, *Octavia Walton Le Vert Journal 1846-1860*, 79.
2. DeLeon, *Belles, Beaux and Brains of the Sixties*, 183.
3. Edwards, *Scarlett Doesn't Live Here Anymore*, 25.
4. Benjamin Buford Williams, *A Literary History of Alabama: The Nineteenth Century* (Rutherford: Fairleigh Dickinson University Press, 1979), 64.
5. Chadwick Stephens, "Madame Octavia Walton LeVert," 83.
6. Chadwick Stephens, "Madame Octavia Walton LeVert," 82.
7. Brewer, "*Alabama.*"
8. DeLeon, *Belles, Beaux and Brains of the Sixties*, 184.
9. Chadwick Stephens, "Madame Octavia Walton LeVert," 83.
10. Chadwick Stephens, "Madame Octavia Walton LeVert," 84.
11. Wells, *Women Writers and Journalist in the Nineteenth-Century South*, 78.

12. Gamble, *Alabama Catalog*, 304-305. Note: LeVert House and Office (AL-29), 151, 153 Government Street (southwest corner Government and St. Emanuel Streets.)

13. Forrest, *Women of the South Distinguished in Literature*, 23.

14. "Mary Forrest," *Morning Democrat*, February 9, 1856, 4, Newspapers.com.

15. "Mardi Gras Eve Masquerade at the St. Charles Hotel," *Times-Picayune*, February 6, 1856.

16. *Houma Ceres*, March 20, 1856, Newspapers.com.

17. Roberts, *Confederate Belle*, 5.

18. *Octavia Walton LeVert to Miss Booth, March 14, 1870.* Letter. New York Public Library, *Astor, Lenox, and Tilden Foundations.*

19. Satterfield, *Madame LeVert*, 173.

20. Chadwick Stephens, "Madame Octavia Walton LeVert," 89-90.

21. *Washington Irving to Octavia Walton LeVert, July 6, 1856.* Letter. In "Madame Octavia Walton LeVert 1810 – 1877," ed. Caldwell Delaney (Master's Thesis, University of Alabama, 1952), 79-80. Note: Delaney states he found this letter in the Dyer Collection. It is missing as of 2020.

22. *Daily National Intelligencer*, June 13, 1856, Newsbank, *America's Historical Newspapers.* University of South Carolina, *The Simms Initiatives.*

23. *William Gilmore Simms to Madame LeVert*, November 24, 1856. Letter. In *The Letters of William Gilmore Simms Vol. 6*, ed. Mary C. Simms Oliphant and T. C. Duncan Evans (Columbia: University of South Carolina Press, 2012) 172-173.

24. *William Gilmore Simms to Madame LeVert*, November 24, 1856. Letter. In *The Letters of William Gilmore Simms Vol. 6*, ed. Mary C. Simms Oliphant and T. C. Duncan Evans (Columbia: University of South Carolina Press, 2012) 174-175.

25. Horton, "Madame LeVert and Her Friends," 1.

26. *Edward Everett to Octavia Walton LeVert*, May 8, 1856. Letter. University of West Florida Archives, *Satterfield Collection.*

27. *Octavia Walton LeVert to Anna Cora Ogden Mowatt*, January 25, 1857. Letter. University of West Florida, *Satterfield Collection.* Note: Author consulted digital copy of records in her files.

28. Note: Images of Octavia, Diddie, and Sally referenced are in the collection of the History Museum of Mobile.

29. Horton, "Madame LeVert and Her Friends," 1.

30. "Arrivals at the Principal Hotels Yesterday," *Times-Picayune*, February 19, 1857, Newspapers.com

31. "Continentals Anniversary Ball," *Times-Picayune*, February 24, 1857, Newspapers.com.

32. "Address of Madame LeVert," *Times-Picayune*, April 22, 1857; "Parade of the Mobile Continentals," *Times-Picayune*, April 22, 1857; "Preparation of a Flag by the Ladies," *Times-Picayune*, April 22, 1857.

33. "Address of Madame LeVert," *Times-Picayune*, April 22, 1857; "Parade of the Mobile Continentals," *Times-Picayune*, April 22, 1857; "Preparation of a Flag by the Ladies," *Times-Picayune*, April 22, 1857.

34. *Edward Everett to Octavia Walton LeVert*, July 22, 1857. Letter. Washington Library, *Digital Collection*.

35. *Octavia Walton LeVert to Henry Wadsworth Longfellow*, August 20, 1857. Letter. Harvard University, *Longfellow Papers*.

36. *George Walton Jr. to Octavia Walton LeVert*, August 24, 1857. Letter. Private Collection of Reab Berry, Augusta, Georgia. Note: There is no indication of who Andrew is. It is possible that he could be a servant but records do not indicate.

37. *George Walton Jr. to Octavia Walton LeVert*, August 24, 1857. Letter. Private Collection of Reab Berry, Augusta, Georgia.

38. "Souvenirs of Travel," *Charleston Daily Courier*, September 9, 1857, Newspapers.com.

39. "Souvenirs of Travel," *Charleston Daily Courier*, September 9, 1857, Newspapers.com.

40. William Perry Fidler, "Augusta Evans Wilson as Confederate Propagandist," *The Alabama Review* (January 1949): 33.

41. Forrest, *Women of the South Distinguished in Literature*, 25.

42. Satterfield, *Madame LeVert*, 183.

43. Catherine Kunce, *The Correspondence of Sarah Helen Whitman and Julia Deane Freeman: Writer to Writer, Woman to Woman* (Newark: University of Delaware Press, 2014), 53.

44. Satterfield, *Madame LeVert*, 189.

45. *Edward Everett to Octavia Walton LeVert*, October 28, 1857. Letter. Washington Library, *Digital Collection*.

46. *George Walton Jr. to Octavia Walton LeVert*, November 2, 1857. Letter. Private Collection of Reab Berry, Augusta, Georgia. Note: Andrew is mentioned again. It is unknown if he is a slave or a friend.

47. *Octavia Walton LeVert to Susan L. Pellet,* January 31, 1858. Letter. Washington Library, *Digital Collection.*
48. *Octavia Walton LeVert to Susan L. Pellet,* February 17, 1858. Letter. Washington Library, *Digital Collection.*
49. "Mrs. Octavia LeVert," *Charleston Daily Courier,* March 11, 1858, Newspapers.com.
50. Delaney, "Madame Octavia Walton Le Vert," 100.
51. "Mrs. Octavia LeVert," *Daily Constitutionalist and Republic,* March 19, 1858, Newspapers.com.
52. *Octavia Walton LeVert to George W. Riggs,* July 22, 1858. Letter. Washington Library, *Digital Collection.*
53. "From an Occasional Correspondent," *Charleston Daily Courier,* August 31, 1858, Newspapers.com
54. *Octavia Walton LeVert Journal Excerpt,* August 27, 1858. Journal/Diary. In *Madame LeVert* ed. Frances Gibson Satterfield (Edisto Island: Edisto Press, 1987), 202.
55. "Madame Octavia Walton Le Vert," *Wabash Express,* December 1, 1858, Chronicling America.
56. "Fashionable News," *Yazoo Democrat,* October 9, 1858, GenealogyBank.
57. "From Life Illustrated: An Evening with Madame LeVert," *Daily Constitutionalist and Republic,* February 20, 1859, Newspapers.com.
58. "From Life Illustrated: An Evening with Madame LeVert," *Daily Constitutionalist and Republic,* February 20, 1859, Newspapers.com.
59. "From Life Illustrated: An Evening with Madame LeVert," *Daily Constitutionalist and Republic,* February 20, 1859, Newspapers.com.
60. "Distinguished Arrivals," *Richmond Enquirer,* October 29, 1858, GenealogyBank.
61. *Octavia Walton LeVert to Mary Morris Hamilton,* November 9, 1858. Letter. Washington Library, *Digital Collection.*
62. "Mobile," *Times-Picayune,* November 23, 1858, Newspapers.com.
63. *Edward Everett to Octavia Walton LeVert,* November 29, 1858. Letter. Washington Library, *Digital Collection.*
64. "The Continental's Ball," *Times-Picayune,* February 23, 1859, Newspapers.com.
65. "Madame LeVert Admires Edwin Booth," *Newbern Daily Progress,* March 1, 1859.
66. "The St. Charles Ball," *Times-Picayune,* March 3, 1859, Newspapers.com.

67. "Visit of the Firemen to Mobile," *New Orleans Daily Crescent*, April 14, 1859, Chronicling America.

68. LeVert, *Octavia Walton Le Vert Journal 1846-1860*, April 23, 1859 - 81.

69. LeVert, *Octavia Walton Le Vert Journal 1846-1860*, May 3, 1859 - 81.

70. *Independent Monitor*, June 25, 1859, Newspapers.com.

71. *Octavia Walton LeVert to George W. Riggs, November 29th, 1858.* Letter. Washington Library, *Digital Collection*. Note: To Mr. George Riggs, Treasurer of the Mount Vernon Association.

72. "Madame LeVert," *Daily Confederation*, September 8, 1859, Newsbank, *America's Historical Newspapers*.

73. "Mr. Fillmore coming South," *Augusta Chronicle*, November 24, 1859, 2.

Chapter 11

Society and Sacrifice

Oh, it is hard to take to heart
The lesson that such deaths teach;
But let no one reject it,
For it is one that all must learn,
And is a mighty, universal truth.[1]

Mobile grew into a cosmopolitan Southern city, and it culturally complemented her larger sister, New Orleans. The introduction of books with abolitionist themes and free discussion of issues brought new societal norms. The dreaded institute of slavery, for example, challenged owners in such places as Mobile, whose citizens struggled with continuing to care for their enslaved or setting them free.

Octavia and her family moved away from the ownership of slaves, and they did not cling to the belief that slavery was in their best interest.[2] When asked by Fredericka Bremer, an abolitionist, concerning her enslaved, Octavia told her she had inherited them as part of the family for over two hundred years. She also made clear she was not interested in participating in the practice any longer, indicating her generation would be the last slave owners. When the Civil War began, the family had four slaves; Betsey Walton was rumored as Octavia's half-sister.

Henry possibly had the three remaining slaves, all-male, helping him in his medical office or around the home. He was still a practicing physician with his nephew, Dr. Claudius Mastin, but he appeared to be close to retiring, and now he had more freedom to accompany Octavia, who used the pseudonym, Madame LeVert, as she promoted *Souvenirs of Travel* and raised funds for the Mount Vernon Association.

Octavia was like many southern women who opposed the formation of the Confederacy and African-American women, like Betsey, let it be known where their loyalties lay early in the conflict.[3] It is not clear if Octavia saw how the upcoming war affected her daily life simply because she chose to ignore it like many other citizens in Mobile. The city, still growing, was so far south from the heart of the conflict in Washington, DC, that it made those who lived there disconnected from that reality.

Despite the distance, Mobile was growing into the "Athens of the South," with Octavia as one of its shining stars. According to the *Daily Crescent*, "A fair Southern city of the extreme South, a queen of the Gulf - our peculiar Southern sea - noted for the pubic spirit, the refinement and the wealth of her citizens, and the elegance of her society, Mobile adds to these attributes of a polite and enlightened community, strong and sufficient claims to be considered a favored haunt of the muses and a stronghold of the republic of letters." [4]

Photo of Octavia, Diddie, and Sally Walton taken shortly before the Civil War. 2021. Photograph. *A Mobile Sextet*, by Caldwell Delaney.

In the throes of her successful book, Octavia still maintained the measure of success she had since she was the "Rose of Florida," but nothing compared to her role as

Octavia's close friend, Edward Everett. *Edward Everett / From the Original Painting by Chappel in the Possession of the Publishers.* Photograph. Washington, D.C., 1863. Library of Congress.

the matronly Madame LeVert. Poems were written about her,[5] a group of young ladies formed the LeVert Literary Society, and educational institutions for women were named in her honor, including the LeVert College in Talbotton, Georgia.[6]

Octavia always had an interest in politics, and with the death of the Whig Party, the LeVerts political stance changed to the Constitutional Unionist Party. This new party, formed in 1859, was a moderate alternative to the Democrat and Republication parties. They nominated John Bell for President and Octavia's friend, Edward Everett, for Vice-President.[7] In May of 1860, Henry LeVert was identified as one of the Vice Presidents in Mobile's local group.[8]

Family politics soon became overshadowed by health concerns within the family. By June of 1860, Henry had his first known attack of Erysipelas, a bacterial infection in the skin. Octavia's mother, Sally, was also ill and experienced early signs of edema, swelling from fluid developing in the extremities. Henry's attack had more impact on Octavia. It was severe enough to require her to take over the correspondence with his oldest brother, Francis LeVert. Octavia informed Francis of one of Henry's attacks during a family visit to Bladen Springs, a watering resort just north of Mobile. Dr. Cladius Mastin and family friend Mr. Scott rushed to Bladen when they learned of his illness, and their visit eased Octavia's anxiety. They stayed until they were able to bring Henry back home.[9]

Paula Lenor Webb

Image of Octavia used in Mary Forrest's book, *Women of the South Distinguished in Literature. Octavia Walton Le Vert, 1810-1877.* Photograph. New York, n.d. New York Public Library.

Henry's health resulted in unplanned delays, including completing her next book, *Souvenirs of Distinguished People*. Mary Forrest wrote, "As soon as she is sufficiently recovered to endure the fatigue of traveling her faithful physician, Dr. LeVert - prescribes a tour of the Holy Land. This most interesting journey accomplished, we shall look confidently, not only for another book of travels but for the postponed work, whose material is already in her hand in the affluent pages of her diary." [10]

When the family could travel once more, they traveled to St. Louis, Chicago, Detroit, Niagara Falls, and finally to St. Catherine's Well in Canada.[11] They then traveled to Boston, New York, Saratoga, and Newport.[12] In New York, the family stayed at the 5th Street Hotel, enjoying the attention she received because of her fame. By September, Henry decided to return home to Mobile, leaving Octavia, Diddie, and Cara Netta to continue partaking in New York society.[13]

Octavia extended their stay when she learned the eighteen-year-old heir to the British throne arrived in Detroit in September 1860 to tour America. When Prince Edward VII, British Queen Victoria's son, came to New York, he visited the University of New York, the Astor Library, and Cooper Institute. At Mayor Fernando Wood's residence, Edward was present when a coalition was formed that included former President Millard Fillmore, Archbishop Hughes, Bishop Potter, John Jacob Astor, George Law, Jas. Gordon Bennett and Madame Octavia Walton LeVert. The evening ended with Edward attending the Prince's Ball.[14]

The Prince of Wales tour of America concluded with a trip to Boston, where celebrations continued, and it featured the season's event, the Boston Ball. The Prince invited Octavia and her daughter, Diddie, to his theatre box at the Ball, and both enjoyed the attention received.[15] Prince Edward then left for Portland, Maine, on October 20th and sailed for England.

The Prince, a reputed playboy, became associated with Octavia when he invited her to use his theatre box. However, Octavia had a spotless reputation, and gossip about the event left her offended and quick to report what happened to the *Saturday Press* editor, Henry Clay, Jr. She shared, "The day before I left for NY. I heard that some persons in Boston believed that I had asked permission of the Prince of Wales to occupy his Royal Box. I was horrified at the malicious story... During the visit of the Prince to NY. I had seen and conversed with him several times, and he had brought me a flattering message from the Queen concerning my mention of her in the '*Souvenirs of Travel*.' Early in the evening of the Ball, I met him, and he received me in the most cordial manner, and after conversing a while, he spoke of the beautiful coup d'eil from his box, and said, 'Madame, will you do me the honour to occupy my box. I regret I cannot accompany you, but I have a long list of dances and must remain.' I thanked him for the courtesy, deeming it only of a gentleman to a lady who had been a guest of his Royal Mother. Imagine then, dear Mr. Clapp, my horror to hear it was said in Boston that I committed the great breach of etiquette in asking the Prince to allow me to enter his box.

Only think of such a malicious story. I who have been so often the associate & guest of crowned heads of Europe, to commit such a terrible breach of etiquette - it is false - utterly false, I assume you on my honour as a gentle-woman, and as an American lady. Should you hear it spoken of among my acquaintances do me the justice to correct it. I do not wish to make any publication in your paper about it, but I wish you to correct this wicked story, if you hear it mentioned in the social circles of Boston, where I have always received such kind attentions. I am now in route for my southern home." [16]

It is strange how events that appeared most important to Octavia, such as sharing a theatre box, became trivial compared to the dramatic events that soon overtook her. According to Peter J. Hamilton's book, *Mobile of the Five Flags*, detailed Mobile's response to the 1860 Presidential election, "The Democrats were themselves divided between two candidates, Breckinridge and Douglas, while conservative men united in a Union Party to put up Bell and Everett...Douglas visited Mobile during the campaign and in an address at the courthouse told the people, that, while slavery must be safeguarded under the conditions at the South, it was not favored by modern civilization. 'Gentlemen,' he said, rising on his tip toes until he seemed almost a large man, 'on this issue the world is against you.'... Excitement ran very high, but the division of the Democrats enabled the Republican ticket to obtain the majority of the electoral votes, although the majority to the actual votes were opposed to Lincoln." [17]

The "Athens of the South" quickly progressed to separating itself from the rest of the United States. On January 4th, 1861, the state government ordered the capture of Forts Morgan, Gaines, and the arsenal at Mount Vernon by secession forces.[18] Mobile sent a group of officials to the state capitol, Montgomery, to hear advocating for separate succession. On January 11th, 1861, the state of Alabama voted to succeed from the United States.[19]

Streets in Alabama filled with people celebrating. In Mobile, citizens tended to see things differently; many of its residents did not see secession as the answer. However, they did not question the need for some sort of revolution. In Octavia's house, they rejected secession completely.

When the war began, the 'Iron Days' also threatened to return to Octavia and the family. On January 14th, 1861, only days after Alabama declared secession, Sally Minge Walton, not only Octavia's mother, but her closest companion, died.[20] She recently experienced heart trouble, and no one thought it serious. She passed away on a Monday night. Octavia wrote the memorial placed on her gravestone in Magnolia Cemetery:

Beside her repose, her noble son and lovely
Little grand-children, who proceeded her
Through the gates of death to their eternal rest.
Her only daughter, Octavia Walton LeVert,
Erects this memorial to the fondest and best of Mothers.[21]

Sally's loss was dramatic for the family, and Octavia's grief great. Newspapers throughout the North and South received the funeral notice. The *New York Herald* reported, "A deep gloom hung over Mobile on the

The headstone of Sally Minge Walton in Magnolia Cemetery, Mobile, Alabama. 2021. .

morning of the 14th instant, when it was announced that this esteemed and eminent lady had 'passed to that bourne whence no traveler returns,' and her friends and those of her distinguished daughter, Madame Levert, throughout America and Europe will drop the silent tear of sympathy at this bereavement." [22]

Her mother's death was soon followed by strained communication with her father, George Walton, Octavia's father, living in Petersburg, Virginia, as governmental changes to the Postal System slowly began to affect communications between states, even in the South. Octavia received the last known letter from her father, Colonel George Walton, on February 22nd, 1861. He shared with her the upcoming conflicts in Virginia. His final message to his daughter said, "My own angel child - I know how agonizing how intensely you suffer the view you take was due to yourself & your angel & to society. I bless you and worship you for it - it will prolong my days & when I know that you are now content & cheerful I can pass off this stage without a murmur of regret." [23]

While many people celebrated the secession, Octavia could not hold back her sorrow from those who visited her home. Elizabeth Lyle Saxon, a close friend of Octavia's and fellow Unionist who remained in Alabama, called on her in Mobile on March 4th, 1861; she said, "I recall the day of Lincoln's inauguration, March 4th, as a memorable one in my life. I had that day spent many hours with Mme. Octavia Walton LeVert, so well known for many years as a charming society woman. ...Whatever one may hear or know of this lovely woman, one fact remains irrefutable: She was the most generous and helpful spirit to every young aspirant to fame and fortune that I ever knew. The tears flowed down her cheeks as we talked of the then existing condition of affairs. With deep interest we discussed the outlook, and her views were gloomy in the extreme. Younger and with less of life's larger interest to lose (for her friends were legion all over the Union), I saw things through more hopeful glasses. Nevertheless, her gloom depressed me greatly." [24]

Octavia continued to write her journal, as she had throughout her life, but the war left her unable to carry on with her literary career. Much like many other southern female writers at the time, communicating with publishing houses in the North was nearly impossible.[25]

Instead, the LeVert family started to see their role as helpers to the friends and family in the city who sided with the Confederacy. Their daughters, Diddie and Cara Netta knew they represented their family honor and helped at the LeVert Hospital, where officers went for treatment of war injuries.[26]

Despite early military actions, Mobile was far removed from the direct action of the Civil War. City residents continued their daily lives, much like previous to the war. The LeVert family lived as they always had as well. Octavia's Salon remained open to entertaining well-known visitors to the city, only now the parties visiting were limited to the bounds of the Confederate borders.

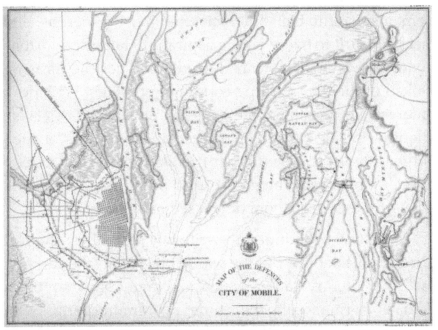

Map of the Defences of the City of Mobile. [1862-64]. Photograph. Washington, D.C., 1866. Library of Congress Geography and Map Division Washington, D.C. 20540-4650.

Unable to leave the South due to the War, Octavia and her family became more and more disconnected from the world they knew in New York and Boston. Those thirsty to learn about Octavia became distracted by concerns for loved ones. They sought newspapers for battle reports, injuries, and deaths. The interest in Society was no longer a concern.

Mobile's location so far within the deep South kept the city secluded. If it was attacked, then it would more than likely be by sea before by land. Mobile was fortified in all directions. According to Peter J. Hamilton, "The city itself was surrounded by three lines of earthworks...The one closest in passed from the Bay at Frascati through the pine forest east of Ann Street until it rested on One Mile Creek. This left many residences outside the line, and later Maury thought it necessary to cut down the beautiful oaks and shrubbery on Spring Hill Avenue. All in all, Gen. Joseph E. Johnston pronounced Mobile the best-fortified city in the Confederacy." [27]

Octavia, Henry, Diddie, Cara Netta, and Betsey saw all this activity around their home and tried to make the best of the situation. Everyone initially felt that the war could not last longer than three months, but this proved untrue.[28] By June, Henry LeVert and Claudius Mastin opened a private infirmary on the Northeast Corner of Conception and Lipscomb streets.[29] Dr. Mastin soon joined the Confederate Army and appointed the Surgeon for the Provisional Army of the Confederate States. He was ordered to report to General Leonidas Polk in Memphis, Tennessee. He left Dr. LeVert, one of the few medical professionals, to remain in the city due to his age and illness.[30]

As the war progressed, Octavia's standing in society diminished on the national front. However, signs of her activities did rise in various places. John Newland Maffitt, the Confederate ship captain, *Florida*, received Octavia, Diddie, and many of her friends on board while stationed at Mobile Bay. Word of Octavia's condition made it North in early 1862, sharing that she was in excellent health, but Diddie was suffering from inflammation of the eyes. The *Home Journal* reported, "She is, however, sorely pained in mind by the condition of our country, and although by birth, education and residence a southern woman, cannot, and will not, forget her love and allegiance to the United States." [31]

New Orleans surrendered to Union Admiral David Glasgow Farragut. *Admiral David Glasgow Farragut.* Photograph. Washington, D.C., 1860. Library of Congress Prints and Photographs Division Washington, D.C. 20540 USA https://hdl.loc.gov/loc.pnp/pp.print.

Farragut placed General Benjamin Butler in charge of the city of New Orleans. *[Benjamin F. Butler, Maj. Gen.].* Photograph. Washington, D.C. , 1860. Library of Congress Prints and Photographs Division Washington, D.C. 20540 USA https://hdl.loc.gov/loc.pnp/pp.print.

The Civil War impacted Mobile's life on January 26th, 1862, when its sister city, New Orleans, surrendered to Admiral David Glasgow Farragut. Three days later, he put General Benjamin Butler in command of the city.[32] Butler garnished no favors from and order he made to treat ladies like prostitutes. According to Mary P. Ryan, "The action that provoke this international squabble was General Butler's infamous General Order Number 28, which held that those women of New Orleans who insulted Union soldiers in the city streets were liable to be prosecution as common harlots." [33]

Union General Nathaniel P. Banks was sent to replace Butler, but he soon ordered thousands of those still loyal to the Confederacy out of New Orleans. According to *Mobile Under Siege*, "He wanted them out so desperately that he loaded them on a ship with the promise that it would take them directly to Mobile. The trip went only as far as Pascagoula, Mississippi, where the loyal rebels and their families were put to shore and ordered to get to Mobile any way they could. When the people of Mobile heard of this, they sent private carriages and wagons to bring them into the city." [34] These unexpected new residents in Mobile were not as tolerant of Octavia's perspective of the war and would influence the public opinion of Octavia in the days to come.

One of the most notable people to influence the LeVert household during the war years was Octavia's personal friend, the famous General Pierre Gustave Toutant-Beauregard, known for leading the attack on Fort Sumter. He left his command due to a throat ailment and

GENERAL BEAUREGARD.—[FROM A PHOTOGRAPH FURNISHED BY E. ANTHONY.]

Octavia and Henry's friend, General Pierre Gustave Toutant Beauregard. *[Pierre Gustave Toutant Beauregard, Full-Length Portrait, Standing, Facing Front, Wearing Uniform]*. Photograph. Washington, D.C., 1861. Library of Congress Prints and Photographs Division Washington, D.C. 20540 USA http://hdl.loc.gov/loc.pnp/pp.print.

went to Bladen Springs, near Mobile, to recover.[35] Due to changes in control, Beauregard spent the summer of 1862 in Mobile and Bladen Springs while waiting for orders.[36] In September, he left Mobile for his new command in Charleston.[37]

As the war Between the States progressed, Mobile filled with evacuees afraid of what was to come. Octavia feared an attack any day from Union forces and expected Mobile to fall like New Orleans and be under Beast Benjamin Butler's command.[38] Beauregard, aware of her concerns, assured her in a letter, "I regret to hear that you are in a state of agitation at the demonstration of the Yankees in front of your bay. They will not do much until their 'ironclads' are ready, i.e. winter. Then you will have to be on the look out, but not to tremble; for by that time Mobile could be made next to impregnable." [39]

Not only was Octavia concerned with battleships in Mobile Bay, within walking distance of her home, but she also worried about the health of Henry. He gradually had become more paralyzed with Erysipelas.[40] Unfortunately, the "Iron Days" kept coming into the lives of the LeVerts.

On January 3rd, 1863, her father, George Walton Jr., seventy-four years old, died in Petersburg, Virginia, and Octavia could not attend the funeral at Blandford Cemetery.[41] She wrote Francis LeVert soon after, "My beloved Papa died at Petersburg of Congestion of the Brain on January 3rd. It is a bitter bitter anguish to me that I was not near him in his last moments. But, his disease only lasted 48 hours. Thus I am left more desolate, still, the friend remaining on earth who loved me best appreciated me most has passed away from my love and my care. My brother, my children, my Darling Mamma, my beloved Papa, all are gone from me." [42]

Octavia also shared her concerns about Henry's health, "I am glad to tell you that dear M.D. appears much better of lately. His health is perfect, and his mind clear. His lameness, however, is quite hinders him from going his usual modes of practice. This troubles him dreadfully as we have no income independent of his practice. As soon as the weather is warming he is going to the Arkansas Hot Springs, feeling immersed in their water will cure him. As he has such an entire faith I am sure they will restore him to health and usefulness." [43]

The LeVert home and Salon, where many came to visit when they were passing through, felt the effects of the war. Octavia wrote, "Never was I so much in need of sympathy as now for sorrow seems established as a permanent guest in our household. The trials and troubles of everyday life induced by this frightful war are burdens difficult to support where to them is added the griefs I am called upon daily to endure. I assure you, at times, my courage fails me, and but for the promptings of duty, I should sink beneath the dark waves of anguish which surge around me. I cannot bear to add to dear M.D.'s discomfort by complaining and repining. I must be calm for his sake and appear as content as possible. M.D.s's state of health is excellent, but his lameness evidently increases. He was all ready to leave on the 15th of this month for the Arkansas Springs, but the Army being before Vicksburg has hindered him. A friend of ours, Captain Robert ... is still here waiting to accompany him as some of the route is clear of Abolitionists, they will leave here for the Springs M.D. is certain those baths will cure him of the paralysis of his legs. He has no other malady. Like yourself, I do not see any indication of peace. We, however, feel very secure and do not believe the US. Fleet will come here." [44]

Towards the end of 1863, Henry's health declined further. Octavia's continuing denial was shared with a friend, "Dr. LeVert continues in excellent health, but entirely paralyzed, and not, enabled to walk one step. It is a sad spectacle to behold, this strong, robust looking man, bound, as though, with, chains of iron and utterly powerless to rise out of his bed. But for Octavia (Diddie), who is my angel of consolidation, I don't know how I should endure the hard and wearing existence to which I am henceforth doomed." [45] She hoped for his recovery, but the reality was different.

Despite the LeVert's tragedies when they were restricted to Mobile, Octavia did not close her Salon. Instead, she continued to welcome Confederate soldiers, friends, and those who came to her with a letter of introduction. The popularity of her Salon in Mobile made it a destination in the city. While no definite proof of Octavia's involvement as a Union spy during the Civil War, it is possible that Confederate spies utilized her Salon. It was still active in November of 1863 as a possible location to exchange information. While it cannot be proven, a notable Confederate spy, Miss Belle

Edmondson, was in Mobile on multiple occasions and spent time at Octavia's Salon with many other prominent men and women in the area.[46]

In 1864, Octavia's role in the family changed quickly. As Henry's illness became worse, she became

Henry S. LeVert's gravestone at Magnolia Cemetery, Mobile, Alabama. 2021. Photograph.

responsible for protecting and feeding her family. Her role as the head of the family increased, and those in the household witnessed a change in how she took over tasks that generally fell to Henry. She had to ensure the survival of Diddie, Cara Netta, Betsey, and anyone else who was a part of the household.[47]

It was common knowledge that Henry was very ill. The disease didn't seem fatal, so his death on March 15th, 1864, surprised family and friends. The people in the medical field paid tribute to his memory by wearing a black armband, and Octavia placed on his gravestone in Magnolia Cemetery, "Mark the perfect man, and behold the upright, for the end of that man is peace."[48] She shared her loss with many close friends, including General Beauregard, who had just lost his wife.[49]

The last year of the war brought the most significant struggle to Mobile and its residents. Ladies continued normal activities such as shopping, riding around town using carriages until the horses were needed for the war effort, and deliveries of food, cloth, and other goods gradually became less and less. Tea and coffee, a luxury for all, practically disappeared and was replaced with local substitutes.[50]

On August 5th, 1864, the Battle of Mobile Bay guaranteed Mobile's city would fall into Union hands eventually, but when was still unknown.[51] Yet, the Confederate commanders refused to give up the fight, and the same spirit ran among their sympathizers. Despite the

Mobile Bay activity in the city's site, many continued their activities as if nothing had happened.

The Battle of Mobile Bay. *Surrender of the TENNESSEE, Battle of Mobile Bay (5 Aug. 1864).* Photograph. Washington, D.C. , 1894. Library of Congress Prints and Photographs Division
Washington, D.C. 20540 USA.

Octavia's friend, General Beauregard, returned once more to Mobile and visited her Salon to build morale and recruit troops. His message ran rapidly throughout the North; according to the *Chicago Tribune*, "The reports that Mobile had been evacuated are entirely without foundation. On the contrary, from all I can learn, they are determined to make a stubborn resistance. Beauregard made a speech there lately at the residence of a Madame LeVert and expressed confidence that the city would be successfully defended. Where are Corinth and Savannah,

Nashville and Atlanta? If Toutant could only move armies as he does his tongue he could overwhelm the world by prodigious feats of valor." [52]

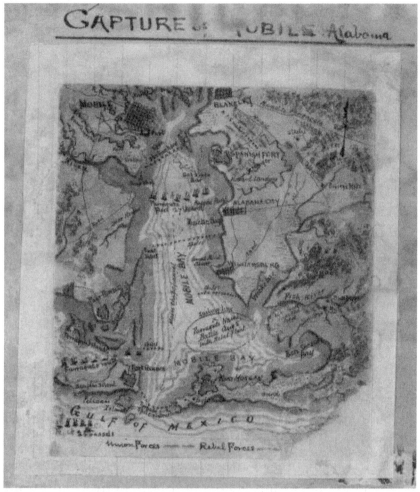

The Capture of Mobile, Alabama. Sneden, Robert Knox. *Capture of Mobile, Alabama*. Photograph. Richmond, Virginia, 1865.

While spirits were high in Mobile, the ability of the Confederates to hold the city was not. They left the early morning of April 12th, 1865, and Union troops moved in that afternoon. Immediately after the surrender of Mobile by Mayor Slough, at a location just south of the city, Union General Gordon Granger sent Octavia a note, politely offering a guard to protect her person and property should she desire it.[53]

Confederate Admiral Raphael Semmes. *Capt. Semmes, of the Pirate "Alabama".* Photograph. Washington, D.C., 1862. Library of Congress Prints and Photographs Division

Cranger sent Octavia a note, offering protection of her property. *Gen. Gordon Granger*. Photograph. Washington, D.C., 1860. Library of Congress Prints and Photographs Division Washington, D.C. 20540 USA https://hdl.loc.gov/loc.pnp/pp.print.

It is rumored, when she learned of the surrender, she flew to the home of Admiral Raphael Semmes, still occupied by his family. When she exclaimed, 'Joy, Lee has surrendered!' Electra Semmes, his daughter, requested she leave the house at once.[54] It is also rumored those enslaved who remained with Octavia throughout the war did not want to leave when they were set free. According to Mildred Lewis Rutherford, "After her slaves were freed, they begged her to allow them to stay and work for her as they had always done. 'We do not want freedom,' they said, 'if it takes us from you.' Betsey never would leave her." [55]

Mobile's transition from the occupation of Confederate forces to Union troops was quick, far faster than many of those who lived in the city that was under siege could handle. On April 12th General Granger entered Mobile, and by April 14th, Octavia began hosting at her home again, only this time it was General Edward Canby and other Union officers.[56] They had enacted strict Marshal Law and fearing the possible arrest of women in Mobile, like in New Orleans, Octavia used her Salon to help ease the restrictions placed on the citizens.[57]

Henry Alfred Schroeder, a resident who remained in Mobile when Union troops entered the city wrote to his son, Gilliat, of the situation there, "All goes on far better than we had any right to expect. Perfect order reigns in the city." African-Americans, newly free, were leaving families constantly. He was concerned the assassination of Mr. Lincoln would do much harm. He called it an atrocious crime and reprobated by every true Southerner.

He continued to share how the churches were open as usual, and they prayed for all in authority.[58]

It was important to note that Schroeder mentioned the ladies walked around as usual with no impropriety. He was concerned the ladies of Mobile were to repeat the ladies of New Orleans' rude behavior and be arrested. He shared, "Perhaps they did not want a repeat of the situation in New Orleans." [59]

Martha Schroeder, Henry's wife, wrote to her son about the celebration the Northerners brought to the city. She told him, "I have not seen city demonstrations of rejoicing, but hear very distinct the hurrahs and bands of music as the troops entered, it was very humiliating to hear *Yankee Doodle* instead of *Dixie* altho' I hear they play that often." [60]

Mrs. Schroeder continued to talk about the homes occupied by Union commanders. General Canby and two of his staff were staying at the Ketchum house. His staff occupied the Stewart house. Mrs. Schroeder, too, distinctly felt the impact of Lincoln's death, "The flags are all half-mast, and the officers of the staff have crape on their arms for Lincoln; if he had died a natural death or been killed in battle I would rejoice, but I have a horror of murder." Martha shared how the Yankees were grateful to the noble ladies for their dignified and ladylike behavior. She had heard of only one person arrested, a girl named Adel, because she clapped her hands and cheered at

General Edward Canby. *Canby*. Photograph. Washington, D.C., 1860. Library of Congress Prints and Photographs Division Washington, D.C. 20540 USA https://hdl.loc.gov/loc.pnp/pp.print.

Lincoln's death, she was at once released by an apology by Dr. Josiah Nott.[61]

Octavia never denied she was a Constitutional Unionist during the entire war and everyone in Mobile seemed tolerant of her decision. This sentiment was changing, judging from what Mary Schroeder, Martha's daughter, wrote on April 26th, 1865. She shared, "I know no lady who has received Federals, unless forced to do so, except Mrs. LeVert and we did not expect anything else from her." [62] It appeared to Octavia the war was over, and her home could return to the country it was before the war. She could return to some semblance of life before when her family was intact, and there was not so much suffering; for her it was a time to forgive.

Despite the desperate conditions in the city, people tried to resume life as before by holding a reception at the Battle House; according to the *Times-Picayune*, "Mobile was always notable for its social hospitalities, and the elegant and general courtesies of life. These for some time past must have been sadly disturbed and interrupted, and we are glad to observe, as we do, on pursuing the last number of the Mobile News, that the old order of things is beginning to be restored, in our pleasant sister city. Mrs. Parker, the lady of our popular Postmaster, who is now doing for Mobile what he did so well for us, in that capacity, being on a short visit there, held a reception at the Battle House."[63]

While there were those in Mobile, like Octavia, who sought to smooth the city's transition back into the United

States, many strongly opposed working with the Union forces at all. The *Mobile Register* shared the perspective of a citizen who struggled with the concept, "There is a great dread among some of the people of the South, of losing caste in society by affiliating with the people of the loyal States, whom they are pleased to term Yankees! It is all the same, New Englander, New Yorker Westerner, Southerner, if you will - by the criterion of these self-made aristocrats, all are classed as Yankees, and are considered plebeians, who favor the Government of the United States, and repudiate the Confederacy. But this is changing very rapidly, and it will soon (if it is not already) become as much a term of reproach to be classed as "secesh" or "rebel" as it was two years ago to be branded as a Yankee! Yankee arms and armies, Yankee pluck and prowess, Yankee money, and Yankee bonds are all quoted as "advancing" in our home and foreign markets. It will soon be "unfashionable" to be known as anything else than as a TRUE, LOYAL AMERICAN, in this country or any other. Then everybody will claim precedence as such, and desire to forget they were ever anything else." [64]

Octavia, Diddie, Cara Netta, and Betsey continued to spend time with the occupying Union soldiers. Union Brevet Major-General Thomas Kilby Smith was at their home recovering from illness when he learned about the capture of Confederate President Jefferson Davis and how he was sent to Washington under guard. Everyone was unsure of what the new United States President Andrew Johnson would do. Smith wondered if Davis would go to trial for treason, made a martyr, or permitted to go free. [65]

Octavia treated Smith with extreme kindness as he was nursed back to health. She must have spent a good bit of time telling him stories of her life before the war because a letter to his wife is descriptive. He even shares that he was sleeping upon a bed and bedstead that General Jackson slept in and once in the home of Sally Walton. They moved the bed to the LeVert house when Sally died. He concluded his letter by stating, "What I have hastily written and more hastily selected, may serve to give you some faint idea of this most charming lady. It is a good thing to have a sensible, well-educated sweet woman for one's friend, and I thank God, who has vouchsafed to me one or two such in the course of my pilgrimage." [66]

Efforts to develop peace between those in Mobile and Union troops continued. Major General Banks' wife, Mary Theodosia Palmer Banks, held parties and took a trip to New Orleans with a group of Mobile ladies. Despite their efforts to move beyond the war, not everyone was receptive. Animosities increased towards those ladies and most of all towards Octavia. The accusations of being a trader and spy ran rapidly through the streets.

One of the greatest tragedies in the history of Mobile, Alabama, could have been the deciding factor in Octavia taking her family and leaving her home for safer places. On May 25th, 1865, an incredible explosion destroyed a large portion of the city. According to *Mobile of the Five Flags*, "While General Maury had carried away all stores possible, on the surrender of General Dick Taylor at Meridian and other commanders in the Southwest, much of every kind, especially ammunition, fell into the hands of the Federals and was brought by river and rail to Mobile and stored into cotton warehouses. The city, in this way, became a great arsenal. Suddenly on May 25th in the afternoon, the city was shaken as if by an earthquake. Warehouses were demolished, residences and public buildings injured all over town, and men and animals killed by the shock. Men and women fled to safety and for some time no one knew what had happened, except that those who had looked to the North had seen, as one boy recollects seeing, a vast column of fire and smoke ascending and branching out on all sides like a huge umbrella, surpassing any that ever hung over Vesuvius; and it then settled down as a pall upon the town. Military guards were at once placed around the centre of the disturbance. It was found that the ammunition stored in Pomeroy's Warehouse on Beauregard near Water street had exploded, and with such force that there was no trace left of the building, - all that represented the warehouse was a great hole in the ground."[67]

For Octavia and her family, it was too much. They could not handle yet another tragedy, and with the help of Union officers, maybe General Canby, they were able to do what many in Mobile could not do - leave. Octavia, Diddie, Cara Netta and maybe, Betsey, soon found themselves on a steamer headed to New Orleans.

When she boarded the steamer, did Octavia watch in sadness as the city slowly faded from sight, knowing she was leaving her life behind? There are not any documents or writings about this pivotal moment in her life. What is known is that she had to start over, reinvent herself, and become the decision-maker in their small family – leave a life that was so much more fulfilling before the war. How were they to survive? Only time would tell.

Works Cited and Notes

1. *Daily Delta*, January 22, 1861, 7, Newspapers.com.
2. Edwards, *Scarlett Doesn't Live Here Anymore*, 78.
3. Edwards, *Scarlett Doesn't Live Here Anymore*, 67.
4. "A Southern Book," *Daily Crescent*, September 25, 1860.
5. *Yorkville Enquirer*, February 2, 1860, Newspapers.com.
6. "Correspondence of the Richmond Dispatch: Letter from Farmville," *Richmond Dispatch*, March 7, 1860, Newspapers.com.
7. The Editors of Encyclopedia Britannica, "Constitutional Union Party," *Encyclopedia Britannica*.
8. "Constitutional Union Meeting in Mobile," *Times-Picayune*, May 22, 1860, 3, Newspapers.com.
9. *Octavia Walton LeVert to Francis LeVert*, June 27, 1860. Letter. Southern Historical Collection, University of North Carolina, *LeVert Family Papers, 1760-1888*. Note: Letter from Traci LeVert Fowler.
10. Forrest, *Women of the South Distinguished in Literature*, 26.
11. "The Mobile Tribune, of Wednesday contains the following paragraph," *Times-Picayune*, July 12, 1860, 1, Newspapers.com.
12. "Personal," *Times-Picayune*, September 1, 1860, 2, Newspapers.com.
13. "Matters and Things in New York," *Times-Picayune*, September 11, 1860, 1, Newspapers.com.
14. "The Prince in New York," *Richmond Dispatch*, October 15, 1860, 1, Newspapers.com.
15. "Winding Up of the Prince's Visit," *Times-Picayune*, October 25, 1860, 1, Newspapers.com.
16. Satterfield, *Madame LeVert*, 212.
17. Hamilton, *Mobile of the Five Flags*, 291.
18. Hamilton, *Mobile of the Five Flags*, 292.
19. Hamilton, *Mobile of the Five Flags*, 293.
20. Satterfield, *Madame LeVert*, 214.

21. Satterfield, *Madame LeVert*, 218.

22. Martin, *Divided Mastery*, 161; *New York Herald* Issue 8903, January 24, 1861, 8, GenealogyBank. Note: It was documented that Sally owned 13 slaves at her residence. It is suggested that they did not live at her residence, but were rented out. In Mobile at this time, it was not unusual for slaves to not live with their owners, but were free to live elsewhere and get their own employment. They would bring to their owners a part of their salary once a year. According to *Divided Mastery*, "Some slaves who were hired out in the South decided on their own where to work, how long to stay with their higher s, and even what prices to charge. The practice occurred all over the South but predominated in cities and towns, where slaves were sent out to live on their own and to roam the streets looking for work. Self-hired slaves paid over a stipulated sum to their owners by the week or month and sometimes they kept any money they earned beyond their set hire." (Divided Mastery by Martin page 161.)

23. *George Walton Jr. to Octavia Walton LeVert,* February 22, 1861. Letter. Private Collection of Reab Berry, Augusta, Georgia.

24. Elizabeth Lyle Saxon, *A Southern Woman's War Time Reminiscences* (Chapel Hill: Documenting the American South), 23.

25. Wells, *Women Writers and Journalist in the Nineteenth-Century South,* 91.

26. Roberts, *Confederate Belle*, 4.

27. Hamilton, *Mobile of the Five Flags*, 295.

28. T. C. DeLeon, *Four Years in Rebel Capitals: An Inside View of Life in the Southern Confederacy from Birth to Death* (Mobile: Gossip Print Co., 1890), 27.

29. "Private Infirmary," *Mobile Advertiser and Register*, June 7, 1861, Newspapers.com.

30. "Dr. Claudius Henry Masdtin, Sr. (1826-1898)," Memorials, Find a Grave, last modified March 11, 2013.

31. "Madame Le Vert, of Mobile," *Daily Louisville Democrat*, January 5, 1862, Fultonhistory.com.

32. DeLeon, *Four Years in Rebel Capitals*, 170-171.

33. Mary P. Ryan. *Women in Public: Between Banners and Ballots: 1825 – 1880* (Baltimore: John Hopkins University Press, 1992), 130.

34. Paula L. Webb, *Mobile Under Siege: Surviving the Union Blockade* (Charleston: The History Press, 2016), 21.

35. Benjamin F. Butler, *Autobiography and Personal Reminiscences of Major-General Benjamin F. Butler: Butler's Book* (Boston: A. M. Thayer, 1892), 458, Google Books.

36. T. Harry Williams, *P.G.T. Beauregard: Napoleon in Gray* (Baton Rouge: LSU Press, 1995), 160.

37. Williams, *P.G.T. Beauregard*, 163.

38. *Octavia Walton LeVert to Ellen Long*, October 5th, 1862. Letter. Florida Memory State Library and Archives of Florida.

39. *Pierre Gustave Toutant Beauregard to Octavia Walton LeVert*, October 5, 1862. Letter. In *Madame LeVert* ed. Frances Gibson Satterfield (Edisto Island: Edisto Press, 1987), 223.

40. *Octavia Walton LeVert to John Walton*, December 20, 1862. Letter. In *Madame LeVert* ed. Frances Gibson Satterfield (Edisto Island: Edisto Press, 1987), 227.

41. "George Walton, Jr.," US, Find a Grave Index, 1600s-Current, Ancestry.com.

42. *Octavia Walton LeVert to Francis Walton*, January 22, 1863. Letter. University of North Carolina, *LeVert Collection*. Note: Collected by Traci LeVert Foster.

43. *Octavia Walton LeVert to Francis Walton*, January 22, 1863. Letter. University of North Carolina, *LeVert Collection*. Note: Collected by Traci LeVert Foster.

44. *Octavia Walton LeVert to Brother*, February 28, 1863. Letter. University of North Carolina, *LeVert Collection*. Note: Collected by Traci LeVert Foster.

45. *Octavia Walton LeVert to Friend*, December 9, 1863. Lawson McGhee Library. *McClung Collection*. Note: Author consulted copy at the University of West Florida Archives.

46. Belle Edmundson, *Travels in Dixie*, November 23, 1863. Journal. In *A Lost Heroine of the Confederacy: The Diaries and Letters of Belle Edmundson*, ed. William Galbraith, and Loretta Galbraith (Jackson: University of Mississippi Press, 2009).

47. Roberts, *Confederate Belle*, 772.

48. Ma Stephens, *Madame Octavia Walton LeVert*, 25. Note: Engraved on Dr. Henry S. LeVert's tombstone, Magnolia Cemetery, Mobile, AL. Psalm 37, verse 37.

49. *Pierre Gustave Toutant Beauregard to Octavia Walton LeVert*, April 5, 1864. Letter. In *Madame LeVert* ed. Frances Gibson Satterfield (Edisto Island: Edisto Press, 1987).

50. Hamilton, *Mobile of the Five Flags*, 306.

51. Webb, *Mobile Under Siege*, 31.

52. "Mobile News," *Chicago Tribune*, March 4, 1865, Newspapers.com.

53. *Times-Picayune*, April 21, 1865, Newspapers.com.

54. Satterfield, *Madame LeVert*, 241.

55. Mildred Rutherford, *American Authors: A Handbook of American Literature from Early Colonial to Living Writers* (Atlanta: The Franklin Printing and Publishing Co., 1894). Note: There are not any original documents to support this. It is rumored, but it is a well-known rumor.

56. Hamilton, *Mobile of the Five Flags*, 336.

57. Williams, *A Literary History of Alabama*, 65.

58. *HAS to Gilliat Schroeder*, April 1865. Letter. *Civil War Letters, from April 1861, to April 1865, April 22nd, 1865*. Note: Author owns copy.

59. *HAS to Gilliat Schroeder*, April 1865. Letter. *Civil War Letters, from April 1861, to April 1865, April 22nd, 1865*. Note: Author owns copy.

60. *HAS to Gilliat Schroeder*, April 1865. Letter. *Civil War Letters, from April 1861, to April 1865, April 22nd, 1865*. Note: Author owns copy.

61. *Martha Schroeder to Gilliat Schroeder*, April 1865. Letter. *Civil War Letters, from April 1861, to April 1865, April 22nd, 1865*. Note: Author owns copy.

62. *Sister Mary to Gillie Schroeder*, April 26, 1865. Letter. *Civil War Letters, from April 1861, to April 1865, April 22nd, 1865*. Note: Author owns copy.

63. "Social Life in Mobile," *Times-Picayune*, May 11, 1865, Newspapers.com.

64. *Mobile Register*, May 13, 1865, Minnie Mitchell Archives, *LeVert Collection*. Note: This paper states it is Octavia Walton LeVert. It is not. The person who wrote it had a husband who was still fighting for the Confederacy. Octavia's husband, Dr. LeVert, died in 1864.

65. *Thomas Kilby Smith to Wife*, May 17, 1865. Letter. In *Life and Letters of Thomas Kilby Smith, Brevet Major-General, United States*, ed. Walter George Smith (New York: G.P. Putnam's Sons, 1898), 397.

66. *Thomas Kilby Smith to Wife*, May 17, 1865. Letter. In *Life and Letters of Thomas Kilby Smith, Brevet Major-General, United States*, ed. Walter George Smith (New York: G.P. Putnam's Sons, 1898), 397.

67. Hamilton, *Mobile of the Five Flags*.

Paula Lenor Webb

Chapter 12

Times Moves On

Too late I stayed - forgive the crime
Unheeded flew the hours,
How noiseless falls the foot of time,
That only breaths on flowers.[1]

Along with Ditty and Cara Netta, Madame Octavia Walton LeVert left Mobile around June 25th, 1865, and became guests of Louisa Hawkins Canby, General Edward Canby's wife quartered in New Orleans. The residence located on the corner of St. Charles and Julia Streets proved to be a refreshing reconnection to the world outside of the blockaded Mobile. With Octavia's social standing, she feared for the health of herself and of her daughters, who would be in danger if they had stayed in Mobile any longer. In New Orleans, it was discovered they were in excellent health and enjoyed relief from worry that had plagued them since the beginning of the war.[2]

After a short time to recover in New Orleans, Octavia and her two daughters traveled on the steamer,

North Star, to New York, the place they stayed so often before war divided the nation. When they arrived, the LeVert family shared some of their experiences with the local press; one story told of how, on the Fourth of July, African-American societies and Sunday schools had celebrated the day by stopping at their home and saluting it with three cheers.[3]

General Beauregard received word the LeVerts left Mobile because of rumors of treason. Among them was that Octavia was a Union spy and during his last visit to the city she went through his official papers.[4] He wrote to her, "You qualify properly those idle reports relative to yourself at the time of my visit to Mobile. 'Ils m'entrait par une oreille et soient par l'autro' [in one ear and out the other] the best proof of which is, that I accept 'sans ceremonie" [without ceremony] your kind offer of services, by sending you the enclosed papers, which will explain themselves. I have endeavored in writing them to be as cool and collected as my temper and the nature of the outrage permitted. I would consider it a great favor if you could have without too much trouble my baggage and papers returned to me. Also, if you can procure me a pass to leave our beloved country. I feel that I can no longer remain in it, not-with-standing my great desire to do so. Indeed, I was only waiting to hear positively that my Seniors, Generals Lee and Johnston had applied for their pardons, to do likewise, but the treatment I have received at the hands of the Federal authorities has made me change my intention and I now prefer expatriating myself, at least for a few years."[5]

Beauregard was having trouble getting an official pardon from the United States government, but Octavia and the girls were accepted back into Northern society with open arms. The welcoming atmosphere led to their decision to remain in New York for an extended period of time. She realized that her family could live there cheaper than in Mobile, where food was scarce and expensive. They were comfortable and did not have to worry about the transitional chaos in the South. Octavia wrote to a relative, "We are floating on the 'crest of the wave' enjoying the Present, trying to forget the painful Past and never thinking of the uncertain future. I have suffered so fearfully during four years past that I am banqueting, if I may use the word in the actual absence of care and trouble and trial. It is really a time of Peace to me, and I enjoy it intensely, and thank the good God every day for the blessing of Peace."[6]

Octavia lacked funds to take care of herself and her family. Four years of war turned their wealthy estate into nearly nothing. She was dependent on friends' help, so what happened to Betsey in this stage of Octavia's life is questionable. It is suggested she left Mobile with Octavia, but no indications of where she went exists. What is known is that she was finally a free woman and able to make her own decisions. She possibly remained in New Orleans, returned to where her family originated in Augusta, Georgia, or was in New York.

Octavia found New York full of recently released Confederate officers who were treated well in the city. She noticed how differently Union and Confederate officers and soldiers related, "The Confederates are dined and supped by the very men they fought against. Everyone expresses the highest admiration of the Confederates, and I have not yet heard one word of bitterness against the South."[7]

When two publishers learned the author, Madame Octavia Walton LeVert, had returned to New York from her experiences in the South and intended to write about them, they visited her to learn more. She planned to call the book *Souvenirs of the War,* and they offered her a much-needed sum of money if she published it. She told her friend, "I have serious thoughts of doing so. I assure you I will do justice to the heroic Southern soldiers. I often feel it is my duty to let the world know that the annals of all times do not hold a parallel to the self-sacrifice and heroism of the Southern soldiers. They were cursed in many of their leaders, but ennobled in others."[8]

Old friends sought out the LeVert's at their hotel and invited them to dinners and parties. Everyone was happy to see the family in New York again after such a long absence. Octavia expressed her hope that God would grant that there never be another revolution in the South. Seeing the need, a friend of Colonel Walton's offered to take Octavia, Diddie, and Cara Netta to Europe for three months, all expenses paid, but they preferred to remain in New York, still recovering from the stress of the last four years.[9]

A photo of Octavia (Diddie) Walton LeVert. 2019. Photograph. Copy in possession of Stacey Plooster.

A photo of Cara Netta (Henrietta) LeVert. 2019. Photograph. Copy in possession of Stacey Plooster.

A photo taken of Diddie and Cara Netta for a magazine. 2019. Photograph.
Copy in possession of Stacey Plooster.

In a market eager for new accounts of the late war, Octavia still talked about writing a book about her experience in Mobile. Many were curious about what she witnessed during the siege, battles and the final capture of

Mobile by Union troops.[10] By October, people in New Orleans were reading about her intentions in the *Times Democrat*, "Her book will fill up a blank in history which is much needed, as Mobile was very secluded, though interesting spot during the war. Of course Madame will write gossip, but it will be interesting as history, because social life at Mobile from 1861 to 1865 was intimately blended with military existence. It is reported, doubtless on the authority of Madame and her publishers, that the authoress will be very severe on Jeff. Davis."[11]

If Octavia intended to be critical of Jefferson Davis, or if that was a bit of journalist gossip, it was not well received in the South. When it was reported about the possible position she could take was to favor the North. Those at the *Selma Messenger* shared their disregard, "We cannot believe that the lady in question could be so unlike her Southern sisters, could so unsex herself, as to publish a book containing abuse of a man whom all the Southrons love and admire. If she does, we shall buy one and Burn it."[12] Mobilians were unhappy she with her writing a book of their war experience.[13]

Octavia decided to stay in New York to work on her book, but she needed income to support her family in the meantime. She was now the leading provider and was responsible for caring for Diddie, twenty-nine years old, and Cara Netta, who was nineteen years old. She added to her income by renting her home in Mobile to Judge Richard Busteed of New York. He was designated the Judge of the United States District Court of Mobile.[14] Also, the LeVert home continued to be used by Union officers after the war.[15]

Octavia had a generous nature, ever a person who helped friends out when possible, she used her connections to arrange a meeting with President Andrew Johnson. She sought to solicit Executive Clemency for her life-long friend, General Beauregard.[16] According to T. Harry Williams, "She went to Washington to request Johnson to pardon Beauregard and other leaders. The President was supposed to have told her that he could not exonerate Beauregard at present but that he hoped the general would not go abroad, as the country needed such men."[17] It was reported he further told her it was impossible because so many Northern people were opposed to it.[18] A letter from John Van Buren, son of former President Martin Van Buren, seems to indicate that he even offered to buy Beauregard's passage to any port he liked.[19]

The LeVert family continued to live in New York into the next year and traveled to fashionable watering-places as before the Civil War. Octavia, so far, had not completed the books she promised the year before, but she was able to arrange a reprinting of her first book, *Souvenirs of Travel*, and it opened doors to Northern society. The family took full advantage of the opportunity.

Although Octavia and the girls left Mobile in the poorest of circumstances, the local papers still wrote of her actions, but it was probably not received well. Many people in the city were experiencing recovery and reconstruction of their lives, and reports of Octavia attending balls and parties only increased the animosity. When it was reported she attended a dance at the National Hotel in Washington D.C. with two men well-known and not liked in Mobile, Major General Nathaniel Banks and Major General Benjamin "Beast" Butler, claimed the fame Octavia once had was gradually fading.[20]

Beauregard reached out to the family again in March of 1866 and shared his experience. He still wanted his baggage and papers, but they were seized to be examined for evidence of treason, but it didn't exist. Instead, they contained mainly notes from his female admirers.[21] He waited patiently for his pardon but became concerned as others he fought beside in the Confederate army were pardoned, but his was not accepted. He told Octavia he was living from hand to mouth, but he hoped to do better before long.[22] He eventually left for Europe on business with a railroad company, without the pardon.[23]

Octavia also wrote articles and stories for local publications such as the *Philadelphia Home Weekly*.[24] At fifty-six years old, it was time for her to rebuild her career as a writer, but nowadays, it was out of necessity. She needed to support Diddie, who did not seem interested in getting married, and her youngest daughter, who did. Until things changed, they both were under her care. The Civil War left many southern women having to create an occupation to survive.[25]

In April 1866, Octavia, Diddie, and Cara Netta wanted to return to Niagara Falls, much like they did

Photograph of Octavia Walton LeVert after the Civil War. 2019.
Photograph. Copy in possession of Stacey Plooster.

before, but this time their circumstances were very different; they needed money to do so. Octavia reached out to various friends and connections to help with their costs. She wrote to a friend, Mr. Bush, "You were always too kind to us, that I am ever beholden to write, and, ask, the favor of you, to make some inquiries about the price of board at Niagara Falls, whether on the American or Canadan side. We cannot return to the South this summer, our account of the small pox, and it is too expensive to remain at the Hotel all the summer, besides being unhealthy." Octavia made it clear to Mr. Bush that she did not have enough funds to stay at the 5th Street Hotel, but with his help, she could share a room with Diddie and Cara Netta and they desired a quiet place to visit.[26]

The LeVerts returned to the Fifth Avenue Hotel in August of 1866[27,] and they were able to meet with Beauregard once more. He returned from his employment with the railroad in Europe and dined with the LeVerts at their hotel and a small group of his old friends. Word quickly spread that he was at the hotel and visiting in the drawing-room, which led to the hotel's corridors becoming packed with spectators. The owners didn't mind. They provided wine for all of Octavia's guests, free of charge.[28]

Beauregard left this meeting and went to Washington, D.C., where he met with President Johnson but did not secure a pardon, nor did he acquire his papers. He returned to New Orleans and remained in the United States. He was finally pardoned on July 4th, 1868.[29]

Octavia and her daughters decided to return to the South towards the end of 1866 when they were invited to stay with her friend, Mrs. Adelica Hayes Acklen, the owner of *Belmont*, an impressive mansion in Nashville. According to Lauren K. Lessing, "The estate had several formal gardens, numerous fountains, a water tower, conservatory, deer park, art gallery, and zoological garden. The house itself is Italianate in style, finished with reddish-brown stucco and white trim. Lacy, cast-iron balconies originally extended above the recessed entrance nd along the second story of each wing."[30]

Belmont Estate in Nashville, Tennessee. *Belmont, Belmont Boulevard & Wedgewood, Nashville, Davidson County, TN*. Photograph. Washington, D.C. , 1933. Library of Congress Prints and Photographs Division Washington, D.C. 20540 USA http://hdl.loc.gov/loc.pnp/pp.print.

When Octavia arrived at Belmont, she took a moment to write to Eugene LeVert, to let him know how they were doing. She told him that Diddie and Cara Netta were enjoying themselves, and many people were calling on them. She told him of the home, "Adelicia Acklen has the most delightful home. It is a Villa, built in the Italian style of architecture immensely large and superbly furnished. She has the Drawing rooms and the Hall and Commodes filled with splendid paintings and magnificent statues. In the center of the Grand Hall is the exquisite marble statue...It is really one of the most beautiful works of art I have ever seen."[31]

During the visit, Adelicia gave a reception in honor of Madame LeVert, which caused a great deal of excitement in Nashville. According to *The Queens of American Society*, "It was called 'the forerunner of a new regime of entertainments, combining intellectual and artistic enjoyment with perfect taste.' The observatory, groves, and parterres were illuminated, and the effect of the light among the statues, shrubbery, and flowers, with music from the portico, was fairy-like. The beautiful hostess wore the dress of pearl-colored satin, trimmed with the richest point d'Alencon, in which she had been presented at the French court, with a coronet of diamonds, and diamond necklace and bracelets. Ladies were there from Memphis and from Kentucky; and the sister and nieces of the hostess were greatly admired."[32]

After the grand ball, Octavia and the girls planned to visit Belle Vue, their family home in Augusta, Georgia, where their Aunt Anna Robinson lived. They also planned to follow this visit with their first trip to Mobile since they left.[33]

It seems the intent is there on behalf of Octavia and the family to return to Mobile, and she shares this in a letter to Frances LeVert. She regretted not visiting him when she left Nashville, but she might not have been able to handle the stress of seeing Henry LeVert's family. She still seemed determined to go on to Mobile, and Octavia wrote, "We leave here on Monday 4th of February for Mobile. We shall board at the Battle House as our own dwelling is rented out for a year. We shall find a sad change in our situation. In place of going home to a comfortable and pleasant house with darling mamma and beloved M.D. to welcome us, we are going to a Hotel and not one of our own Kindred to receive us. But we must be reconciled 'God doeth all things well.'"[34] Yet, maybe Octavia, Diddie, and Cara Netta were not reconciled. It is possible the family could not emotionally handle the visit, much like the others. There were clearly plans to visit Mobile, but no records exist to support their arrival or departure from the city.

The LeVerts were rediscovered in August of 1867, but they were spending the summer at the Clifton House in Niagara Falls, as they had in the past.[35] During this visit, Octavia sprained her foot while descending a stairway at Niagara Falls and spent the majority of the time recovering in her room.[36]

Octavia recovered in time to travel with the family to return to the *Belmont Mansion* in Nashville to attend Adelicia Acklen's wedding to a physician, William Archer Cheatham. She might have wished she had not attended the event due to the ridicule that followed. It was reported in *The Home Journal*, "A friend amused us with the following which he got from a witness on the occasion...Madame Acklen, a very wealthy lady residing about three miles from Nashville, Tenn., was recently married to a man by the name of Cheatham. A very large and gay assembly attended the wedding, and every thing was done up the most costly and stylish manner imaginable. Madame LeVert was also present...At the banquet, after all parties had done perhaps more than justice to the delicious viands, etc., Madame LeVert, who sat near the head of the table, took up a little silver bell and rung it, thereby attracting the attention of the guests, and remarked, 'Any young gentlemen wishing to converse with my daughters in Spanish, Italian, or French can now have the opportunity by withdrawing to the parlor.' No one responding the drinking and jokes went on for a while longer, when the brother of the groom, another Mr. Cheatham, all at once took up his cane and gave several loud raps on the floor, bringing the whole assembly to a dead calm, and exclaimed, 'Any young lady wishing to converse with me in the English language can now have the opportunity.' The roars of laughter that followed this admirable hit may possibly prevent the Madame from indulging in such another freak of vanity."[37] The embarrassing exchange humbled Octavia, and while she still mingled with high society, she was not quite as vocal.

However, she was a viable part of the New York literary community and should have access to related events, even if she was a woman. During this time, there were many clubs where men-only literary groups gathered and did not welcome women regularly. This led to the formation of the first Woman's Club.

How the first Woman's Club was created was rather simple. After completing a tour of the United States, Charles Dickens was a guest of the New York Press Club, a mens'-only club, at the famous Delmonico's restaurant. According to the book, *Madame LeVert*, "Mr. D.G. Croly, then managing editor of the New York World, was on the executive committee that was in charge. His wife, also a journalist, applied for a ticket at the same price the men were paying ($15), saying the dinner was offered to the press of New York in honor of one of the most distinguished members of the profession, and that she was a member of the press in good standing and wished to attend. Most of the committee were inclined to take the request as a joke, but Mr. James Parton took it seriously and approved it. At the next meeting he presented a similar request from his wife, a writer known as 'Fanny Fern.' Other applications followed." This was too much for the men, and they refused to let ladies attend. The ladies then formed their own club, the Sorosis Club, with the first meeting also at Delmonico's on April 20th, 1868.[38]

The club, called both the Sorosis and the Blue Stocking Club, included Octavia and the most prominent and popular female writers in the United States. Among them were: Mrs. D.G. Croly (Jennie June), Mrs. James Parton (Fannie Fern), Mrs. Elizabeth Stoddard, Mrs. Ann S. Stephens, Alice, and Phoebe Cary, Miss Mary L. Booth, Miss Dunning (Shirley Dare), Mrs. Elizabeth Cady Stanton, Miss Susan B. Anthony, Miss Cara Jennings, and

Miss Clara Louise Kellogg. These ladies and many others were known for their literary ability and reputation. When the men excluded them, it required action, and they took it.[39] Octavia became involved with the club, connecting with other writers with like minds and traveling, with her daughters, from one home to another, visiting with friends at their country houses.

Soon things changed in the LeVert household. During the previous visit to Augusta, Georgia, or sometime soon afterward, Cara Netta was introduced to Lawrence Augustus Rigail Reab of Augusta, Georgia, and fell in love. He was a distant cousin and lived with their Aunt, Anna Rigail Tabitha Robinson.[40]

Octavia shared happy news with Dr. Mastin, Henry LeVert's former partner, in September 1868, "As you are one of the family I will tell you that Cara Netta will be married in a few months. She has made an excellent selection from several suitors. I will write to you when the time is appointed."[41]

Octavia also wrote a letter to Francis LeVert, announcing the good news, "I write to inform you of the engagement of my darling Cara Netta to Raigail Reab, the adopted son of my Aunt Mrs. Robinson. They are to be married on the 16th of December. The match is very agreeable to me, for the young man is intelligent, handsome and industrious."[42]

If Rigail Reab and Cara Netta LeVert expected a nice, simple wedding, their hopes were to be dashed, for nothing was simple with Octavia Walton LeVert. In

Trinity Church, where Cara Netta was married. *Trinity Church, New York City*. Photograph. Washington, D.C. , 1920. Library of Congress Prints and Photographs Division Washington, D.C. 20540 USA.

addition, this would probably be the only wedding for her family since her oldest daughter, Diddie, was beyond the marriageable age of thirty-two.

The wedding was held on December 16th, 1868, at Trinity Church in New York. The guests numbered into the hundreds for the wedding and were considered one of the season's social events. When the bridal party entered the church, Diddie was first in line and led by a Mr. Jefferson. Her dress was rose-colored silk, and her dark hair was trimmed with roses.[43]

Dr. Skillen, a nephew, led Octavia, who followed her daughter. She must have missed Henry at such a moment. She was dressed in a rose-colored silk dress with short puffed sleeves edged with lace. At her throat was fastened a cluster of diamonds. Her hair was puffed, and a lace shawl fell from her shoulders.[44]

Cara Netta and Rigail followed Octavia, and they both captured the attention of all present. Rigail, with his mustache and blue eyes, was dressed in the customary black suit. However, Cara Netta was the one to attract all the attention. According to the *New Orleans Crescent*, "His Bride, Miss Cara Netta, was very handsome, in an elaborate muslin dress, with an immense train, edged with 3 rows of fluting. The skirt was composed of alternate narrow tucks and puffings of insertion. The waist was décolleté, and edged with lace. A lace underwaist fastened at the throat. A wide, white satin sash passed around the waist, and fastened behind."[45]

In Cara Netta's hands, she held a large bouquet, and orange blossoms encased a wreath on her head. The blossoms in memory of her former home in the South and

Inside Trinity Church. *Interior, Trinity Church, New York, N.Y.*
Photograph. Washington, D.C. , 1907. Library of Congress Prints and
Photographs Division Washington, D.C. 20540 USA
http://hdl.loc.gov/loc.pnp/pp.print.

the sisters she lost so early. Dr. Skillern also stood in for
Cara Netta's father and gave the bride away. The
reception was held at the Coleman House, where many

beautiful ladies and their dresses were on display. The couple also received many gifts, but there was one that touched everyone the most and was on the grandest display.[46] It was her special wedding gown.

Octavia later wrote to Dr. Mastin of what transpired, "The dress was beautiful. It was made by my dear Betsey, and was her present to my dear Netta. It was exquisitely embroidered, puffed and tucked. Caroline, a little house girl, sent a beautiful embroidered chemise and drawers. Was that touching? They could not be at the wedding but they entreated that their dear Miss Netta should wear the articles made by their faithful hands."[47] In their honor, Cara Netta had put aside the elegant trousseau that was already prepared, and chose the dress that loving fingers had prepared for her.[48]

Through the sadness and the tears, Octavia Walton LeVert was striving in her new world of independence. The family had been through difficult times together. Now her youngest daughter was married and in good hands. Cara Netta had found a dedicated and loving man in Rigail Reab. Octavia and Diddie missed Cara Netta in their daily lives, but the family grew, which meant hope. The future was unknown.

Works Cited and Notes

1. *Edgar Allen Poe Journal July 23, 1827*. Journal/Diary. Columbia University, *Edgar Allan Poe Papers, 1827-1908*.
2. *Times-Picayune*, June 25, 1865, Newspapers.com.
3. *Buffalo Commercial*, July 31, 1865, Newspapers.com; "Letter from Madame Levert," *Tri-Weekly News Winnsboro*, August 6, 1865, Newspapers.com.; "Letter from Madame Levert," *Tri-Weekly News Winnsboro*, September 12, 1865, Newspapers.com.

4. Delaney, "Madame Octavia Walton Le Vert," 108.
5. Delaney, "Madame Octavia Walton Le Vert," 108.
6. *Octavia Walton LeVert to Julia LeVert*, September 25, 1865. Letter. In "Madame Octavia Walton LeVert 1810 – 1877," ed. Caldwell Delaney (Master's Thesis, University of Alabama, 1952), 109-110. Note: Delaney cites the letter as belonging to the Harralson.
7. "Letter from Madame Levert," *Tri-Weekly News Winnsboro*, September 12, 1865. Newspapers.com.
8. "Letter from Madame Levert," *Tri-Weekly News Winnsboro*, September 12, 1865. Newspapers.com.
9. "Letter from Madame Levert," *Tri-Weekly News Winnsboro*, September 12, 1865. Newspapers.com
10. *Norfolk Post*, August 9, 1865, Newspaper.com.
11. "Mme. Levert's Book," *Times Democrat New Orleans*, October 3, 1865, Newspapers.com.
12. *Daily Mississippian*, November 1, 1865, Newspapers.com.
13. "A Southern History of the War Wanted," *Daily Evansville Journal*, November 21, 1865, Newspapers.com.
14. "Judge Busteed," *New Orleans Times*, October 4, 1865, GenealogyBank.
15. "Military Changes", *Nashville Daily Union*, June 7, 1866, GenealogyBank.
16. "Madame Levert Interceding for Beauregard," *World*, October 6, 1865, GenealogyBank.
17. Williams, *P.G.T. Beauregard*, 260.
18. "The New York correspondent of the Baltimore Gazette writes," *Plain Dealer*, October 18, 1865, GenealogyBank.
19. *John Van Buren to Andrew Johnson*, October 9, 1865. Letter. National Archives, *The Papers of Andrew Johnson*. Note: John Van Buren was the son of President Van Buren.
20. "Society in Washington," *Mobile Daily Times*, March 1, 1866, Newspapers.com.
21. Williams, *P.G.T. Beauregard*, 259.
22. *Letters to and from Madame LeVert*, March 23, 1866. Letter. Minnie Mitchell Archives, *LeVert Collection*. Note: Author referenced a copy from the University of West Florida Archive.
23. Williams, *P.G.T. Beauregard*, 260.
24. Charles R. Rode, *American Literary Gazette and Publisher's Circular* 6, Philadelphia Home Weekly.

25. Wells, *Women Writers and Journalist in the Nineteenth-Century South*, 142.
26. *Octavia Walton LeVert to Mr. Bush*, April 15, 1866. Letter. Department of Special Collections, Memorial Library, University of Wisconsin-Madison. Note: From New York, 5th Avenue Hotel, April 15, 1866, Dear Mr. Bush.
27. "Personal Intelligence," *New York Herald*, August 29, 1866, GenealogyBank.
28. "Gen. Beauregard," *Chicago Daily Times*, October 5, 1866, GenealogyBank.
29. Williams, *P.G.T. Beauregard*, 260.
30. Lauren K. Lessing, "Angels in the Home: Adelicia Acklen's Sculpture Collection at Belmont Mansion" (Spring 2011), Colby Digital Commons @ Colby, *Faculty Scholarship*.
31. *Octavia Walton LeVert to Eugene LeVert*, November 29, 1866. Letter. Private Collection of Staci Plooster. *Walker Family Cemetery Collection*.
32. Ellet, *Queens of American Society*.
33. *Octavia Walton LeVert to Eugene LeVert*, November 29, 1866. Letter. Private Collection of Staci Plooster. *Walker Family Cemetery Collection*.
34. *Octavia Walton LeVert to Francis Walton*, February 2, 1867. Letter. Private Collection of Traci LeVert Foster. Note: Sent from Belle Vue Cottage, near Augusta, Georgia. Note: Traci LeVert Foster obtained letter from Chapel Hill.
35. *Times-Democrat*, August 11, 1867, Newspapers.com.
36. *Public Ledger*, August 31, 1867, Chronicling America.
37. "A Good One," *The Home Journal*, January 2, 1868, Chronicling America.
38. Satterfield, *Madame LeVert*, 254.
39. "Blue Stocking Club," *Buffalo Daily*, April 17, 1868, Newspapers.com.
40. Delaney, "Madame Octavia Walton Le Vert," 111.
41. *Octavia Walton LeVert to Doctor (probably Dr. Mastin)*, September 18, 1868. Letter. Minnie Mitchell Archives, *LeVert Collection*.
42. *Octavia Walton LeVert to Anne*, October 3, 1978. Letter. University of West Florida, *Satterfield Collection*.
43. "The LeVert-Reab Wedding in New York," *The New Orleans Crescent*, December 23, 1868, Newspapers.com.

44. "The LeVert-Reab Wedding in New York," *The New Orleans Crescent*, December 23, 1868, Newspapers.com.
45. "The LeVert-Reab Wedding in New York," *The New Orleans Crescent*, December 23, 1868, Newspapers.com.
46. "The LeVert-Reab Wedding in New York," *The New Orleans Crescent*, December 23, 1868, Newspapers.com.
47. *Octavia Walton LeVert to Dr. Claudius Matin*, December 30, 1868. Letter. University of North Carolina Library, *LeVert Family Papers, 1760-1888*. Note: Author obtained copy of the letter from the private collection of Staci Plooster.
48. *Weekly Standard*, December 30, 1860. Newspapers.com.

Paula Lenor Webb

Chapter 13

Will thou Remember Me?

Farewell! Forget me not, when others gaze
Enamored on thee with the looks of praise,
When weary leagues before my view are cast,
Forget me not may joy thy steps attend;
With care unsullied by thy every thought.
And in thy dreams of home forget me not.[1]

Octavia's life became less complicated after her youngest child's marriage. This new family, Cara Netta and L.A.R. Reab settled in Augusta and shared the large family home, Belle Vue, with Aunt Robinson. Her oldest daughter, Diddie, who chose to remain unmarried, spent her time between the Belle Vue estate in Augusta and living with Octavia in New York.

Octavia also moved on from the life she left in Mobile, removing connections she once held dear. Since Octavia realized she could not be buried in Magnolia Cemetery with her husband, brother, mother, and children., she made arrangements for using her gravesite.

Col. Henry "Harry" Maury, once a familiar figure in her salon, passed away on February 23rd, 1869. He had no family. So, Octavia gave him her burial plot in the LeVert section of the cemetery.[2]

Octavia had to let go of other things, too, such as the project she was dedicated to before the war, the efforts to restore Mount Vernon, George Washington's home. She worked hard to return the sacred place to its former glory. Now she was barely able to earn enough to sustain her family. Much to her disdain, she was officially removed as the Vice-Regent for the state of Alabama because she no longer lived in Alabama.[3]

Although rumors circulated that Octavia saved much of her fortune by sending it to the Bank of England during the Civil War, anyone close to her knew this wasn't true.[4] She had to work to survive. She wrote articles for publication to earn some income. For example, she wrote for *Hearth and Home* and shared her experience meeting the Pope in Rome and the meeting of Robert Browning and his wife, Elizabeth Barrett Browning, in Europe years before when she last visited.[5]

Strangely enough, Octavia, herself, seemed to be an ideal subject of books and articles post-Civil War. Her grandfather's role in helping shape the United States and her adventures made her life story famous. She was a part of the book, *The Living Writers of the South*, written by James Wood Davidson, and was published in 1869.[6] This summary of her life was to become the standard format many later writers would follow in years to come. She was also interviewed in 1872 by Elm Orlou for the article, "Deserving Women of Alabama," in *Pomeroy's Democrat.*[7]

Meanwhile, in January 1870, Octavia and Diddie were living in Belle Vue cottage in Augusta. Octavia described it as a perfect gem of comfort and neatness. Her Aunt never allowed any article of furniture to be removed from the position by her grandmother, Eliza's orders.[8] The cottage was a place of familiarity and comfort for the LeVerts.

Diddie made a trip to their former home in Mobile in the Spring of 1870. Octavia shared the adventure with Miss W.E. Bush in New York, "You will be surprised to hear that my darling Octavia has been in Mobile for the past month. The imperious demands of business required the presence of one of us in Mobile, and my unselfish child insisted upon going herself as I was so happy here with my Cara Netta and my dear old Aunt. Octavia being the businesswoman of our family. I readily consented. She has been much occupied, she writes, and her health has greatly improved. All our former slaves flooded around her when she arrived with perfect adoration, and my faithful Betsy accompanied her back to see me and Cara Netta. Betsy was the servant who made and sent Cara Netta her beautiful Bridal dress as a wedding gift. She was Cara Netta's nurse, and her devotion to her is unbounded." [9]

In 1870, Regail Reab and Cara Netta had a son. Octavia, still in Augusta, shared the news with her Portrait of Regail and Cara Netta after their wedding. 2021. Photograph. *Madame*

LeVert A Biography of Octavia Walton LeVert, by Frances Gibson Satterfield.
The location of the original photograph is unknown.

nephew, Dr. Claudius Mastin, "Our dear Baby is beautiful. He is a perfect LeVert in features, and we are very proud of this, for the LeVerts are a handsome race of people. He knows us perfectly and is so engaging and lovely. I don't know how I shall ever tear myself away from him."[10]

Betsey, who came back to Augusta with Diddie, decided to stay in town. On May 17th, 1871, she married Richard Lamar. The ceremony was officiated by pastor Henry Watts at Springfield Baptist Church. Richard was possibly the man she cared for when she was interviewed by Fredrika Bremer in Mobile.[11]

Octavia and Diddie continued to spend time traveling between New York and Augusta. Cara Netta gave birth to another child in April 1871, but the child died. Her health was notably delicate, so she needed her family near.[12] Family tragedy required them to stay in town longer than planned.

In June 1871, Octavia's first grandchild, Rigail LeVert Reab, passed away at eight months old. She wrote Miss Bush of the event, "He died on Sunday morning May 7th - after a brief illness. He was in glowing radiant health only a few hours before he was seized by the fatal malady which terminated his precious life. He was so beautiful, bright, and loving that we worshipped him. Amid our happiness, he was snatched away from us, and our hearts are bleeding & quivering with agony. The poor little child's mother is overwhelmed at this her first sorrow, but bravely does she bear up for the sake of her husband, who is so utterly wretched since our darling has gone home with the angels. As for myself, dear friend, I am like one bereft of all joy. This child was my idol, and God has taken him from me so intensely has been my grief that a most dangerous illness has been the result, and our Physician says nothing will restore me but change of scene and change of climate. I am so utterly prostrated by this great sorrow that I cannot travel and shall remain all this summer." [13]

The next year Cara Netta was expecting another child. Octavia and Cara Netta, in New York again, were called back home by Rigail. Fearful of a miscarriage, the doctor restricted Cara Netta to bedrest. Rigail rented a house in Augusta, close to Belle Vue, so that Cara Netta could have her own home's comforts during her pregnancy. Diddie and Betsey prepared the place and brought Cara Netta there. She recovered with their care and was able to walk around her bedroom.[14]

The only known picture of Betsey Walton Lamar. Taken with George Walton Reab, Cara Netta's son. *Madame LeVert A Biography of Octavia Walton LeVert*, by Frances Gibson Satterfield. The location of the original photo is unknown.

Diddie was incredibly dedicated to her sister, cooking dishes to tempt Cara Netta's appetite to help her grow more robust. On June 4th, 1872, George Walton Reab came into the world. However, his mother was very sick, vomiting, and bleeding badly. The doctor was so concerned he did not leave the house for over twenty-four hours. Octavia remained close, anxious over her child's health. Diddie continued to live in the Reab's new home, helping to care for her sister and the new baby.[15]

In April 1873, Octavia was once more in New York and held her first parlor readings. After not earning an income while in Augusta caring for Cara Netta, she returned to New York and tried to bring in additional funds. The reading was described in the *Herald*, "The friends of Madame LeVert in New York have invited her to give parlor reading under the direction of a committee of fashionable ladies, who desire thus to show their regard for this talented and estimable lady, she will give her first reading tonight at the residence of Madame Mears." [16]

This presentation was a repeat of her experiences in Europe and her interview with Pio Nono at the Vatican with descriptions of a bullfight in Spain.[17] The success of the first reading led to a second a week later, and she expanded her subjects to her interview with the Brownings and what she recalled when she visited Baden Baden.[18] Additional invitations for readings were to follow.

OCTAVIA WALTON LE VERT
[The grand-daughter of George Walton.]

Octavia Walton LeVert during her parlor readings. *Octavia Walton Le Vert, 1810-1877*. Photograph. New York, 1873. New York Public Library Digital Collections.

Many of her friends were aware of Octavia's situation and did what they could to help. In April 1863, the *Daily Graphic* described their efforts as follows, "A very successful matinee, dramatic and musical, was given yesterday at the residence of Mrs. Delamater, in West Twentieth street, for the benefit of Madame LeVert, at which the lady and Grace Greenwood were the principal attractions. At two o'clock, the parlors, which are exceptionally adapted to such purposes, were filled with a brilliant company of ladies. The entertainment commenced with a piano solo by Professor Feoderline. Miss Kate Willard followed with a recitation of her poem, the "Sparrows;" and music and recitations occupied the intervening space until Grace Greenwood appeared with her popular rendering of the "Old Maid" and in response to encores gave Bret Harte's "Tim Flynn" and "Cicely." Mme. LeVert read her account of her interview with Mrs. Elizabeth Barrett Browning in an easy, natural, unaffected style, which was most agreeable, and gave indications of talent other than literary, which would find fitting occupation in the reader's desk, if not upon the stage." [19]

For the next few years, Octavia continued to earn additional income through her parlor readings at the invitation of friends she knew before the war. According to Corinne Chadwick Stephens, "In 1874, when at the age of sixty-three, she attempted a career as a public reader and traveled about Georgia...she was in financial distress, being at this time dependent on the charity of her cousins, the Reabs of Augusta." [20]

In February of 1875, Octavia appeared before the Forty-Third Congress seeking back rent for the Union forces using the LeVert Hospital in Mobile and damages to the property that once belonged to Henry LeVert and Dr. Claude Mastin.[21]

The Mayor of Mobile, C.T. Moulton, provided testimony on Octavia's behalf. He stated that he knew Dr. LeVert fifteen years before his illness as a thorough Union man. When Moulton referenced Octavia, he said no lady in America surpassed her in a real love of the Union, and none but herself and her God could know the sufferings Octavia endured.[22]

Moulton testified as to why she should receive compensation. Octavia was asking for rent from April to October 1865 in the amount of $936.67. "On April 12th, 1865, as General Granger entered Mobile, at the head of the U.S. forces, her house was open for his reception, it being the only instance of hospitality being offered to Union officers then in the city...later Justice Chase and his daughter were entertained by Madame LeVert and her daughters...For her Union sentiments and hospitality to Federal officers, and especially to Justice Chase, she and her two daughters have been virtually driven from their home, and suffered the torments of social ostracism and rebel persecutions, which must be experienced to be known." [23]

Mouton continued, "Slander and persecution, because of her faithfulness to the cause of the Union, have done its work. She is driven from...the society she once adored...She is now in need and the payment of her just claim against the government would go far to relieve her present condition of want." [24]

When this Bill came before Congress, Octavia also had the support of General Canby, who agreed she was due rent for the use of the LeVert Hospital, but Chief Quartermaster, Col. Wickersham, did not. He felt Mobile was a hostile city captured by Union troops, which was a prize of war, much like Atlanta. However, Congress was reminded this bill was not about the war but about compensating Octavia and her children. Unfortunately, they decided against paying Octavia rent for the use of the hospital and considered her loss a part of the misfortunes of war.[25]

Soon journalists became aware of how badly Octavia lacked money; it was reported, "The Madame LeVert who entertained the titled and distinguished in her Southern home - and who, till the first year of the war, gave grand levees to the wealth and fashion of New York, wherein she would carry on a sparkling conversation in half a dozen languages at the same time, and the Madame LeVert of today, "penniless," no longer young, trudging over the long spaces of the capital on the little feet that, till of late, never had need to touch the ground, an umbrella for a staff, and her pockets full of tickets that are to earn her bread, are one, the same - Nothing could be more changed than the condition of her lot, while she is utterly unchanged, unbroken, undimmed, loving, enthusiastic, and ever delightful."

"'I saw you lift up that little finger to stop a car,' said her friend, Mrs. Paren Stevens, to her not long since. 'As you got into the car you smiled as if you were perfectly happy, and I asked myself, what in this world now can she find to smile about -- this woman who has lost fortune, friends, everything that makes life delightful. Tell me. I want to know. Were you as happy as you looked? It seems impossible.'"

"'I was,' said the little lady, 'just as happy as I looked. It was so delightful to have just five cents left to take me home in a car.'" [26]

In 1875 Octavia took her parlor talks outside of New York and the surrounding area, traveling to other states. She went to St. Louis, Missouri;[27] Denver, Colorado;[28] San Francisco, California[29]; Salt Lake City, Utah;[30]

The Salt Lake City parlor talk seemed to be different from the others. She did her regular parlor readings, but then she talked about something exceptional. According to an article, "Then followed her 'Personal Souvenirs of Distinguished Americans,' in which she gave personal recollections of Jackson, Clay, Webster, Calhoun, Preston, of South Carolina, and McDuffie, which her audience listened to with almost breathless interest. Her 'Episode of My Early Life' was a glowing resume of her first acquaintance with one of the most distinguished literary men of America. This effort disclosed the lady's wonderful powers of description, and involved dramatic effects rare and enchanting." [31] It seems Octavia did complete her book, *Souvenirs of Distinguished People*, and was sharing it with this audience, but it was never published.

The tour was successful enough that Octavia supported Diddie and herself as they stayed at the Coleman House in New York. She continued to have the parlor talks, but the invitations to talk dwindled, and at sixty-six years old with Diddie, who was forty, she needed to make decisions about where they would live in the future. However, as it often does, life events intervened.

Another tragedy disrupted her life. Octavia described the events best when she wrote to a friend, "I write to you in deepest sorrow and anguish. My precious child, my darling little Cara Netta is dead. She died on December 15th of Bright's Disease... After an illness of only two weeks. As you know we were in New York and on December 6th I gave a superb Reading at 50 West, 55 Street. It was grandly successful and we are so glad & happy that night. After the Reading Miss Keeman had a delightful supper for us, thus it was very late when we reached the Coleman." [32]

She continued, "Octavia (Diddie) seemed better than she had been for months and I said after we retired... It seemed to me that I had scarcely slept an hour when a knock at the door gave me that woeful sound "telegram" aroused me. O. (Diddie) sprung up and there was a dispatch from Rigail saying, 'Come down without stopping at Washington she is sick.' Thus sorrow followed fast from the steps of joy. A wild fear propelled us both but still we did not think the shadow death was over us.

The tombstone of Cara Netta LeVert Reab in the Walker Family Cemetery, Augusta, Georgia. 2019. Photograph.

We hastened to Augusta. Rigail met us at the station, telling us our darling was better. But this improvement was a short duration she grew rapid worse and worse until that supreme moment came when the cord of life was snapt asunder and her pur and finish abounded to the Heavenly Home. which our father has prepared for the pure in heart and life and she was pure and innocent as a little child and of such is the Kingdom of Heaven. I have not one doubt of her perfect belief in that "Betterland." where there is not more pain and suffering. It seems to me that my heart will break! I am so utterly miserable. I have felt the pang of which the human heart may endure. Loss of Mother, Brother, Husband, but the children (only Octavia is left me and she will not long be with me. And then loss of Fortune and the necessity of work & toil for my "daily bread" yet under all these nuisances I bore up bravely... This last, unlooked for and dreadful blow has crushed me to earth. All hope, and happiness in the future seems to have ended in darkness and gloom." [33]

Cara Netta LeVert Reab was only thirty years old when she passed away on December 15th, 1876. They buried her in the Walker Family Cemetery on December 16th, 1876, the eighth anniversary of her marriage to Rigail. They dressed her in a snowy white dress with a japonica on her chest.

Octavia told a relative, "She was beautiful, so beautiful in death. A lovely smile was on her lips as though she already saw the angels and her angelic children who had gone before her. Oh Father of Heaven

The tombstone of Octavia Walton LeVert in the Walker Family Cemetery, Augusta, Georgia. 2019. Photograph.

give me strength to endure this agony. Never can anymore happiness come to me." [34]

After the death of Cara Netta, Octavia and Diddie stayed in Augusta indefinitely. Octavia loved Rigail as if he were her own child, and he needed help with his infant son, George. Diddie took over the housekeeping and devoted her life to raising the boy and helping care for their elderly Aunt Anne, who still owned Belle Vue.[35]

While it seems the Octavia Walton LeVert, the "Rose of Florida," the Queen of Mobile and American Society, did not conclude her life as she expected; she did have a comfortable place to live, her remaining daughter and son-in-law were near, and she was involved in her grandson's life. However, some things are not meant to be.

It was officially announced that Octavia Walton LeVert, died on March 12th, 1877, in Augusta, Georgia, of pneumonia. She was buried in the Walker Family Cemetery, next to the daughter she lost only months before. [36]

Octavia was always a woman of great insight. An entry she made years before when she visited the same cemetery can help put things in perspective: "I knelt by the Graves of those who have been gathered to the Land of Shadows. I press the cold marble, that arose above their ashes, against my heart and ask myself, "Is this all that is left of the loved & idolized?" Ah! It is in moments like these, the world loosed its hold upon our affections. We feel willing to die - we long to lie down by their side, and enjoy everlasting rest. We lift our eyes to the Heaven, where we believe our loved ones are gone, and we pine for wings of the Angels to fly to their blissful Home!" [37]

Works Cited and Notes

1. *Edgar Allen Poe Journal July 4, 1827*. Journal/Diary. Columbia University, *Edgar Allan Poe Papers, 1827-1908*.

2. David A. Bagwell, "Rediscovering That Devil Harry Maury." Manuscript of Lecture.

3. "Alleged Mismanagement of Mt. Vernon," *Cincinnati Semi-Weekly Gazette*, April 19, 1872, GenealogyBank.

4. *South-Western*, June 2, 1869, Newspapers.com.

5. Octavia Walton LeVert, "An Hour with the Pope of Rome," *Yorkville Enquirer*, July 1, 1869, Library of Congress, *Chronicling America*; Octavia Walton LeVert, "Elizabeth Barrett Browning, Hearth and Home," *Daily Kansas Tribune*, January 1, 1869, Library of Congress, *Chronicling America*, Newspapers.com.

6. Satterfield, *Madame LeVert*, 192.

7. *Pomeroy's Democrat*, March 23, 1872, GeneologyBank; Elm Orlou, "Chapter VII, Madame Le Vert," in "Deserving Women of America," (*PD*, January 13, 1872).

8. *Octavia Walton LeVert to Mary Booth*, January 20, 1870. Letter. Letter. In "Madame Octavia Walton LeVert 1810 – 1877," ed. Caldwell Delaney (Master's Thesis, University of Alabama, 1952), 112. Note: Delaney states he found this letter in the Dyer Collection. It is missing as of 2020.

9. *Octavia Walton LeVert to Mary Booth*, March 14, 1870. Letter. New York Public Library.

10. *Octavia Walton LeVert to Claudius Matin*, December 10, 1870. Letter. Private Collection of Traci LeVert Foster in Selma, Alabama. Note: Foster obtained her copy of the letter from Chapel Hill.

11. Georgia Marriage Records from Selected Counties, 1828-1978. Springfield Baptist Church.

12. *Octavia Walton LeVert to Mary Booth*, April 4, 1871. Letter. New York Public Library.

13. *Octavia Walton LeVert to Miss Bush*, June 8, 1871. Letter. New York Public Library.

14. *Cara Netta Reab to Octavia Walton LeVert Jr.*, June 10, 1872. Letter. Private Collection of Stacy Plooster in Augusta, Georgia.

15. *Cara Netta Reab to Octavia Walton LeVert Jr.*, June 10, 1872. Letter. Private Collection of Stacy Plooster in Augusta, Georgia.
16. "Musical and Dramatic Notes," *Herald*, April 4, 1873, Genealogybank.
17. "Readings at Madame Meare's House," *Evening Post*, April 5, 1873.
18. "Lectures and Meetings," *New York Tribune*, April 15, 1873, Genealogybank.
19. "The LeVert Reception," *Daily Graphic*, April 29, 1873, GenealogyBank.
20. Chadwick Stephens, "Madame Octavia Walton LeVert," 29.
21. 43rd Congress, 2nd Session, S. 1216, Report No. 593. Note: A Bill for the relief of Octavia LeVert and her children. Copy located in the Minnie Mitchell Archives, HMPS, Mobile, Alabama.
22. 43rd Congress, 2nd Session, S. 1216, Report No. 593
23. "Madame LeVert Asked, Hospital Bill of Congress," *Press Register*, October 4, 1964, Minnie Mitchell Archives, *LeVert Collection*. Note: Clipped copy located in the Minnie Mitchell Archives, HMPS, Mobile, Alabama.
24. "Madame LeVert Asked, Hospital Bill of Congress."
25. "Madame LeVert Asked, Hospital Bill of Congress."
26. "Madame LeVert Asked, Hospital Bill of Congress."
27. Delaney, "Madame Octavia Walton Le Vert," 113.
28. "LeVert," *Brooklyn Daily Eagle*, May 19, 1875, Newspapers.com.
29. "Mme. LeVert," *Birmingham Iron Age*, August 12, 1875, Newspapers.com.
30. *New Orleans Republican*, October 5, 1875, Newspapers.com.
31. "Madame LeVert's Readings," *Deseret News*, September 22, 1875, Newspapers.com.
32. "Mrs. LeVert," *Mobile Daily Tribune*, October 6, 1875.
33. *Octavia Walton LeVert to Rielly (?)*, January 8, 1877. Letter. New York Public Library and Meadow Garden Archives.
34. *Octavia Walton LeVert to Rielly (?)*, January 8, 1877. Letter. New York Public Library and Meadow Garden Archives.
35. *Octavia Walton LeVert to Marie*, December 22, 1876. Letter. Meadow Garden Archives.
36. "Death of Madame LeVert," *Augusta Chronicle*, March 13, 1877, 4, GenealogyBank.
37. LeVert, *Octavia Walton Le Vert Journal 1846-1860* - 54.

Afterword

When Octavia passed away, an endless number of obituaries were written about her life and her legacy. *Such a woman* isn't forgotten; she serves as a reminder of how one person can impact the world. She would probably be surprised to find herself now in the *Alabama Women's Hall of Fame* at Judson College in Marion, Alabama, and to discover one of its graduates writing her story. It is as if everyone said farewell not only to a person but a representative of a way of life that died as time moved on. Yet, Octavia became a legend.

Despite all of this, one problem followed Octavia well beyond her death, her controversial decisions during the Civil War. Plenty of people were quick to judge her welcoming Union troops into her home in Mobile, Alabama. However, it is hard to determine how Octavia felt during this time because she never spoke of it, nor is there a journal entry or a story about what happened.

Some people told unfavorable tales about her, even after her death, those idol-smashers of the American press who had no hesitancy to judge her. The press accused her of, "Asking for money upon some paltry pretext or

Judson College, the home to the Alabama Women's Hall of Fame. 2019.

another, and who lived by maintaining by hook or crook a standing in that society best able to contribute liberally to her attempts at piracy."[2]

Octavia Walton LeVert's plaque in the Alabama Women's Hall of
Fame. 2019.

Yet, this is only one perspective from people who did not know her personally. To balance the picture, it is necessary to look toward someone who did know her and loved her dearly. The answer lies within an article published in the *Augusta Herald*. Simply titled, "An Interesting Incident in the Life of Madame Le Vert." It said, "A word in defense of a once distinguished lady of Society of Mobile may be interesting at this time to her many friends. It is from a conversation between M'me Octavia Walton LeVert and a cherished friend of thirty years standing, of the city of New Orleans."

"In remarking the condition of things in the last year of the war, especially the charged position of this once 'Queen of Mobile,' M'me Levert said: 'I have suffered much wrong from not being rightly understood. I loved, as does every American woman, the country of my birth. My noble father placed his name upon that scroll we were all taught to revere: when, however, the State of Alabama joined the 'secession movement,' I went with it feeling, believing the State to be supporting principles which the constitution of the United States upheld."

"I think still the same; but, sir, when I saw my last dollar spent to give my children bread-although I had property, I could not dispose of it, or could I feed my family - I received an offer from an old Northern friend whom in my flourishing days I had entertained oft times in the very parlors he then wished to rent from me. I accepted. Why should I not? He was no enemy to the South, but had many friends in the army and navy, amongst whom were many of my cherished friends of bygone days."

"Of course they frequently visited my friends, to whom I had rented my parlors, and I again met them. They were truly gentlemen and only a few differed from my own views; they heartily desired to see the matter settled; and I was convinced the time would come when we would again be united. Every courtesy that true gentlemen can offer a lady - their respect and esteem - was proffered to me. Their carriages were at my disposition, and one day I rode out and passing, stopped to glance at a 'review of the troops' then taking place. American ladies are always exhilarated by the shutter of arms (and I confess my weakness there en passant); for with the grace and precision of the manoeuvres I was charmed, and in my ecstasy I waved my handkerchief in approbation, not of the cause they had espoused at that time, for had it been a Confederate review I would have done the same, but from a love for military order."[3]

"Without a word in my own defense, I was 'tabooed' by persons who had ever sought me and my home for pleasure, and I am thoroughly convinced they will yet take by the hand the very representatives they condemn me for receiving. It was the deed, sir, a severe trial. But I leave the whole matter with my Father in Heaven to judge."[4]

"Knowing how very charming M'me Levert was in society; and during the war, how very difficult it was for those, however high in rank in the Federal army, to obtain access into agreeable society, there is no doubt much was done to consolidate the "Queen" of one of our loveliest Southern cities. Love and sympathy for those around her were ever her characteristics, and it was almost impossible for one of such a temperament to have acted differently, even with those whom most of the people of the South then considered their enemies. Yet how grand the life of sacrifice she led! What noble example for her lovely daughter and namesake to follow! M'me Octavia Walton LeVert died as she lived, an embodiment of Christian virtue."[5]

Knowing the true Octavia, her surviving family cherished the good memories and put aside the negative. Cara Netta's husband, L.A.R. Reab, remarried Maria Jenkins and had more children. Diddie inherited Belle Vue when her aunt passed away, and Betsey Walton Lamar moved in with Diddie when her husband passed. George Walton Reab, Octavia's only grandchild into adulthood, fought in World War I and became an editor for the *Augusta Chronicle*. He died single, concluding the family line for George Walton, Sr., Signer of the Declaration of Independence.

Biography & Notes

1. "Broken Idols," *Bozeman Avant Courier*, May 31, 1877, Chronicling America.
2. "An Interesting Incident in the Life of Madame Le Vert," *Augusta Herald*, January 26, History Museum of Mobile Research Library, *Josephine Walton Collection*.
3. "An Interesting Incident in the Life of Madame Le Vert."
4. An Interesting Incident in the Life of Madame Le Vert."

Paula Lenor Webb

About the Author

The author, Paula Lenor Webb, has a Master's in Library and Information Science from the University of Alabama. She is currently a tenured Librarian at the University of South Alabama, in Mobile. Ms. Webb has always enjoyed research and documented her local history findings in her first book, *Mobile Under Siege: Surviving the Union Blockade*, in 2016. She has continued pursuing this avenue of research with her latest book, *Such a Woman: The Life of Octavia Walton LeVert*.

Made in the USA
Columbia, SC
18 June 2021